AF849675

Transforming Risk

AI Applications in Modern Insurance

Editor

Hamed Taherdoost

Department of Arts, Communications and Social Sciences
School of Arts, Science and Technology
University Canada West, Vancouver, Canada

GUS Institute, Global University Systems, London, UK

College of Technology and Engineering
Westcliff University, United States

Gisma University of Applied Sciences, Germany

Research and Development Department
Hamta Business Corporation, Canada

CRC Press
Taylor & Francis Group
Boca Raton London New York

CRC Press is an imprint of the
Taylor & Francis Group, an **informa** business
A SCIENCE PUBLISHERS BOOK

Cover credit
The image for the cover is provided by AliReza Rafiea, Q Minded | Quark Minded Technology Inc., 1132 Haro St., Vancouver, BC V6E 1C9 Canada.

First edition published 2026
by CRC Press
2385 NW Executive Center Drive, Suite 320, Boca Raton FL 33431

and by CRC Press
4 Park Square, Milton Park, Abingdon, Oxon, OX14 4RN

© 2026 Hamed Taherdoost

CRC Press is an imprint of Taylor & Francis Group, LLC

Reasonable efforts have been made to publish reliable data and information, but the author and publisher cannot assume responsibility for the validity of all materials or the consequences of their use. The authors and publishers have attempted to trace the copyright holders of all material reproduced in this publication and apologise to copyright holders if permission to publish in this form has not been obtained. If any copyright material has not been acknowledged please write and let us know so we may rectify in any future reprint.

Except as permitted under U.S. Copyright Law, no part of this book may be reprinted, reproduced, transmitted, or utilised in any form by any electronic, mechanical, or other means, now known or hereafter invented, including photocopying, microfilming, and recording, or in any information storage or retrieval system, without written permission from the publishers.

For permission to photocopy or use material electronically from this work, access www.copyright.com or contact the Copyright Clearance Center, Inc. (CCC), 222 Rosewood Drive, Danvers, MA 01923, 978-750-8400. For works that are not available on CCC please contact mpkbookspermissions@tandf.co.uk

Trademark notice: Product or corporate names may be trademarks or registered trademarks and are used only for identification and explanation without intent to infringe.

Library of Congress Cataloging-in-Publication Data (applied for)
ISBN: 978-1-041-01677-9 (hbk)
ISBN: 978-1-041-02826-0 (pbk)
ISBN: 978-1-003-62111-9 (ebk)

DOI: 10.1201/9781003621119

Typeset in Times New Roman
by Prime Publishing Services

Preface

The world of insurance is rapidly evolving, and at the forefront of this transformation lies artificial intelligence (AI), a powerful tool that is reshaping how the industry assesses risk, makes decisions, and serves customers. "Transforming Risk: AI Application in Modern Insurance" delves into the cutting-edge applications of AI in the insurance sector, offering both a comprehensive overview and forward-thinking insights into how these technologies are revolutionizing the industry.

This book is structured to provide readers with a well-rounded understanding of AI's role in insurance, from foundational concepts to the challenges the industry faces as it integrates these advanced technologies. We begin with a deep dive into the fundamentals of AI, examining the core principles of machine learning and big data that drive AI innovations. The journey continues with an exploration of AI's pivotal role in risk assessment and underwriting, followed by a look at how AI enhances diagnostic capabilities and decision-making processes. As we move through the chapters, we highlight AI-driven predictive analytics and customer behavior analysis, which are now integral to developing personalized and efficient insurance solutions.

In the later chapters, we tackle the specifiic applications of AI in property and casualty insurance, one of the most complex and dynamic areas of the industry. While AI brings tremendous potential, the book also doesn't shy away from the obstacles that organizations face in its integration. We examine the technological and organizational challenges that have impeded AI adoption, and the hurdles companies must overcome to fully unlock its benefits.

A key feature of this book is the focus on advanced AI technologies such as Generative Adversarial Networks (GANs), Explainable AI (XAI), and Deep Learning. These innovations are being used to mitigate financial fraud and predict future trends in the insurance market, presenting both opportunities and risks in the coming years. Finally, we conclude by discussing the broader barriers to AI adoption, offering a critical look at what the insurance industry needs to address to move forward successfully.

Whether you're a practitioner within the insurance industry, an academic interested in the intersection of technology and business, or someone eager to learn how AI is shaping the future of risk management, this book serves as a comprehensive guide. It is our hope that by the end of this book, readers will gain a deep understanding of AI's potential to transform the insurance sector, as well as the challenges and strategies that come with its integration.

Welcome to an exciting exploration of AI's transformative power in the world of insurance.

Acknowledgements

I would like to express my sincere gratitude to everyone who has contributed to the development and completion of this book. Without the support and expertise of many individuals, this project would not have been possible.

First and foremost, my heartfelt thanks go to the authors and contributors, whose deep knowledge and dedication have brought this work to life. Their insightful research, thoughtful perspectives, and commitment to excellence have made this book a comprehensive and invaluable resource for anyone interested in the intersection of artificial intelligence and the insurance industry.

I would also like to extend my gratitude to the peer reviewers, whose critical feedback and suggestions have played an essential role in improving the quality and clarity of this book. Your expertise and attention to detail have been invaluable in shaping the final manuscript.

A special thank you to the team behind the scenes, including editors, designers, and all those who assisted with the technical aspects of publishing. Your hard work and professionalism ensured that the vision for this book came to fruition.

To my family and friends, thank you for your unwavering support and encouragement throughout this journey.

This book is a collective effort, and I am deeply grateful to everyone who has played a part in its creation. I hope it serves as a valuable resource and a source of inspiration for those exploring the role of AI in transforming the future of insurance.

Contents

1

AI Fundamentals: Machine Learning and Big Data

Mahmood Seyyedzadeh, Pooya Zeynali, Amir A. Ghavifekr, and Alireza Tajdid*

INTRODUCTION

Modern data-driven research and applications increasingly rely on the interplay between artificial intelligence (AI), machine learning (ML), and big data. Big data provides the massive, diverse datasets needed for training intelligent systems, while machine learning offers computational techniques to extract patterns and insights. In turn, AI encompasses a broader spectrum of cognitive abilities ranging from problem-solving and reasoning to perception and natural language understanding that are enabled by ML methods. Together, these fields drive innovations in decision support, smart manufacturing, and intelligent services across industries (Gandomi et al. 2022, Roh et al. 2019).

Artificial Intelligence

AI refers to the capacity of machines to perform cognitive functions traditionally associated with human intelligence, such as reasoning, learning, problem-solving, and decision-making. Certain scholarly perspectives suggest that AI should extend beyond emulating human thought processes to include the ability to act rationally (Kühl et al. 2022). Although AI and ML are occasionally conflated in practical contexts, many researchers assert that ML constitutes only a subset of AI. The broader scope of AI encompasses additional domains, including knowledge representation, natural language processing, robotics, and other related fields (Khanzode and Sarode 2020).

Machine Learning

ML, a specialized subfield of AI, concentrates on the development of algorithms that enable computers to learn from data and enhance their performance over time without explicit programming. Early definitions in the discipline underscore the significance of experiential learning to improve capabilities in tasks such as classification or prediction (Das et al. 2015). ML methodologies include several

Faculty of Electrical and Computer Engineering, University of Tabriz, Iran
* *Corresponding author:* mahmood.seyyedzadeh@ieee.org

DOI: 10.1201/9781003621119-1

approaches: supervised learning, which relies on labeled data; unsupervised learning, which uncovers hidden patterns within unlabeled data; reinforcement learning (RL), which involves iterative learning through trial and error guided by reward signals; and recommender systems, which personalize content based on user preferences. The substantial expansion of digital data, with up to 90% being newly generated, has posed increasing challenges to traditional ML techniques, particularly due to issues of scalability and the prevalence of unstructured formats. To overcome these obstacles, advanced ML algorithms have been engineered to support distributed processing and facilitate real-time analytics.

Big Data

Big data refers to datasets that are large in volume, high in velocity, and wide in variety. These datasets are critical for uncovering hidden patterns, making predictive decisions, and driving innovations in fields ranging from healthcare and cybersecurity to astronomy and marketing. Big data analytics involves the use of advanced algorithms and high-performance computing to process and analyze these large datasets, making it possible to extract meaningful insights that would be infeasible with traditional data processing methods.

Data collection is recognized as a significant challenge in big data analytics, particularly within the ML domain. With the widespread adoption of ML, new applications frequently emerge without sufficient labeled data. Furthermore, the popularization of deep learning techniques, which automatically generate features and save feature engineering costs, has increased the demand for substantial labeled datasets. This necessity presents a bottleneck in big data analytics, primarily due to the high costs and domain expertise required for manual data labeling. Recent research addressing data collection challenges spans multiple disciplines, including ML, natural language processing, computer vision, and data management, emphasizing the critical need for accurate and scalable data collection methods. These methods typically involve three key operations: data acquisition, data labeling, and data or model improvement. Effective management of these operations significantly enhances the efficiency of processing and analyzing big data, facilitating more robust and accurate insights across various applications (Roh et al. 2019).

Integration of AI, Machine Learning, and Big Data

The integration of AI and big data is fundamental to the advancement of applications such as intelligent manufacturing, smart cities, and Industry 4.0. Big data serves as the foundational resource for training ML models, while AI frameworks use these models to emulate cognitive functions and facilitate decision-making processes.

Research on data acquisition for ML, particularly from the perspective of integrating big data and AI, underscores the critical role of acquiring, labeling, and refining data in the development of robust ML systems. These processes necessitate methodologies capable of managing the extensive scale and intricate nature of big data.

AI and ML facilitate the automation of intricate decision-making tasks and boost operational efficiency across a wide range of applications, including web search engines, spam filtration, intelligent tutoring systems, and customer service platforms (Das et al. 2015, Khanzode and Sarode 2020). The incorporation of big data analytics empowers these systems to learn from vast datasets, thereby augmenting the precision and reliability of their predictive capabilities.

Within the framework of Industry 4.0, the combination of AI and big data drives advancements in areas such as predictive maintenance, quality assurance, and process enhancement. For instance, ML algorithms analyze real-time data from the Industrial Internet of Things (IIoT) sensors to forecast equipment malfunctions and streamline production workflows (Jagatheesaperumal et al. 2021).

As ML models increase in complexity, comprehending their decision-making mechanisms—frequently characterized as "black-box" models—becomes increasingly difficult. This opacity can undermine the trustworthiness and ethical deployment of AI systems.

AI and Big Data in Industries

AI and big data are widely recognized as transformative forces reshaping modern industries. They enable real-time analytics, automation, predictive decision-making, and enhanced personalization, helping organizations optimize operations, reduce costs, and innovate products and services. Across diverse sectors—including healthcare, finance, manufacturing, retail, and transportation—AI and big data confer significant competitive advantages by enhancing processes from supply chain management to customer relationship management. In the insurance industry specifically, AI and ML have emerged as critical tools, revolutionizing traditional operations. Insurers leverage these advanced technologies extensively for claims processing, underwriting, fraud detection, and improving customer service. AI-powered chatbots, capable of natural language interactions, have been adopted by major insurers such as Lemonade, Allstate, and Lincoln Financial to enhance client experiences and operational efficiency. Notably, the insurance company Lemonade demonstrated the potential of AI by successfully settling a claim within three seconds using a chatbot. AI also significantly enhances claim management by analyzing historical data, sensor information, and photographic evidence to evaluate damage severity accurately and predict repair costs efficiently. Additionally, AI empowers insurers to capitalize on vast big data repositories to create personalized services, develop targeted marketing strategies, and deploy predictive risk management solutions. The integration of AI and ML technologies facilitates a paradigm shift from traditional reactive models ("detect and repair") to proactive risk management frameworks ("predict and prevent"), enabling insurers to mitigate risks before claims occur. Despite these substantial benefits, integrating AI technologies into existing systems poses various challenges, including data quality management, cybersecurity threats, and legacy system compatibility. Nonetheless, ongoing technological advancements ensure AI and big data continue to serve as pivotal drivers of innovation and competitive advantage, not only in insurance but across all industry sectors (Kumar et al. 2023).

Importance of AI and Big Data in the Insurance Industry

The insurance industry has experienced a radical transformation due to the digital revolution. From the early 2000s onward, the massive increase in digital data (from less than 1% digital in the late 1980s to 99% by 2012) has provided insurers with unprecedented volumes of data. This growth is supported by advances in storage technology and data processing, enabling the creation of robust data-driven models (Belhadi et al. 2023). New technologies have accelerated the speed at which data is collected and processed. Insurance companies now capture and analyze data in seconds rather than in traditional intermittent cycles, which is critical for timely risk assessment and decision-making. Big data has multiplied the data collection rate dramatically up to 50 times from 2010 to 2020 facilitating instantaneous data processing and analysis critical to operational effectiveness and accuracy. Figure 1 illustrates the dramatic increase in data collection speed over the past decade, reinforcing the role of big data in real-time analytics.

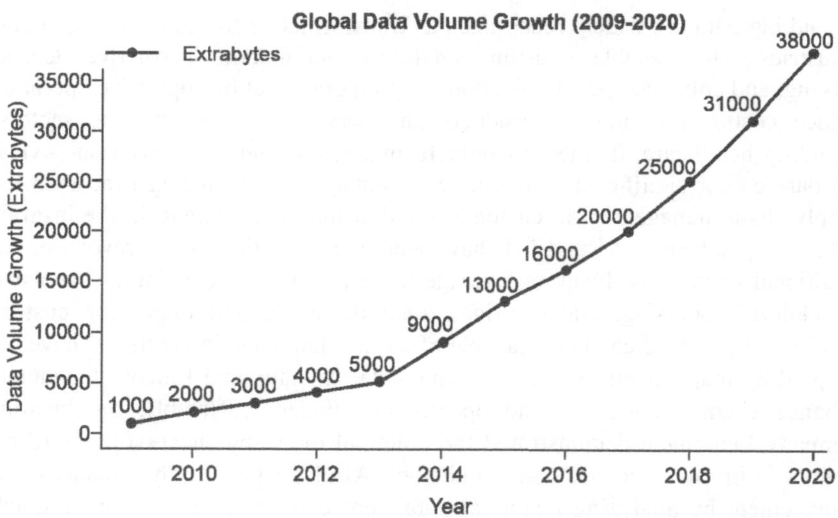

Fig. 1. The Evolution of Data Collecting Speed Between 2010 and 2020 (Belhadi et al. 2023)

AI models utilize historical claims data along with real-time inputs to expedite claims processing, detect fraudulent activities with higher accuracy, and even anticipate risk events before they occur. Advanced algorithms such as anomaly detection and statistical modeling have resulted in improved fraud detection rates, sometimes up to 60% better than traditional methods. Big data analytics enhance insurers' capabilities by leveraging unstructured data sources such as social media, emails, and multimedia content, significantly increasing the effectiveness of fraud detection through methods like text mining and predictive analytics. By using big data, insurers can extract patterns and trends that enable highly accurate risk assessment and dynamic pricing. The use of advanced classification models allows companies to segment policyholders and tailor policies based on individual risk profiles. AI techniques, such as ML algorithms and anomaly detection, have significantly enhanced claims processing and fraud detection. These systems analyze historical and real-time data to flag suspicious claims and reduce the manual effort required in investigations. The integration of connected sensors in cars and health insurance has further allowed personalized risk assessment, enabling insurers to offer real-time customized pricing and preventive services based on detailed behavioral analytics.

AI-powered solutions such as chatbots and virtual assistants provide 24/7 customer service. Additionally, data-driven personalization allows insurers to offer products that match the specific needs and behaviors of policyholders, thereby enhancing customer satisfaction and loyalty. According to industry reports, insurers using AI-driven personalization have witnessed improvements in customer retention, satisfaction, and acquisition, establishing AI and big data as critical elements in competitive strategy development (Belhadi et al. 2023). As AI and big data become integral to insurance operations, ethical considerations are paramount. Frameworks such as the Ethical Hierarchy Model provide guidelines for ensuring that data is used responsibly across the entire value chain—from acquisition to algorithm application and final product delivery. Regulatory bodies such as the European Insurance and Occupational Pensions Authority (EIOPA) have developed ethical frameworks addressing complex ethical issues arising from the use of AI and big data, emphasizing the importance of transparent and responsible practices.

The ability to access and effectively use big data is becoming a critical competitive factor. Insurers that cannot integrate these technologies risk losing market share to tech giants (e.g. Google, Apple, Facebook, Twitter, Amazon) that control significant portions of the data value chain. This dynamic pressures traditional insurers to innovate or face potential obsolescence (Belhadi et al. 2023). Insurers without sufficient access to technology and analytical skills face substantial competitive disadvantages, potentially leading to significant market disruption or acquisitions by these major tech platforms.

FUNDAMENTALS OF MACHINE LEARNING

ML is the study of algorithms and models that enable computers to learn from data and improve their performance over time without explicit programming. It is often formulated as a nonlinear optimization problem where network parameters (weights) are adjusted to minimize an error function (e.g. mean squared error (MSE)) on training examples. Learning methods are broadly categorized as:

a. *Supervised Learning:* Utilizes labeled data to guide training. Errors are calculated by comparing predicted and actual outputs. Supervised learning is a closed-loop feedback system where the error functions as feedback, adjusting network parameters through methods such as gradient descent. Supervised learning is widely applied in classification, approximation, control, signal processing, and optimization.

b. *Unsupervised Learning:* Finds hidden structures within unlabeled data, focusing on tasks such as clustering and feature extraction. Unlike supervised learning, unsupervised learning operates solely based on the correlations within input data, without external guidance. Popular approaches include Hebbian learning, competitive learning, and self-organizing maps (SOM).

c. *Reinforcement Learning:* Involves agents making sequential decisions and learning by receiving rewards or penalties based on their actions. It seeks to maximize the cumulative expected reward. RL algorithms are commonly employed in control systems and robotics, adapting their actions based on the received external reinforcement signals rather than explicit correct answers (Du et al. 2013).

Figure 2 clearly illustrates the differences between supervised, unsupervised, and RL methodologies, enhancing the conceptual understanding of these learning categories.

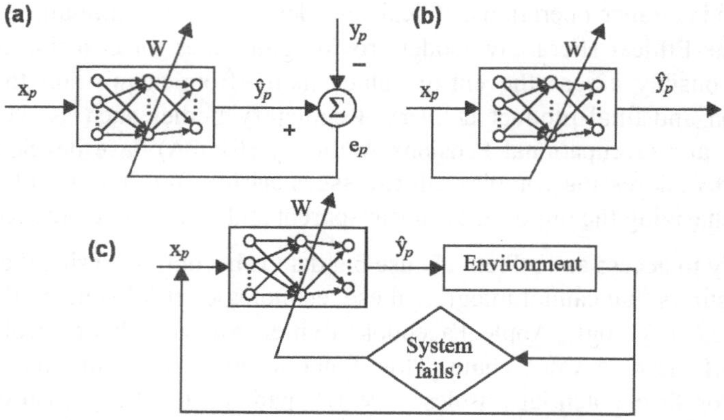

Fig. 2. Learning Methods: (a) Supervised Learning. (b) Unsupervised Learning. (c) RL (Du et al. 2013)

A key goal is to achieve good generalization on unseen data. Techniques such as early stopping and regularization are used to prevent overfitting, where a model fits the noise in the training data instead of the underlying pattern.

Types of Machine Learning

Supervised Learning

Supervised learning involves learning a mapping from inputs (features) to outputs (labels) using a training dataset containing input-output pairs. The primary objective is to build a model that generalizes effectively to new, unseen data. Supervised learning tasks typically include:

a. *Classification:* Predicting discrete labels (e.g. distinguishing spam emails from non-spam). Commonly used methods include support vector machines (SVMs), decision trees, random forests, logistic regression, and neural networks. Each method has distinct advantages and limitations. For example, decision trees offer interpretability, while random forests mitigate overfitting by aggregating multiple decision trees. SVMs identify hyperplanes that best separate categories, especially useful in high-dimensional spaces. Neural networks excel at modeling complex, nonlinear relationships (Nasteski 2017).

b. *Regression:* Predicting continuous values (e.g. house prices). Linear regression and its extensions, such as ridge regression, lasso, and elastic net, are common regression methods. These approaches model relationships using linear functions, optimizing parameters to minimize prediction error, commonly measured by MSE (Nasteski 2017).

In addition to these tasks, many modern supervised learning methods are designed to handle high-dimensional data and complex relationships, often using ensemble techniques to improve prediction accuracy (Jiang et al. 2020, Nasteski 2017).

Unsupervised Learning

Unsupervised learning focuses on uncovering hidden structures in data when no explicit labels are provided. The primary goal is to model the underlying probability distribution or to identify meaningful groups and patterns inherent in the data. This form of learning can be motivated through information-theoretic principles and Bayesian inference frameworks (Ghahramani 2003). Common unsupervised techniques include:

a. *Clustering:* This approach involves grouping data points into clusters based on similarity measures. Techniques such as K-means clustering, hierarchical clustering, and Gaussian mixture models (GMMs) are widely utilized. K-means, for example, partitions data into clusters by minimizing within-cluster variance, whereas hierarchical clustering builds clusters by either merging or splitting based on distance metrics.

b. *Dimensionality Reduction:* Methods such as Principal Component Analysis (PCA), Factor Analysis (FA), and Independent Component Analysis (ICA) reduce the dimensionality of data while preserving essential informational content. PCA transforms data into a lower-dimensional subspace using eigenvectors corresponding to the largest eigenvalues of the data covariance matrix. FA models data as linear combinations of latent variables plus noise, whereas ICA seeks statistically independent components by maximizing non-Gaussianity, beneficial for capturing sparse and informative features in datasets.

c. *Mixture Models:* A mixture model such as GMMs, assumes that data are generated from a combination of several underlying probability distributions (components), each representing a cluster or subgroup in the data.

These unsupervised methods are critically important for tasks like anomaly detection, exploratory data analysis, preprocessing data for more complex modeling tasks, and for revealing insights in complex datasets without prior labels. Additionally, advanced unsupervised methods utilize graphical models and inference algorithms like Expectation-Maximization (EM), which iteratively estimates latent variables and parameters to optimize model likelihood, enhancing the flexibility and applicability of unsupervised learning to diverse scenarios (Ghahramani 2003).

Reinforcement Learning

RL differs fundamentally from other ML approaches by focusing on learning through direct interaction with an environment. In RL, an agent learns a policy—a mapping from observed states to actions—to maximize a cumulative reward signal received from the environment. Key characteristics of RL include:

a. *Trial-and-Error Learning:* The RL agent explores various actions, learning optimal behaviors through feedback provided as rewards or penalties. This process involves continuous interaction, where the agent updates its strategies based on outcomes.

b. *Delayed Rewards:* RL often deals with situations where the rewards or penalties for actions are not immediate. This necessitates that the agent must account for the long-term effects of its actions rather than just immediate outcomes.

c. *Model-Free vs. Model-Based:* RL algorithms fall into two main categories, model-free and model-based methods. Model-free approaches, such as Q-learning and State–Action–Reward–State–Action (SARSA), directly estimate the optimal action strategy from interactions with the environment without explicitly modeling it. Conversely, model-based methods, such as certain variants of SARSA, initially learn the environmental model and then derive an optimal strategy from it (Qiang and Zhongli 2011).

Figure 3 shows the interactive loop among the agent, the action, the environment state, and the reward.

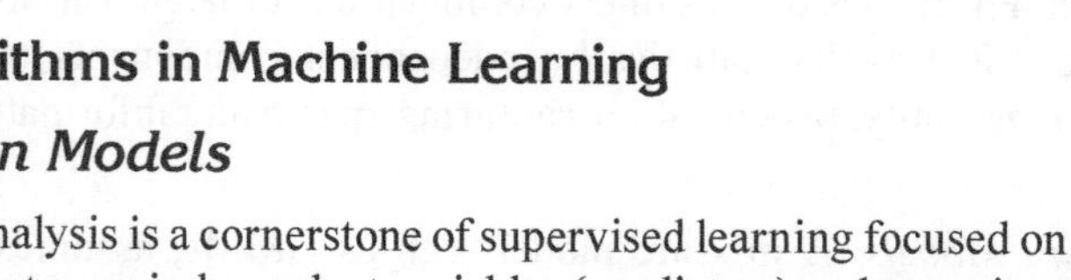

Fig. 3. The Basic Model of RL (Qiang and Zhongli 2011)

Key Algorithms in Machine Learning

Regression Models

Regression analysis is a cornerstone of supervised learning focused on modeling the relationship between independent variables (predictors) and a continuous dependent variable. Common regression techniques include linear regression, logistic regression, polynomial regression, ridge regression, Bayesian linear regression, and Lasso. Linear regression models relationships with a straight-line equation, where y is the dependent variable and x is the independent variable. Regression analysis is fundamental for forecasting trends, quantifying relationships, and supporting decisions in finance, marketing, and economics. For example, regression models can predict product sales based on temperature variations or economic indicators, aiding in efficient resource allocation and strategic planning. Comparative reviews of regression models emphasize the necessity of selecting appropriate regression techniques based on dataset characteristics and application requirements, highlighting differences in model stability and data fitting capabilities (Kumar and Bhatnagar 2022, Rong and Bao-Wen 2018).

Decision Trees

Decision trees are highly interpretable, non-parametric models used for both classification and regression. They operate by recursively partitioning the feature space according to decision rules derived from the input attributes to produce a tree-like structure with internal nodes (representing tests) and leaves (representing outcomes). Algorithms such as ID3, C4.5, and Classification and Regression Trees (CART) exemplify this approach. Their strength lies in the ease of visualization and the straightforward explanation of how decisions are made (De Ville 2013, Navada et al. 2011).

Neural Networks

Neural networks are computational models inspired by the structure and function of the human brain, consisting of interconnected processing units (neurons). These networks adjust connection weights to minimize prediction errors iteratively. Key architectures include feedforward neural networks, convolutional neural networks (CNNs), recurrent neural networks (RNNs), and SOM. CNNs excel in image recognition tasks, while RNNs are suited to sequential data such as language modeling or time series forecasting. Neural networks leverage nonlinearity, parallel processing, and adaptability, significantly enhancing performance in classification, prediction, optimization, and pattern recognition tasks across diverse real-world applications (Gurney 2018, Islam et al. 2019).

Support Vector Machines

SVMs are a family of supervised learning methods primarily used for classification, though they have extensions for regression and other tasks. SVMs work by finding an optimal hyperplane that maximizes the margin between different classes in a high-dimensional feature space. This optimal hyperplane is obtained through convex optimization methods, which provide robustness against overfitting and ensure good generalization performance (Mammone et al. 2009).

BIG DATA: CONCEPTS AND TECHNOLOGIES

Overview of Big Data: Concepts and Technologies

Big data refers to the collection and processing of massive, complex, and heterogeneous datasets that exceed the capabilities of traditional database management systems. It is characterized not only by the sheer size of the data but also by the speed at which it is generated, the wide range of formats in which it exists, and challenges related to its quality and reliability. This new era of data requires novel architectures and technologies to capture, store, process, analyze, and visualize the information so that actionable insights can be derived (Chebbi et al. 2015, Rao et al. 2019, Watson 2014).

Characteristics of Big Data: Volume, Variety, Velocity, Veracity

The four key dimensions that define big data are:

a. *Volume:* This represents the enormous amount of data generated—from petabytes to exabytes and beyond. For example, online transactions, social media posts, sensor logs, and multimedia content contribute to vast data stores.

b. *Variety:* Big data comes in multiple forms, including structured data (e.g. relational databases), semi-structured data (e.g. XML, JSON), and unstructured data (e.g. text, images, videos).

c. *Velocity:* This dimension captures the high speed at which data is produced and needs to be processed in real time or near real time, such as streaming data from sensors or social media feeds.

d. *Veracity:* This refers to the quality and trustworthiness of the data. big data often contains inconsistencies, noise, or biases that must be addressed through robust data cleansing and validation techniques (Charles et al. 2018, Younas 2019).

Sources of Big Data

Big data is generated from a diverse set of sources that include:

a. *Internet of Things (IoT):* Billions of connected devices and sensors continuously produce data on environmental conditions, industrial processes, vehicle telematics, and more.

b. *Transactions:* Digital records from retail, financial services, and online marketplaces contribute large volumes of transactional data that capture customer behavior and business operations.

c. *Telematics:* Data obtained from GPS and vehicle tracking systems provide insights into transportation, logistics, and fleet management.

d. *Social Media:* Platforms like Facebook, Twitter, and Instagram generate a vast amount of user-generated content, including posts, images, videos, and interactions that are valuable for sentiment analysis and trend detection.

e. *Customer Interactions:* Websites, call centers, and mobile applications create data trails through customer service interactions, clickstreams, and feedback, which are essential for improving customer experiences and personalizing services (Khan et al. 2014, Watson 2014).

Storage and Processing Technologies for Big Data

To manage and analyze big data efficiently, several advanced storage and processing technologies have emerged:

a. *Hadoop:* An open-source framework that employs the Hadoop Distributed File System (HDFS) and the MapReduce programming model to store and process large volumes of data across clusters of commodity hardware. Hadoop's scalability and fault tolerance make it a cornerstone technology for big data.

b. *Spark:* An in-memory data processing engine that significantly speeds up data processing tasks compared to disk-based systems. Spark supports batch processing as well as real-time stream processing, and its machine learning library (MLlib) enables sophisticated analytics on large datasets.

c. *Cloud Computing:* Cloud platforms (such as Amazon Web Services, Microsoft Azure, and Google Cloud Platform) offer elastic, scalable, and cost-effective infrastructure for storing and processing big data. They provide managed services that integrate with frameworks like Hadoop and Spark, thus enabling organizations to scale resources as needed without heavy upfront investments (Rao et al. 2019).

BIG DATA APPLICATIONS IN INSURANCE

The integration of big data technologies into the insurance industry has significantly transformed traditional processes and decision-making frameworks. Insurers now leverage extensive and heterogeneous datasets to enhance risk assessment, streamline operations, and deliver personalized products. In this context, big data analytics facilitates automation in claims processing, real-time monitoring of risk factors, advanced customer segmentation, fraud detection, and proactive customer relationship management. These capabilities collectively contribute to cost savings, operational efficiency, improved risk management, and enhanced customer satisfaction (Ellili et al. 2023, Reka et al. 2025).

Claims Processing Automation

The availability of extensive data has allowed insurers to automate claims processing by integrating ML and AI algorithms into their operational workflows. Advanced analytics can extract and interpret information from diverse sources, including images, text documents, and sensor data, facilitating faster and more accurate claim adjudication. Automation reduces manual intervention, substantially decreases processing time, and enhances fraud detection by quickly identifying anomalies and suspicious patterns in claim submissions. Techniques such as natural language processing (NLP), predictive analytics, and image recognition significantly improve the efficiency and accuracy of claims handling, leading to quicker settlements and higher customer satisfaction (Ellili et al. 2023, Reka et al. 2025).

Real-Time Risk Monitoring (Telematics and Wearables)

Insurers increasingly rely on real-time data acquired from telematics devices and wearable sensors to monitor risk continuously. Telematics gathered through devices such as black boxes, dongles, embedded systems, and smartphone sensors provides detailed insights into driving behavior (e.g., speed, braking, and cornering patterns), allowing insurers to adjust premiums dynamically and issue proactive alerts. This real-time risk monitoring not only improves underwriting accuracy but also enhances driver safety and reduces accident-related costs (Arumugam and Bhargavi 2019).

Customer Segmentation and Targeted Marketing

Big data analytics facilitates sophisticated customer segmentation by processing diverse data sources such as transaction records, social media interactions, and customer service logs to identify distinct behavioral and demographic clusters. This segmentation enables insurers to develop targeted marketing strategies and personalized insurance products, improving customer engagement and retention. Predictive models and clustering techniques allow companies to tailor offerings based on risk profiles and purchasing patterns, thereby optimizing product pricing and promotional efforts.

Beyond claims automation, real-time risk monitoring, and customer segmentation, big data applications in insurance extend to fraud detection, underwriting automation, and improved operational efficiency. Advanced analytics enable insurers to uncover hidden patterns that indicate potential fraud and to mitigate risks before they escalate. Moreover, the integration of big data has spurred the development of new business models such as usage-based insurance, which rely on innovative risk classification techniques (Eling et al. 2024, Ellili et al. 2023).

DATA PREPROCESSING AND FEATURE ENGINEERING

Overview of Data Preprocessing and Feature Engineering

Data preprocessing and feature engineering are critical steps in any ML pipeline, especially in domains like insurance where data quality directly affects decision-making. Preprocessing involves cleaning, transforming, and reducing raw data to a form suitable for analysis, while feature engineering extracts or creates meaningful features to enhance model performance. These steps address issues such as noise, missing values, and high dimensionality, ultimately improving the accuracy and efficiency of predictive models. In the context of big data, distributed frameworks (e.g. Hadoop and Spark) further influence these preprocessing tasks by enabling scalable processing of vast, heterogeneous datasets (García et al. 2016).

Handling Missing Data

Handling missing data is a fundamental aspect of data preprocessing. Techniques range from simple deletion methods (listwise or pairwise) to more advanced imputation strategies such as simple imputation (mean, median, mode), regression imputation, and hot-deck imputation. For example, hot-deck imputation replaces missing values by randomly selecting donor values from similar records, thereby maintaining the inherent variability of the data (Emmanuel et al. 2021, García et al. 2016).

Normalization Techniques

Normalization is essential for scaling features so that they contribute equally to the learning process. Techniques include methods such as StandardScaler, which adjusts features to have a mean of zero and a standard deviation of one, and MinMaxScaler, which scales data within a specified range. Additionally, methods like the Normalizer (which scales each row to unit norm) are used to transform data distributions for improved model convergence (García et al. 2016).

Dimensionality Reduction

Dimensionality reduction addresses the "curse of dimensionality" by reducing the number of input features while preserving the most informative aspects of the data. This can be achieved through feature selection (which chooses a subset of the original features) or feature extraction (which transforms the original features into a new set of variables, e.g. using PCA (Jia et al. 2022, Khoei and Singh 2024).

Categorization of Feature Selection Methods

Feature selection techniques are broadly classified into three main categories: filter, wrapper, and embedded methods. Filter methods rank features based on intrinsic data properties using metrics such as information gain, mutual information, and correlation measures. In contrast, wrapper methods evaluate subsets of features using a specific ML algorithm's performance (e.g. via forward selection, backward elimination, or heuristic search strategies), while embedded methods integrate feature selection into the model training process through regularization techniques (Jović et al. 2015).

Feature Selection Process and Evaluation Criteria

The feature selection process generally involves four key steps: candidate subset generation, subset evaluation, stopping criteria, and validation. Filter methods evaluate features independently—using univariate or multivariate measures without involving a learning algorithm, making them computationally efficient but sometimes less effective in capturing inter-feature interactions. On the other hand, wrapper methods, though computationally expensive, assess feature subsets based on the predictive performance of an underlying classifier (Visalakshi and Radha 2014).

Feature Selection Versus Feature Extraction in Pattern Analysis

In pattern analysis, dimensionality reduction can be achieved through two main approaches: feature selection and feature extraction. Feature selection refers to the process of selecting an optimal subset from the original set of features without altering them, thereby preserving their original semantics and interpretability. It focuses on eliminating redundant and irrelevant features to improve computational efficiency, avoid the "curse of dimensionality," and enhance classification accuracy. On the other hand, feature extraction transforms the original features into a new lower-dimensional space, often using techniques such as PCA, ICA, or Linear Discriminant Analysis (LDA). Unlike feature selection, feature extraction combines original features through mathematical transformations, potentially losing direct interpretability but achieving significant reductions in dimensionality and noise, improving the efficiency and performance of classifiers (Ghojogh et al. 2019, Mwadulo 2016).

Feature Selection for Classification Tasks in Practice

In practical classification tasks, particularly in sensitive domains like medical diagnostics, the choice of features critically influences classification accuracy and model interpretability. High-dimensional datasets in these domains typically contain irrelevant and redundant features that negatively impact the classifier's performance, computational efficiency, and interpretability. Effective feature selection methods such as filter methods (e.g. Information Gain, Gain Ratio, Symmetric Uncertainty), wrapper methods (e.g. Genetic Algorithms, Sequential Forward and Backward Selection), and embedded methods have been widely adopted to address these challenges. Filter methods, which assess features based on intrinsic data properties, are computationally efficient and scalable but may ignore feature interactions. Wrapper methods, conversely, evaluate subsets based on the predictive performance of specific classifiers, accounting for feature dependencies but at higher computational costs and potential risks of overfitting. Hybrid methods combine these approaches to balance accuracy and computational efficiency. Recent advances emphasize the integration of multiple feature selection techniques to optimize predictive performance further, manage computational complexity, and ensure robust, interpretable models. These integrated approaches demonstrate significantly improved classification accuracy, especially when handling complex, high-dimensional data such as medical diagnostic datasets, where precision and reliability are critical (Ghojogh et al. 2019, Mwadulo 2016).

MODEL TRAINING, EVALUATION, AND OPTIMIZATION

Training, Validation, and Testing Datasets and Evaluation Metrics

Modern ML practices emphasize the importance of partitioning data into distinct subsets. Typically, datasets are divided into training, validation, and testing subsets.

The training dataset is primarily used for parameter learning. The validation set is employed for hyperparameter tuning and model selection, assisting in optimizing model complexity and performance. Finally, the testing dataset provides an unbiased evaluation of the model's generalization ability on unseen data. Proper data partitioning ensures reliable and reproducible evaluation results, helping prevent issues such as data leakage and overfitting. Commonly employed evaluation metrics for quantifying model performance include accuracy, precision, recall (sensitivity), specificity, F1-score, Receiver Operating Characteristic (ROC) curves, and the Area Under the ROC Curve (AUC). Each metric serves different evaluation purposes; for example, precision focuses on the correctness of positive predictions, whereas recall measures the model's ability to detect positive instances effectively. The F1-score provides a balanced assessment by combining precision and recall into a single metric (Raschka 2018).

Overfitting, Underfitting, and Regularization

Overfitting occurs when a model becomes too finely tuned to the training data, leading to poor generalization on unseen data, while underfitting indicates that the model is too simple to capture the underlying patterns. Robust strategies to counter these issues include regularization methods such as L1/L2 penalties—as well as early stopping, network reduction, and data augmentation (Ying 2019).

Optimization Techniques in Model Training

Efficient training is underpinned by optimization methods that adjust model parameters to minimize a loss function. Common approaches include gradient descent and its variants—stochastic gradient descent (SGD) and mini-batch gradient descent—along with enhancements like momentum and adaptive learning rate techniques (Karthick 2024).

Challenges in Real-World Insurance Datasets

Insurance datasets present significant complexities and noise, often characterized by issues such as missing values, class imbalance, data heterogeneity, and privacy concerns. Missing values are common due to incomplete customer records or limited historical data, requiring techniques like imputation or advanced predictive modeling to address these gaps effectively. Imbalanced classes pose a considerable challenge in insurance data, particularly in fraud detection and rare-event prediction tasks, where instances of interest (e.g. fraudulent claims) constitute a small fraction of the total data. To address class imbalance, resampling methods such as SMOTE (Synthetic Minority Over-sampling Technique) and ensemble approaches like random forests or gradient boosting are frequently used to enhance minority class detection performance. Data heterogeneity arises from integrating data across multiple sources, including structured (transactional data) and unstructured (social media, text, images) forms. Managing this heterogeneity requires sophisticated preprocessing, normalization, and fusion techniques to ensure consistent and reliable inputs for predictive modeling (Kuppan et al. 2024).

Additional Perspectives on Model Evaluation and Hyperparameter Tuning

Beyond basic validation methods, additional methodologies such as K-fold cross-validation, nested cross-validation, and bootstrap methods play a pivotal role in achieving robust performance estimation and reliable hyperparameter optimization. K-fold cross-validation splits the dataset into 'K' distinct subsets, repeatedly using each subset as a validation set while training on the remaining subsets, thereby providing stable performance metrics and preventing model selection bias. Nested cross-validation takes this a step further by embedding an additional cross-validation loop within the hyperparameter tuning process, offering an unbiased assessment of model generalization by ensuring hyperparameter selection and performance estimation are independently conducted (Muhamedyev 2015, Simon and Aliferis 2024). Bootstrap methods are another critical technique, especially effective for estimating the variance and stability of model predictions by repeatedly sampling from the dataset with replacement. This method not only quantifies uncertainty but also addresses potential issues of data variability, enhancing the robustness and reproducibility of the final model. These advanced validation techniques are particularly valuable in contexts characterized by data complexity and variability, such as real-world insurance datasets, where they help mitigate biases and ensure that predictive models are reliable and generalizable (Liu and Panagiotakos 2022).

BIG DATA ANALYTICS AND MACHINE LEARNING INTEGRATION

Using Big Data with Machine Learning

The explosive growth of digital data—from social media, IoT devices, and transactional systems—has created unprecedented opportunities for ML to uncover detailed patterns and actionable insights. Modern ML and deep learning (DL) architectures, such as CNNs, RNNs, and transformer models, are particularly effective at handling high-dimensional, unstructured data. CNNs excel at spatial data like images, RNNs specialize in sequential data processing for applications such as language modeling, and transformers have revolutionized tasks involving sequential and context-sensitive data due to their self-attention mechanisms. By automatically learning robust data representations, these techniques significantly enhance predictive accuracy and enable automated feature extraction, leveraging the intrinsic diversity and volume of big data. Furthermore, ML models continuously improve in predictive power as they process increasingly larger datasets, capturing more nuanced insights and adapting dynamically to new information (Rane et al. 2024).

Distributed and Parallel Learning for Large-Scale Model Training

Handling massive data volumes poses significant computational challenges that traditional, centralized ML approaches cannot overcome. To address these issues, distributed and parallel computing strategies have been developed. Distributed learning frameworks partition the data across multiple workstations, enabling scalable training by concurrently processing data subsets. Parallel ML further exploits multicore processors and cloud-based infrastructures to accelerate model training, reduce memory constraints, and lower energy consumption (Qiu et al. 2016, Zhou et al. 2017).

Cloud-Based AI and Big Data Platforms

Cloud computing platforms such as Hadoop, Spark, and other distributed storage and processing systems provide the scalable infrastructure needed for modern AI applications. These cloud-based systems enable the deployment of ML and DL models over vast datasets by offering on-demand computational resources and parallel processing capabilities. They not only support the distributed training of models but also facilitate real-time data integration, streaming analytics, and the rapid scaling of applications across diverse domains—ranging from healthcare to finance. Moreover, advancements in edge computing and emerging technologies like quantum computing are beginning to complement cloud-based solutions, further enhancing the efficiency and responsiveness of ML systems (Rane et al. 2024, Zhou et al. 2017).

Integrating Heterogeneous Data in Big Data Analytics

Effective big data analytics often depends on the integration of heterogeneous data sources, which can include structured records, unstructured texts, images, and sensor data. Integrative ML models employ various strategies such as early integration (feature concatenation), intermediate (joint learning), and late integration (ensemble fusion) to combine complementary information from multiple origins. Bayesian methods and Bayesian networks play a crucial role in this context by incorporating prior domain knowledge and handling data uncertainty (Li and Ngom 2015).

MACHINE LEARNING APPLICATIONS IN INSURANCE

Risk Assessment and Predictive Modeling

ML techniques have increasingly been adopted in insurance to improve risk assessment and underwriting accuracy. Traditional actuarial models based on generalized linear models (GLMs) have been enhanced by non-linear models such as neural networks and ensemble methods, which can automatically learn complex interactions from historical data. For example, recent reviews on risk prediction in life insurance highlight how predictive models not only classify customers by risk level but also support premium calculation by incorporating customer demographics, clinical history, and external data (e.g. credit, lifestyle) to refine risk classification. Several studies demonstrate that hybrid ML approaches—combining supervised and unsupervised learning—yield more accurate risk predictions and reduce processing time in underwriting decisions (Baruah and Singh 2023, Christopher 2020, Varadarajan and Kakumanu 2024).

Fraud Detection and Anomaly Detection

Fraud detection is another critical application of ML in the insurance sector. Traditional manual methods for identifying fraudulent activities are often imprecise, time-consuming, and costly. Systematic literature reviews have shown that classification methods—particularly SVMs and artificial neural networks (ANNs)—are among the most popular techniques used to detect financial fraud. These methods are capable of analyzing vast volumes of transaction data, recognizing subtle patterns and anomalies that may indicate fraudulent behavior (Ali et al. 2022).

Personalized Pricing and Policy Recommendations

Personalization in insurance is driven by recommender systems that aim to match customers with products best suited to their needs and risk profiles. Advanced systems deploy ML techniques to analyze customer portfolio data along with external marketing information, thereby generating tailored recommendations for additional coverage or policy upgrades. In one study, a system was developed using Bayesian networks to model relationships among customer attributes and existing coverage; DL approaches were also explored for cases where only external data were available. These systems help insurers offer personalized pricing and policy recommendations, improving both customer experience and operational efficiency (Qazi et al. 2020).

Additional Insights and Challenges

Beyond risk assessment and fraud detection, the literature emphasizes that the integration of hybrid ML algorithms is essential to overcome the limitations inherent in standalone models. Combining methodologies—for example, fusing supervised techniques with unsupervised learning for feature extraction—enhances model robustness and predictive performance. Other relevant challenges include handling imbalanced datasets, ensuring model interpretability, and integrating heterogeneous data from multiple sources (Nthenge et al. 2023, Varadarajan and Kakumanu 2024).

Case Study on Vehicle Insurance

Introduction

Insurance claim prediction is a critical task for the motor insurance industry, aiming to improve risk assessment and optimize policy pricing. In this study, we develop and evaluate a machine learning pipeline designed to predict claim amounts using motor insurance data. The approach combines extensive data preprocessing, feature engineering, and the application of five different algorithms—K-Nearest Neighbours (KNN), Gradient Boosting, LightGBM, XGBoost, and Random Forest—to capture complex relationships within the dataset. This work not only provides insights into the factors influencing claim payments but also compares model performance using various evaluation metrics.

The dataset, sourced from the Ethiopian Insurance Corporation, comprises 16 features including policy details, vehicle characteristics, and financial metrics. Key attributes include:

- **Policy and Vehicle Information:**
  - Dates of insurance (INSR_BEGIN, INSR_END)
  - Vehicle production year (PROD_YEAR)
  - Vehicle type (TYPE_VEHICLE), make (BRAND), and engine capacity (CCM_TON)
- **Financial Data:**
  - Insured value (INSURED_VALUE)
  - Annual premium (PREMIUM)
  - Claim amounts (CLAIM_PAID) – the target variable

Dataset

This dataset contains vehicle insurance policy records with 16 columns of features: SEX, INSR_BEGIN, INSR_END, EFFECTIVE_YR, INSR_TYPE, INSURED_VALUE, PREMIUM, PROD_YEAR, SEATS_NUM, TYPE_VEHICLE, CCM_TON, MAKE, USAGE, CLAIM_PAID, POLICY_DURATION, and VEHICLE_AGE (*https://www.kaggle.com/datasets/imtkaggleteam/vehicle-insurance-data*).

The dataset utilized in this study comprises a comprehensive collection of vehicle insurance records, capturing detailed policy and vehicle information over multiple years. It includes 16 key attributes that describe the insured vehicles, policy details, and associated financial metrics, making it a valuable resource for predictive modeling and insurance analytics. The data appears to span several years (e.g. 2011 to 2015 based on the sample), with each row representing an individual insurance policy tied to a specific vehicle. The dataset includes a mix of numerical, categorical, and temporal data, presenting opportunities for feature engineering and preprocessing. In Figure 4, a histogram shows the count of different data types in the dataset. The dataset has more float64 (7) and object (6) types than int64 (3), indicating a mix of numerical and categorical data.

This dataset is well-suited for regression tasks, such as predicting CLAIM_PAID based on vehicle characteristics, policy details, and usage patterns. Its temporal features (INSR_BEGIN, INSR_END, PROD_YEAR) enable the derivation of additional variables like policy duration and vehicle age, enhancing predictive power. The categorical variables (TYPE_VEHICLE, MAKE, USAGE) allow for segmentation and comparative analysis across vehicle types and purposes, while financial metrics (INSURED_VALUE, PREMIUM) provide insights into risk assessment and pricing strategies.

The dataset is split into labeled and unlabeled data based on the presence of the target variable (CLAIM_PAID). This separation allows the model to focus on the labeled data for training while keeping the unlabeled data for future predictions.

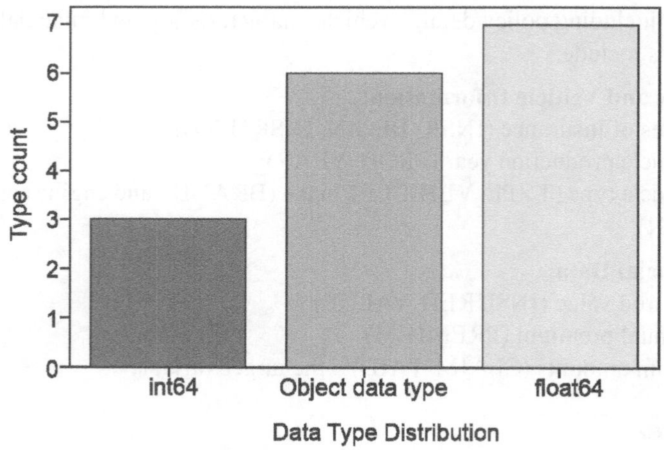

Fig. 4. Data Type Distribution

Figure 5 is a histogram with an overlaid density curve showing the distribution of claim paid amounts. The distribution is right-skewed. Most claims are below 150,000, peaking around 100,000–125,000 (~800 frequency). Few claims exceed 200,000, with outliers up to 350,000. The majority of claims are small, with a long tail of larger claims, reflecting a typical skewed distribution in insurance data.

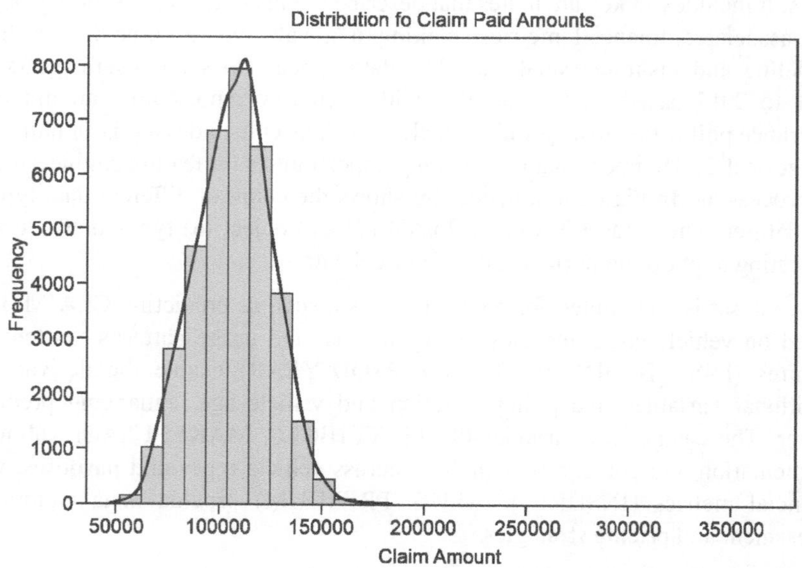

Fig. 5. Distribution of Claim Paid Amounts

Methodology

The methodology follows a comprehensive ML pipeline, comprising the following key steps:

- **Data Loading and Exploration**
  - The analysis begins with loading the dataset using pandas, followed by a preliminary exploration to understand its structure, including data types and distributions. To gain deeper insights, visualizations such as histograms (e.g. Figure 4, which illustrates the distribution of data types) and count plots are employed, effectively highlighting data imbalances and potential outliers that could influence subsequent modeling steps.
- **Data Preprocessing**
  - In the preprocessing phase, missing values are addressed by imputing them with the mode for relevant columns, ensuring the dataset remains complete and usable for analysis. The data is then split into labeled subsets containing the target variable and unlabeled subsets, enabling a focused approach to supervised learning tasks and optimizing the models' ability to learn from available claim data.
- **Feature Engineering and Handling Categorical Variables**
  - Feature engineering enhances the dataset by introducing new variables, such as policy duration, calculated as the difference between INSR_END and INSR_BEGIN, and vehicle age, derived from the difference between the insurance start year and production year, both of which provide temporal context to claim predictions. Additionally, mean encoding is applied to categorical features like TYPE_VEHICLE, replacing each category with the average claim amount for that group, effectively capturing its influence on the target variable CLAIM_PAID in a numerically meaningful way. Also, categorical variables such as SEX are transformed into numerical formats using mapping techniques to make them compatible with ML algorithms.
- **Outliers**
  - To mitigate the impact of extreme values, the Interquartile Range (IQR) method is utilized for outlier detection, either capping or removing these anomalies to stabilize model performance and reduce skew from unusual claim amounts.
- **Model Training and Tuning**
  - Five ML models—KNN, Gradient Boosting, LightGBM, XGBoost, and Random Forest—are trained on the preprocessed dataset to predict CLAIM_PAID. Hyperparameter tuning is conducted using GridSearchCV and RandomizedSearchCV, systematically exploring combinations to optimize each model's performance for accuracy and generalization. Prior to training, the dataset is smoothed with an Exponential Moving Average (EMA) using a span of 150, reducing noise and enhancing the models' ability to detect underlying trends in the data.
- **Feature Importance and Learning Curves**
  - To evaluate model behavior, learning curves for each algorithm (e.g. Figures 6-10) are visualized, showing how performance metrics evolve as the training data size increases, offering insights into potential overfitting or underfitting.

Feature importance is also assessed and displayed through horizontal bar plots (e.g. Figures 11-14), highlighting which variables, such as insured value or vehicle type, most strongly drive predictions, thus aiding in model interpretation and refinement.

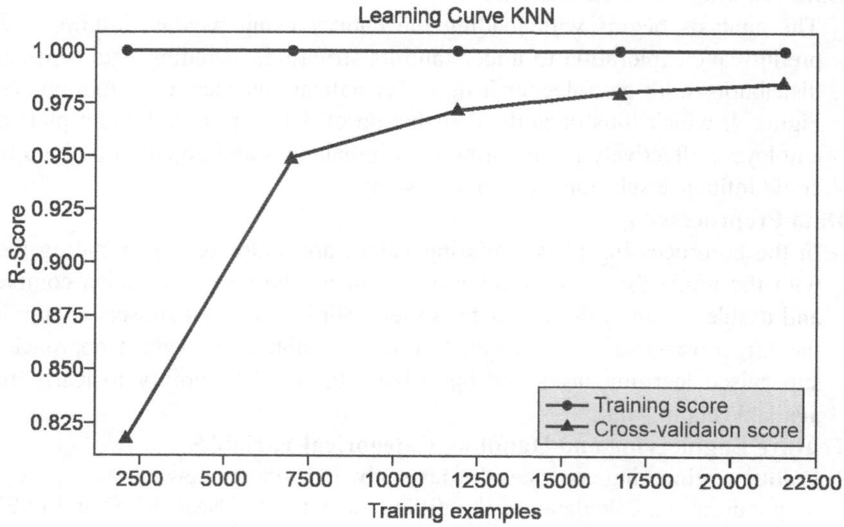

Fig. 6. Learning Curve KNN

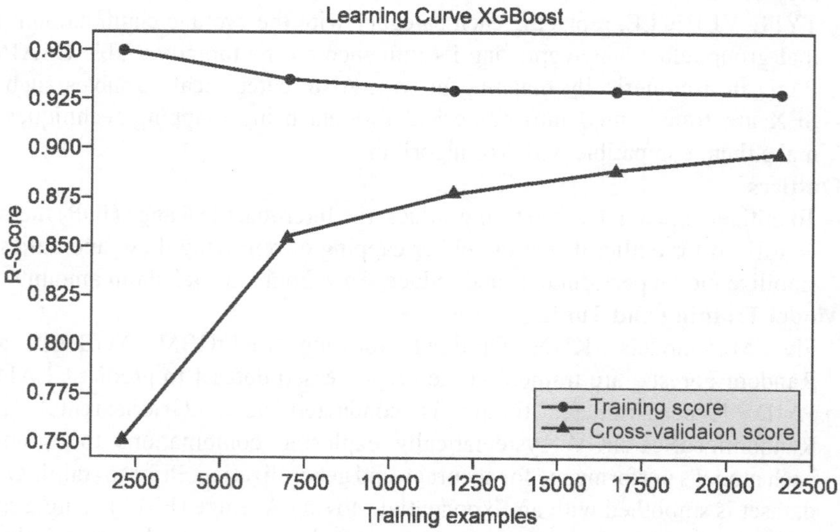

Fig. 7. Learning Curve XGBoost

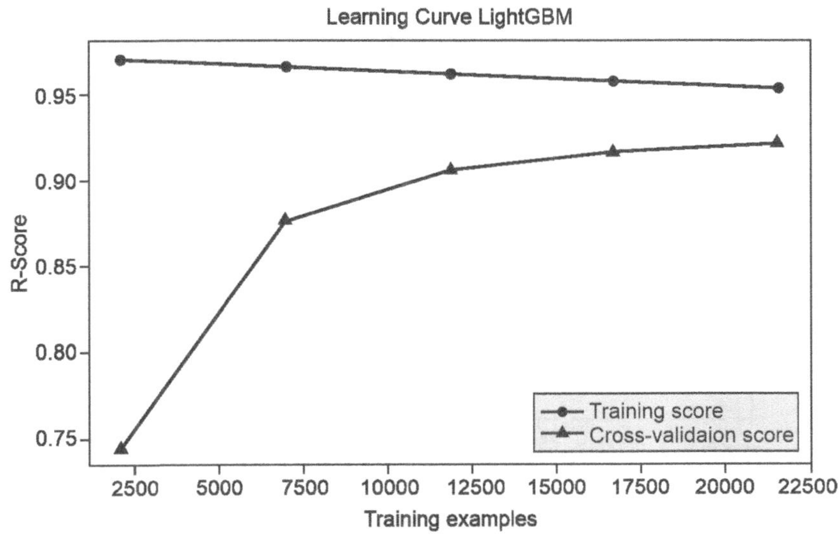

Fig. 8. Learning Curve LightGBM

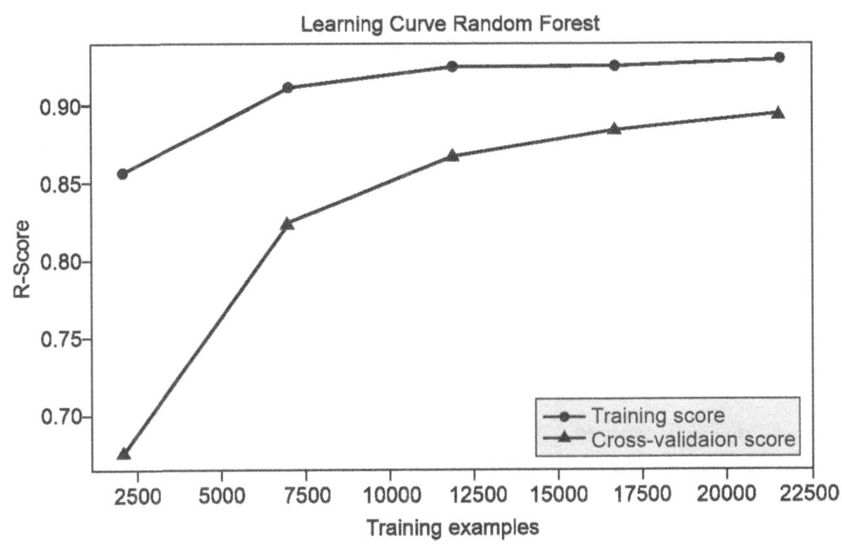

Fig. 9. Learning Curve Random Forest

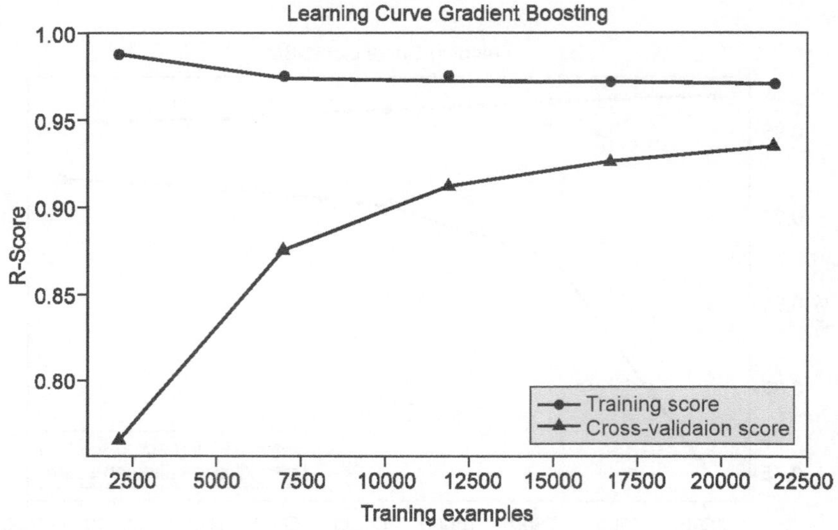

Fig. 10. Learning Curve Gradient Boosting

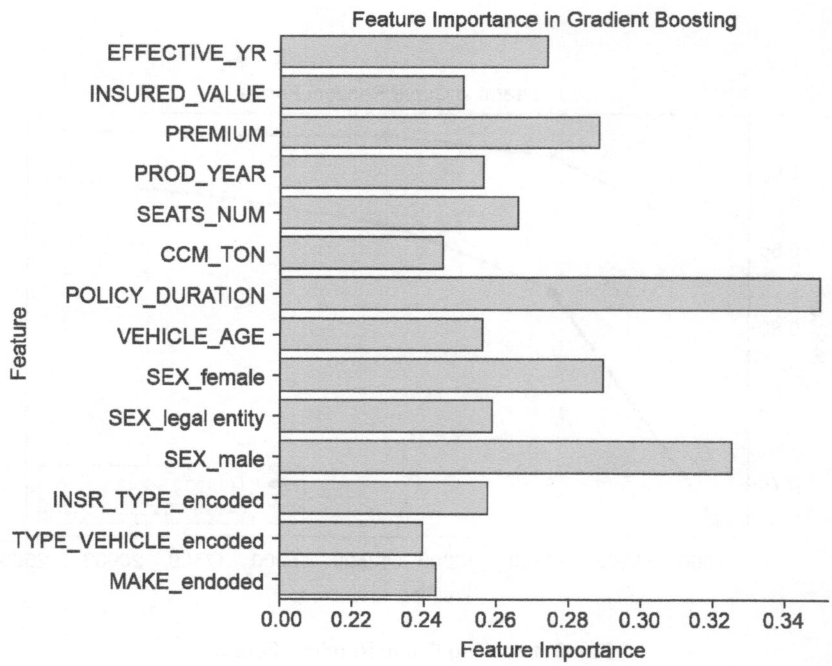

Fig. 11. Feature Importance in Gradient Boosting

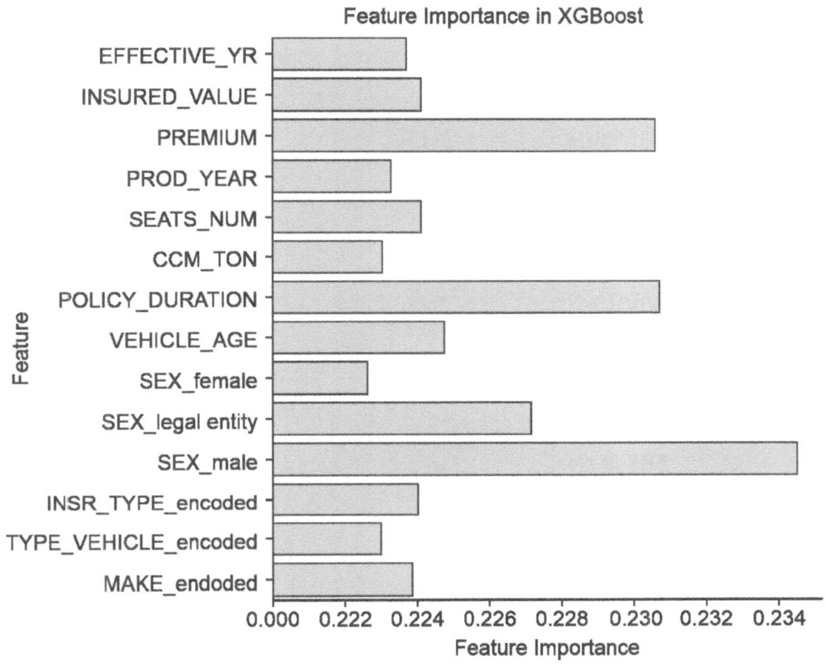

Fig. 12. Feature Importance in XGBoost

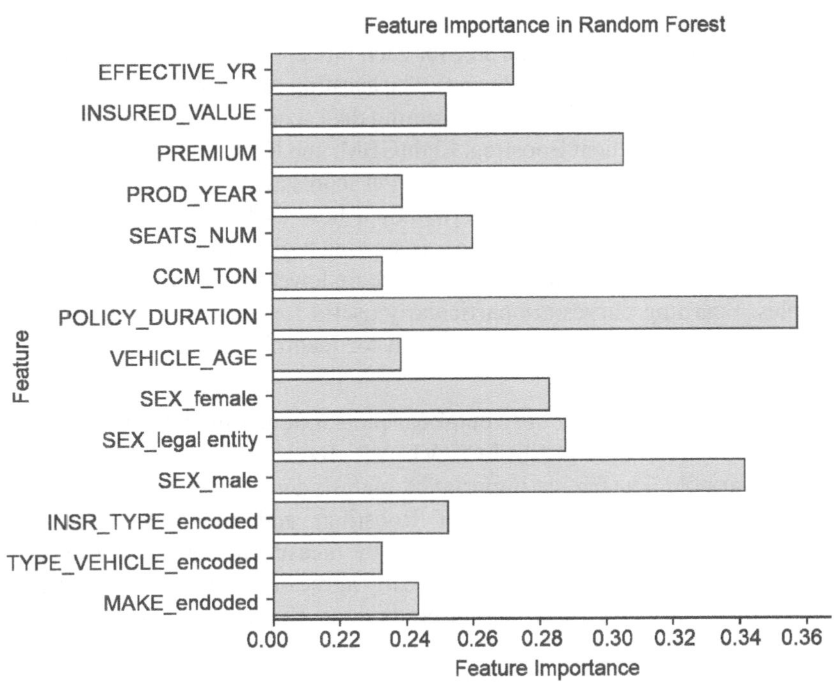

Fig. 13. Feature Importance in Random Forest

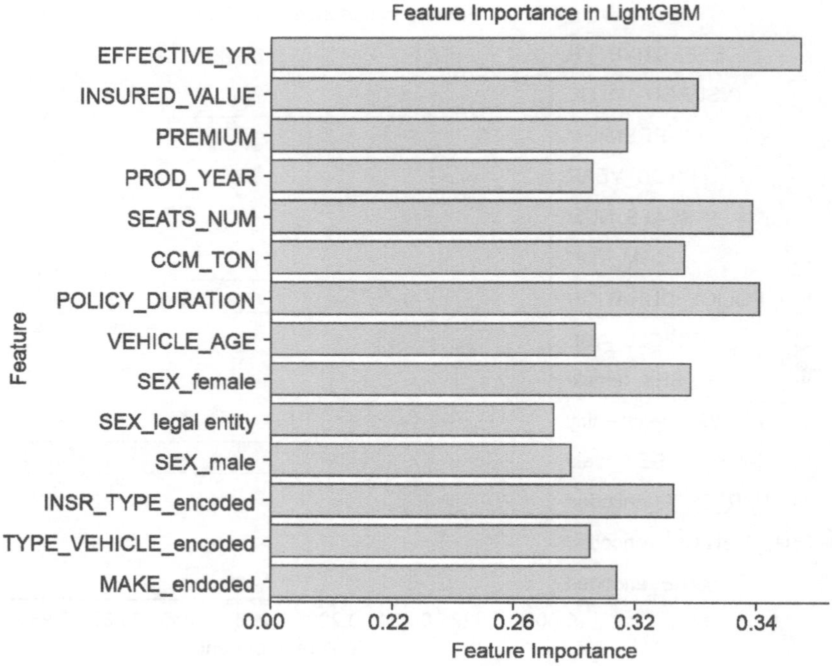

Fig. 14. Feature Importance in LightGBM

In Figures 6-10, the line plots showing training score (e.g., R^2) and cross-validation score vs. increasing training data size for each model (KNN, XGBoost, LightGBM, Gradient Boosting, and Random Forest). The learning curve plot analyzes how model performance evolves with increasing training data size for five algorithms (Random Forest, XGBoost, Gradient Boosting, LightGBM, and KNN). This visualization tool plots both training scores and cross-validation scores against the number of training examples, revealing important patterns about how each model learns from data. The curves typically show training scores starting high and gradually decreasing as more data is added, while validation scores begin lower and improve with additional examples. Learning curves are particularly useful for diagnosing whether models would benefit from more training data and for identifying potential overfitting or underfitting issues.

In Figures 11-14, a series of horizontal bar plots (one per model) show the relative importance of features (e.g. EFFECTIVE_YR, INSURED_VALUE) in predicting the target variable. The feature importance analysis across four tree-based models—Random Forest, XGBoost, Gradient Boosting, and LightGBM—shows how different predictors affect model decisions by measuring their importance. Each method works a bit differently, but they mostly agree on which features matter most, meaning these variables are strong for predictions. Features with lower importance scores still play a role but have a noticeably smaller effect on the model's decisions. Seeing the same trends in all models makes the findings more trustworthy for understanding results and choosing useful features.

Results

The performance of the five ML models—KNN, XGBoost, LightGBM, Gradient Boosting, and Random Forest—is evaluated using several metrics to assess their predictive accuracy and generalization capability on the insurance dataset. These metrics include Training R^2, Test R^2, Mean Absolute Error (MAE), and MSE, providing a comprehensive view of each model's strengths and limitations in predicting the CLAIM_PAID target variable. Table 1 and Figure 15 display these metrics.

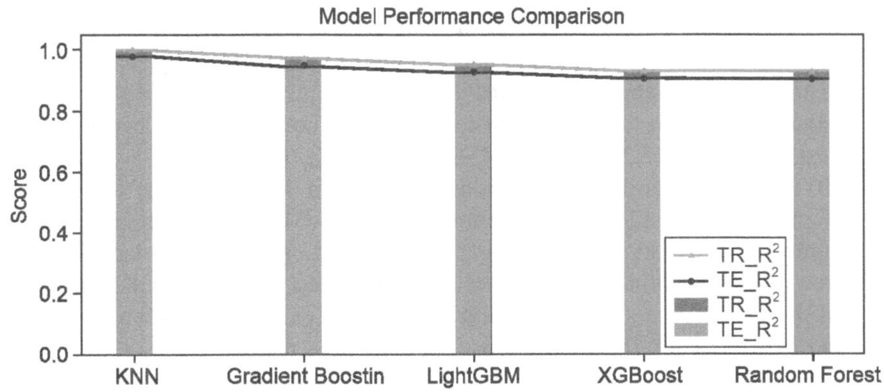

Fig. 15. Model Performance Comparison

Table 1 Simulation Results

Model	TR_R²	TE_R²	TR_MAE	TE_MAE	TR_MSE	TE_MSE
KNN	1.000000	0.987565	0.000000	1504.375183	0.000000e+00	5.006091e+06
Gradient Boosting	0.971194	0.944177	2551.117058	3635.933705	1.140064e+07	2.247401e+07
LightGBM	0.952495	0.928416	3380.219554	4155.215037	1.880096e+07	2.881948e+07
XGBoost	0.933100	0.910626	3921.587673	4638.564955	2.647710e+07	3.598150e+07
Random Forest	0.929422	0.904932	3890.172924	4681.902214	2.793279e+07	3.827363e+07

Figure 15 is a bar chart with overlaid line plots. It compares the performance of five ML models—KNN, Gradient Boosting, LightGBM, XGBoost, and Random Forest—using these metrics: TR_R^2 (Training R^2) and TE_R^2 (Test R^2).

Table 1 compares five ML models (KNN, Gradient Boosting, LightGBM, XGBoost, Random Forest) using R^2 (coefficient of determination), MAE, and MSE on training (TR) and test (TE) data.

- **Model Performance**
  - **KNN:** The KNN model achieves a perfect Training R^2 of 1.0, indicating an exact fit to the training data, which is expected given its nature of memorizing data points rather than learning generalized patterns. On the test set, it delivers an impressive Test R^2 of 0.987, showcasing very good predictive performance

on unseen data, suggesting that despite its tendency to overfit, it adapts well to the dataset's structure with minimal loss of accuracy.

- **Gradient Boosting:** Gradient Boosting strikes an effective balance between training and testing performance, with a Training R^2 of 0.971 and a Test R^2 of 0.944, reflecting its ability to capture patterns without overfitting excessively. It also demonstrates lower error rates compared to other models, evidenced by a Test MAE of 3,635.93 and Test MSE of 2.247401e+07, making it a standout choice for accurate and reliable predictions in this insurance context.
- **LightGBM:** The LightGBM model proves to be a strong model with a Training R^2 of 0.952 and a Test R^2 of 0.928, offering good accuracy on test data alongside its reputation for fast training and scalability. This efficiency, driven by its histogram-based approach, makes it a practical option for handling the dataset, balancing high performance with computational cost, as seen in its competitive Test MAE of 4,155.22 and Test MSE of 2.881948e+07.
- **XGBoost:** XGBoost performs admirably with a Training R^2 of 0.933 and a slightly lower Test R^2 of 0.911 compared to LightGBM, yet it remains a strong contender due to its robust boosting framework. Leveraging regularization and tree pruning, it produces stable results, with a Test MAE of 4,638.56 and Test MSE of 3.598150e+07, highlighting its reliability even if it doesn't reach the top tier of accuracy in this evaluation.
- **Random Forest:** Random Forest delivers a Training R^2 of 0.929 and a Test R^2 of 0.905, performing similarly to XGBoost in terms of stability and robustness, though it is slightly less accurate overall. Its ensemble averaging approach ensures dependable predictions, as reflected in a Test MAE of 4,681.90 and Test MSE of 3.827363e+07, positioning it as a solid, straightforward model despite not leading the pack in precision.

Table 2 Sample of the Insurance Policy Records

	INSR_TYPE	INSURED_VALUE	PREMIUM	TYPE_VEHICLE	MAKE	CCM_TON	CLAIM_PAID
1	Commercial	285451.24	3931.23	Pick-up	TOYOTA	2494.0	12152.73
2	Private	807727.15	4603.00	Automobile	DFM	1600.0	58217.74
3	Commercial	3400000.00	21617.71	Truck	IVECO	12880.0	159754.37
4	Private	473778.00	6121.78	Automobile	TOYOTA	2779.0	16100.00

Table 2 presents a sample of the insurance policy records used in our study. Each row in the table corresponds to a unique policy record and contains key attributes that influence the prediction of the claim paid amount. The columns include:

- **INSR_TYPE:** Indicates whether the policy is for a commercial or private entity.
- **INSURED_VALUE:** Represents the value of the insured asset.
- **PREMIUM:** The annual premium paid for the policy.
- **TYPE_VEHICLE:** Specifies the type of vehicle (e.g. Pick-up, Automobile, Truck).
- **MAKE**: Denotes the vehicle manufacturer.

- **CCM_TON:** Indicates the engine capacity, which can be a proxy for vehicle performance or risk.
- **CLAIM_PAID:** The target variable representing the claim amount paid by the insurer.

The models analyze patterns like:

- **How vehicle age (PROD_YEAR) affects claims:** For example, older vehicles like the 2010 Toyota pick-up might have higher maintenance issues, leading to larger claims.
- **Whether commercial vs. private vehicles have different claim patterns:** Commercial vehicles (like the pick-up in the first row, used for "own goods") might have higher claims due to more frequent use compared to private vehicles (e.g., row 2, a private DFM automobile).
- **How insured value correlates with claim amounts:** Policies with higher insured values (e.g., 3,400,000.00 in the third row) might result in larger claims, as seen with the 365,250.00 claim.
- **The relationship between premium costs and claims:** Higher premiums (e.g., 16,438.15 in the first row) might indicate higher risk, correlating with larger claims like 159,754.37.
- **How vehicle type (TYPE_VEHICLE) influences claims:** Different vehicle types (e.g., pick-up in the first row, truck in row 3, automobile in row 2) might have varying claim amounts due to their usage or accident risk.
- **The role of engine capacity (CCM_TON) in claims:** Vehicles with larger engines (e.g., 12,880) might be involved in more severe accidents, leading to higher claims.
- **The influence of vehicle make (MAKE) on claims:** Different makes (e.g., Toyota, IVECO, DFM) might have varying reliability or repair costs, affecting claim amounts.
- **How usage type (USAGE) affects claims:** Usage like "own goods" vs. "private" vs. "general cartage" might lead to different claim patterns due to varying risk levels.

These patterns help the models predict "CLAIM_PAID" for new policies by learning how these features interact and contribute to claim amounts. Table 2 is not just a representation of the raw data—it is a window into how various features interact to determine the claim paid. The diverse nature of the records emphasizes the importance of robust feature engineering and model selection, ensuring that our predictive framework can handle real-world variability in insurance claims.

The ML models—Random Forest, Gradient Boosting, KNN, LightGBM, and XGBoost—predict CLAIM_PAID by analyzing patterns in features like vehicle age (PROD_YEAR), insured value (INSURED_VALUE), premium costs (PREMIUM), vehicle type (TYPE_VEHICLE), make (MAKE), engine capacity (CCM_TON), and usage type (USAGE), uncovering relationships that drive claim amounts. Random Forest constructs an ensemble of decision trees, averaging their outputs to detect complex interactions, such as how older vehicles (e.g., a 2010 Toyota) or higher insured values (e.g., 3,400,000.00) correlate with larger claims due to maintenance needs or asset value. Gradient Boosting refines predictions iteratively by minimizing errors, effectively distinguishing between commercial usage (e.g., "own goods" pick-ups) and private use, where frequent operation often leads to higher claims. KNN relies on feature proximity, excelling when patterns like large engine capacity (e.g., 12,880 CCM) consistently tie to severe accidents and elevated claims, while LightGBM and XGBoost, advanced boosting models, optimize these relationships with speed and regularization, respectively, linking high premiums (e.g., 21,617.71) to increased risk and capturing variations in repair costs across makes like Toyota and IVECO. These models collectively learn that higher insured values often pair with larger claims and that commercial vehicles carry greater risk than private ones, applying these insights to new data.

To illustrate, consider two rows from the dataset (row 3 and row 4): a private Toyota automobile (Private, INSURED_VALUE = 473,778.00, PREMIUM = 6,121.78, TYPE_VEHICLE = Automobile, MAKE = TOYOTA, CCM_TON = 2,779.0, CLAIM_PAID = 16,100.00) and a commercial IVECO truck (Commercial, INSURED_VALUE = 3 ,400,000.00, PREMIUM = 21,617.71, TYPE_VEHICLE = Truck, MAKE = IVECO, CCM_TON = 12,880.0, CLAIM_PAID = 159,754.37). For the Toyota, the model notes a moderate insured value and low premium, signaling lower risk, reinforced by private usage and the reliable Toyota make with a modest 2,779 CCM engine, leading Random Forest to average tree predictions, Gradient Boosting to adjust residuals, or KNN to match similar low-risk policies, all converging on a modest CLAIM_PAID near 16,100.00. Conversely, the IVECO truck's high insured value and premium, coupled with commercial usage and a truck type prone to heavy operation, plus a 12,880 CCM engine linked to costly repairs, prompt LightGBM's optimized splits or XGBoost's regularized trees to predict a much larger CLAIM_PAID around 159,754.37, reflecting the learned association with high-risk features. KNN might find similar high-claim commercial trucks, while Random Forest and boosting models build rules like "commercial trucks with high insured values yield claims 10 times larger than private automobiles," with the stark feature contrast driving the prediction gap, closely approximating the actual values of 16,100.00 and 159,754.37.

EMERGING TRENDS AND FUTURE OUTLOOK

Generative AI and Deep Learning in Insurance

Generative AI and DL are rapidly emerging as transformative forces in the insurance industry. Generative AI creates synthetic data that can simulate various risk scenarios, thereby enhancing model training, especially in cases where real data is scarce or costly to obtain. DL architectures (such as convolutional neural networks and recurrent neural networks) improve predictive modeling capabilities, enabling insurers to detect fraud more accurately, assess risk in real time, and ultimately offer more personalized pricing and policy recommendations (Javeria and Colton 2024).

Quantum Computing and AI-Powered Risk Management

Quantum computing is poised to revolutionize risk management in insurance by offering unprecedented computational power to solve complex optimization problems and run highly detailed predictive simulations. Quantum algorithms, particularly Shor's algorithm, represent a significant threat to conventional encryption methods, highlighting the urgent need for quantum-resistant cryptographic strategies in the insurance industry's cybersecurity frameworks. This emerging technology promises to accelerate the processing of vast and intricate datasets, driving substantial improvements in risk forecasting, claim management, and investment strategies. Additionally, quantum computing's integration with AI enables highly sophisticated real-time threat detection and predictive analytics, strengthening insurers' proactive cybersecurity measures and resilience against sophisticated AI-driven cyber threats like deepfakes and adversarial attacks (Elmisery et al. 2025, Javeria and Colton 2024).

Emerging Trends and Future Outlook

Looking forward, the convergence of generative AI, DL, and quantum computing is set to redefine the insurance landscape. Insurers will increasingly leverage generative AI to simulate diverse risk scenarios, refine underwriting decisions, and bridge gaps in data scarcity through synthetic data generation. Simultaneously, advanced DL models will continuously enhance fraud detection accuracy, automate customer segmentation, and enable highly personalized customer interactions. At the same time, the advent of quantum computing will necessitate the adoption of quantum-resistant cryptographic protocols to safeguard sensitive financial information from quantum-enabled cyber threats. Quantum-enhanced risk analysis will significantly elevate the effectiveness of portfolio optimization and strategic decision-making, reinforcing the industry's operational and competitive advantage. Furthermore, the proactive integration of these technologies will support insurers in maintaining regulatory compliance and addressing evolving international standards concerning cybersecurity and data protection. As insurers embrace a holistic cybersecurity framework that combines AI-driven threat detection with quantum-resistant encryption, they will be better equipped to navigate the increasingly complex and dynamic financial ecosystem, ensuring sustainable growth and enhanced customer trust (Elmisery et al. 2025, Javeria and Colton 2024, Nthenge et al. 2023).

CONCLUSION

This chapter provided a comprehensive overview of AI, ML, and big data, exploring their interconnections and applications with a particular focus on the insurance industry. The foundational concepts of AI and big data have been discussed, examined the key characteristics of big data—volume, variety, velocity, and veracity—and analyzed how advanced storage and processing technologies facilitate the extraction of valuable insights. Furthermore, we mentioned the fundamentals of ML, classifying different types of learning methods and highlighting key algorithms that play an important role in predictive analytics and decision-making.

The integration of AI, ML, and big data is driving a paradigm shift in the insurance industry, enabling more accurate risk assessment, personalized policy offerings, and enhanced fraud detection. We explored specific applications of these technologies, including real-time risk monitoring using telematics and wearable devices, customer segmentation for targeted marketing, and the preprocessing and feature engineering techniques essential for optimizing ML models.

A practical case study on insurance claim prediction demonstrated how ML can be utilized to enhance risk evaluation and optimize policy pricing. Using a dataset sourced from the Ethiopian Insurance Corporation, we implemented a robust predictive pipeline that included data preprocessing, feature engineering, and model training using five ML algorithms: KNN, Gradient Boosting, LightGBM, XGBoost, and Random Forest. Our findings highlighted key insights into the dataset's composition, which included policy details, vehicle characteristics, and financial metrics.

The comparative analysis of model performance demonstrates the strengths and limitations of each algorithm. KNN exhibited a perfect fit on the training set but demonstrated strong generalization on test data as well. Gradient Boosting emerged as a high-performing model, striking a balance between accuracy and generalizability with minimal error rates. LightGBM offered a competitive alternative with fast training times and scalable performance, while XGBoost and Random Forest also provided robust predictions, albeit with slightly lower accuracy. These results emphasize the importance of selecting the appropriate algorithm based on the trade-offs between precision, interpretability, and computational efficiency. The findings of this study reinforce the transformative potential of AI-driven analytics in the insurance sector. By using ML and big data, insurers can refine their predictive models, improve underwriting decisions, detect fraudulent claims, and deliver more personalized services to policyholders. However, the success of AI in insurance heavily depends on high-quality data, proper feature engineering, and continuous model monitoring to ensure accuracy and fairness.

Looking ahead, there are several promising avenues for future research. Incorporating DL techniques, such as neural networks and transformer-based models, could enhance predictive accuracy for complex datasets. Additionally, integrating real-time data streams from IoT devices, telematics, and social media could provide insurers with even more granular insights into customer behavior and risk patterns. Ethical considerations, regulatory challenges, and data privacy concerns must also be addressed as AI-driven decision-making becomes increasingly prevalent in the insurance domain. In conclusion, AI, ML, and big data are reshaping the future of the insurance industry, driving efficiency, accuracy, and innovation. The ongoing advancements in these technologies will further enable insurers to make data-driven decisions, enhance customer satisfaction, and mitigate financial risks, ultimately fostering a more intelligent and responsive insurance ecosystem.

REFERENCES

Ali, A., Abd Razak, S., Othman, S.H., Eisa, T.A.E., Al-Dhaqm, A., Nasser, M., Elhassan, T., Elshafie, H., and Saif, A. (2022). Financial fraud detection based on machine learning: a systematic literature review. *Applied Sciences,* 12(19), 9637.

Arumugam, S., and Bhargavi, R. (2019). A survey on driving behavior analysis in usage based insurance using big data. *Journal of Big Data*, 6(1), 1–21.

Baruah, P., and Singh, P.P. (2023). Risk prediction in life insurance industry using machine learning techniques—A review. *In:* International Conference on Advances in IoT and Security with AI, 323–332.

Belhadi, A., Abdellah, N., and Nezai, A. (2023). The Effect of Big Data on the Development of the Insurance Industry, Sumy State University.

Charles, P.J., Bharathi, S.T., and Susmitha, V. (2018). Big data—Concepts, analytics, architectures—Overview. *Space*, 10, 8.

Chebbi, I., Boulila, W., and Farah, I.R. (2015). Big data: Concepts, challenges and applications. Computational Collective Intelligence. *In:* 7th International Conference, ICCCI, Proceedings, Part II, 638–647.

Christopher, B.W., Cossette, H., Lamontagne, L., and Marceau, E (2020). Machine Learning in P&C Insurance: A Review for Pricing and Reserving, *Risks*, 9(1), 4.

Das, S., Dey, A., Pal, A., and Roy, N. (2015). Applications of artificial intelligence in machine learning: Review and prospect. *International Journal of Computer Applications*, 115(9), 31–41.

De Ville, B. (2013). Decision trees. *Wiley Interdisciplinary Reviews: Computational Statistics*, 5(6), 448–455.

Du, K.L. and Swamy, M. (2013). Fundamentals of machine learning. *In:* Neural Networks and Statistical Learning, 15–65, Springer.

Eling, M., Gemmo, I., Guxha, D., and Schmeiser, H. (2024). Big data, risk classification, and privacy in insurance markets. *The Geneva Risk and Insurance Review*, 49(1), 75–126.

Ellili, N., Nobanee, H., Alsaiari, L., Shanti, H., Hillebrand, B., Hassanain, N., and Elfout, L. (2023). The applications of big data in the insurance industry: A bibliometric and systematic review of relevant literature. *The Journal of Finance and Data Science*, 9, 100102.

Elmisery, A.M., Sertovic, M., Zayin, A., and Watson, P. (2025). Cyber threats in financial transactions—Addressing the dual challenge of AI and quantum computing. arXiv:2503.15678.

Emmanuel, T., Maupong, T., Mpoeleng, D., Semong, T., Mphago, B., and Tabona, O. (2021). A survey on missing data in machine learning. *Journal of Big Data*, 8, 1–37.

Gandomi, A.H., Chen, F., and Abualigah, L. (2022). Machine learning technologies for big data analytics. *MDPI,* 11, 421.

García, S., Ramírez-Gallego, S., Luengo, J., Benítez, J.M., and Herrera, F. (2016). Big data preprocessing: Methods and prospects. *Big Data Analytics*, 1, 1–22.

Ghahramani, Z. (2003). Unsupervised learning. *In:* Summer School on Machine Learning, 3176, 72–112. Springer.

Ghojogh, B., Samad, M.N., Mashhadi, S.A., Kapoor, T., Ali, W., Karray, F., and Crowley, M. (2019). Feature selection and feature extraction in pattern analysis: A literature review. arXiv:1905.02845.

Gurney, K. (2018). An Introduction to Neural Networks. CRC press.

https://www.kaggle.com/datasets/imtkaggleteam/vehicle-insurance-data.

Islam, M., Chen, G., and Jin, S. (2019). An overview of neural network. *American Journal of Neural Networks and Applications*, 5(1), 7–11.

Jagatheesaperumal, S.K., Rahouti, M., Ahmad, K., Al-Fuqaha, A., and Guizani, M. (2021). The duo of artificial intelligence and big data for industry 4.0: Applications, techniques, challenges, and future research directions. *IEEE Internet of Things Journal*, 9(15), 12861–12885.

Javeria, H., and Colton, J. (2024). AI and Quantum Computing for Financial Services: A Proactive Approach to Cyber Security and Sustainable Growth. Preprint in ResearchGate.

Jia, W., Sun, M., Lian, J., and Hou, S. (2022). Feature dimensionality reduction: A review. *Complex and Intelligent Systems*, 8(3), 2663–2693.

Jiang, T., Gradus, J.L., and Rosellini, A.J. (2020). Supervised machine learning: A brief primer. *Behavior Therapy*, 51(5), 675–687.

Jović, A., Brkić, K., and Bogunović, N. (2015). A review of feature selection methods with applications. *In:* 38th International Convention on Information and Communication Technology, Electronics and Microelectronics (MIPRO), 1–6

Karthick, K. (2024). Comprehensive overview of optimization techniques in machine learning training. *Control Systems and Optimization Letters*, 2(1), 23–27.

Khan, N., Yaqoob, I., Hashem, I.A.T., Inayat, Z., Mahmoud Ali, W.K., Alam, M., Shiraz, M., and Gani, A. (2014). Big data: Survey, technologies, opportunities, and challenges. *The Scientific World Journal*, 2014(1), 712826.

Khanzode, K.C.A., and Sarode, R.D. (2020). Advantages and disadvantages of artificial intelligence and machine learning: A literature review. *International Journal of Library and Information Science (IJLIS)*, 9(1), 3.

Khoei, T.T., and Singh, A. (2024). Data reduction in big data: A survey of methods, challenges and future directions. *International Journal of Data Science and Analytics*, 18, 1–40.

Kühl, N., Schemmer, M., Goutier, M., and Satzger, G. (2022). Artificial intelligence and machine learning. *Electronic Markets*, 32(4), 2235–2244.

Kumar, P., Taneja, S., Özen, E., and Singh, S. (2023). Artificial intelligence and machine learning in insurance: A bibliometric analysis. *In:* Smart Analytics, Artificial Intelligence and Sustainable Performance Management in a Global Digitalised Economy, 191–202. Emerald Publishing Limited.

Kumar, S., and Bhatnagar, V. (2022). A review of regression models in machine learning. *Journal of Intelligent Systems and Computing*, 3(1), 40–47.

Kuppan, K., Acharya, D.B., and Divya, B. (2024). Foundational AI in Insurance and Real Estate: A Survey of Applications, Challenges, and Future Directions. *IEEE Access*, 12, 181282–181302.

Li, Y., and Ngom, A. (2015). Data integration in machine learning. *In:* IEEE International Conference on Bioinformatics and Biomedicine (BIBM), 1665–1671.

Liu, F., and Panagiotakos, D. (2022). Real-world data: A brief review of the methods, applications, challenges and opportunities. *BMC Medical Research Methodology*, 22(1), 287.

Mammone, A., Turchi, M., and Cristianini, N. (2009). Support vector machines. *Wiley Interdisciplinary Reviews: Computational Statistics*, 1(3), 283–289.

Muhamedyev, R. (2015). Machine learning methods: An overview. *Computer Modelling and New Technologies*, 19(6), 14–29.

Mwadulo, M.W. (2016). A Review on Feature Selection Methods for Classification Tasks, *International Journal of Computer Applications Technology and Research*, 5(6), 395–402.

Nasteski, V. (2017). An overview of the supervised machine learning methods. *Horizons*, 4, 51–62.

Navada, A., Ansari, A.N., Patil, S., and Sonkamble, B.A. (2011). Overview of use of decision tree algorithms in machine learning. *In:* IEEE Control and System Graduate Research Colloquium, 37–42.

Nthenge, J.K., Musyoka, D.F.M., and Mugo, D.D.M. (2023). Hybrid Machine Learning Algorithms for Risk Assessment in Insurance Industry: Empirical Review. Preprint in Heliyon. Available at SSRN 4498613.

Qazi, M., Tollas, K., Kanchinadam, T., Bockhorst, J., and Fung, G. (2020). Designing and deploying insurance recommender systems using machine learning. *Wiley Interdisciplinary Reviews: Data Mining and Knowledge Discovery*, 10(4), e1363, 1–33.

Qiang, W., and Zhongli, Z. (2011). Reinforcement learning model, algorithms and its application. *In:* International Conference on Mechatronic Science, Electric Engineering and Computer (MEC), 1143–1146.

Qiu, J., Wu, Q., Ding, G., Xu, Y., and Feng, S. (2016). A survey of machine learning for big data processing. *EURASIP Journal on Advances in Signal Processing*, 2016, 1–16.

Rane, N.L., Paramesha, M., Choudhary, S.P., and Rane, J. (2024). Machine learning and deep learning for big data analytics: A review of methods and applications. *Partners Universal International Innovation Journal*, 2(3), 172–197.

Rao, T.R., Mitra, P., Bhatt, R., and Goswami, A. (2019). The big data system, components, tools, and technologies: A survey. *Knowledge and Information Systems*, 60, 1165–1245.

Raschka, S. (2018). Model evaluation, model selection, and algorithm selection in machine learning. arXiv:1811.12808.

Reka, A., Kosova, R., Hajrulla, S., and Kosova, A.M. (2025). The Use of Big Data in Insurance Industry. A Review of Models, Techniques and Factors, *In:* 2nd International Conference on Modern and Advanced Research, 170–177.

Roh, Y., Heo, G., and Whang, S.E. (2019). A survey on data collection for machine learning: A big data-AI integration perspective. *IEEE Transactions on Knowledge and Data Engineering*, 33(4), 1328–1347.

Rong, S., and Bao-Wen, Z. (2018). The research of regression model in machine learning field. *In:* MATEC Web of Conferences, 176, 1–4, EDP Sciences.

Simon, G.J., and Aliferis, C. (2024). Artificial Intelligence and Machine Learning in Health Care and Medical Sciences: Best Practices and Pitfalls, Springer Nature.

Varadarajan, V., and Kakumanu, V.K. (2024). Evaluation of risk level assessment strategies in life Insurance: A review of the literature. *Journal of Autonomous Intelligence*, 7(5), 1–19.

Visalakshi, S., and Radha, V. (2014). A Literature Review of Feature Selection Techniques and Applications: Review of Feature Selection in Data Mining. *In:* IEEE International Conference on Computational Intelligence and Computing Research, 1–6.

Watson, H.J. (2014). Tutorial: Big data analytics: Concepts, technologies, and applications. *Communications of the Association for Information Systems*, 34(1), 65.

Ying, X. (2019). An overview of overfitting and its solutions. *Journal of Physics: Conference Series*, 1168, 1–6.

Younas, M. (2019). Research challenges of big data. *Service Oriented Computing and Applications*, 13, 105–107.

Zhou, L., Pan, S., Wang, J., and Vasilakos, A.V. (2017). Machine learning on big data: Opportunities and challenges. *Neurocomputing*, 237, 350–361.

2

Risk Assessment and Underwriting with AI

Sara Ramzani[*], *Peter Konhaeusner, Ahmad Abu-Alkheil, Phungmayo Horam, Vahab Esfandani, and Mohammad Amin Borghei*

EVOLVING INSURANCE RISK ASSESSMENT: TRANSITION FROM TRADITIONAL TO AI-DRIVEN MODELS

There are many years of experience in the field of manual risk assessment techniques and their application is widespread across the insurance industry; the insurance industry has been using it with emphasis on client demographics, health history and behavioral characteristics. Such traditional methods of underwriting can no longer meet the present underwriting requirements. Under the traditional underwriting approach, decision-making is largely based on the fixed actuarial models as the applicants are separated into cohorts based on factors such as age, sex, occupation, educational level, and location (Maier et al. 2020, Jaiswal 2023, Yang 2021). The current procedure works, but it cannot keep up with the emerging market expectations of rapidity, accuracy, and customization (Fung, et al. 2021).

However, the prevailing methods of risk assessment rely on such large volumes of data that they cannot be processed effectively. Underwriters must rely on small prediction models and historical data that are unable to capture pattern shifts and environmental changes (Kelley et al. 2018). However, the prevailing methods of risk assessment rely on such large volumes of data that they cannot be processed effectively. Underwriters must rely on small prediction models and historical data that are unable to capture pattern shifts and environmental changes (Agu et al. 2022).

With the shift in underwriting methods, artificial intelligence (AI) is beginning to transform risk assessment operations. Unlike fixed statistical approaches, machine learning (ML), natural language processing (NLP), and big data analytics utilize multiple data sources in real time (Maier et al. 2020, Kelley et al. 2018). Based on this data, these models enable the creation of adaptive underwriting frameworks that respond dynamically to the information received during the application process. This means insurers can maintain more standardized and streamlined underwriting operations, enhancing the precision of individualized risk evaluations.

Gisma University of Applied Sciences, Berlin, Germany
[*] *Corresponding author:* sara.ramzani@gisma.com

DOI: 10.1201/9781003621119-2

In underwriting technology, AI is applied to take advantage of the real time behavioral patterns in combination with sensor input features in order to assess the risk models. The main strength of AI-based underwriting is the ability to use ongoing streams of data collected by wearables, smart devices, and digital platforms (Maier et al. 2020, Kelley et al. 2018). However, risk recognition in most instances is only realized after an unfortunate incident has already taken place limiting insurers to post-factum predictions of exposure patterns and subsequent changes in preventive actions and premium policies.

AI-based underwriting automates basic processes, enhancing decision-making. Traditionally, employees filled out paper forms, and individual review processes often produced late or inconsistent results. Insurers now use AI-powered technologies to accelerate underwriting cycles—from weeks to just hours (Agu et al. 2022)—through automated data extraction, anomaly detection, and predictive modeling. However, according to Jaiswal (2023), three main challenges remain: explainability, regulatory compliance, and bias mitigation. Fung et al. (2021) suggest that insurers can adopt Explainable AI (XAI) frameworks to ensure accountability and regulatory compliance when using black-box AI models.

It is not a temporary change in the underwriting process but a seismic shift in the risk-underwriting process. With the help of ML (real time data processing and advance analytics) and eliminating operational inefficiencies, it becomes easier to make more precise underwriting. In addition to that, it can be used as a risk assessment to each individual customer as well. In some cases, insurance companies can use models that use artificial intelligence to reap the benefits of innovation, both aligning the advances in technology with the moral requirements and, as a result, providing a fair and effective underwriting process (Jaiswal 2023, Maier et al. 2020).

LIMITATIONS OF CONVENTIONAL UNDERWRITING METHODS

Traditionally, underwriting has been a manual, human-led process based on static risk models crafted using known variables: age, gender, and occupational status. However, these methods, first adopted decades ago, are no longer compatible with modern data-driven environments due to their many limitations (Jaiswal 2023). These occurrence-based models rely on historical statistics and fail to account for dynamic changes in risk elements. As a result, policies are often mispriced, and premiums are inequitably distributed due to rigid classification systems that ignore current health indicators, behavior, and financial conditions of applicants (Maier et al. 2020, Pereira 2024).

The outcomes produced by manual underwriting are highly variable and prone to human error. The subjectivity involved in evaluating applications and issuing policies increases delays and inconsistency (Maier et al. 2020). This includes pricing discrepancies, conflicting risk evaluations, and related inefficiencies (Pereira 2024). When datasets become large, traditional methods struggle to scale or process information efficiently. While modern insurers do have access to sophisticated data sources—such as digital footprints, health records, and location tracking—as noted by Kelley et al. (2018), their legacy underwriting systems are unable to integrate or analyze this information effectively. Agu et al. (2022) highlight how this inability to process and understand complex data prevents algorithms from identifying risk patterns, thereby weakening fraud detection and overall risk assessment capabilities.

However, static models are not able to respond to the conversion of basic behavior and environmental events that occur in every case of underwriting. Static risk: If there are no changes in personal circumstances, no changes in new risks, nor do new risks change the financial standings and underwriting criteria when those policies are issued (Jaiswal 2023). Although the assessments are old, they are not capable of showing the changing levels of risk exposure over time (Maier et al. 2020). In relation to digital transformation, in terms of the insurance industry, exposure would be concerned with the problems of insurance product consumers when this is normally a manual process of underwriting and customer problems from the market. Because of data, the real-time, real-market risk evaluation for every insurance customer (Maier et al. 2020, Maier et al. 2019) is being forced by modern insurance with data and will continue to be forced until a critical mass of enterprises recognizes the need for it.

Its three specific challenges shall arise due to its outdated models; taxpayer processes; and its inability to explore the current data resources it has access to. AI-powered underwriting is becoming more mainstream, and insurers will have to develop automated real-time adaptive models of risk (Pereira 2024).

KEY DIFFERENCES—APPROACHES AND OUTCOMES

More than in the traditional way, the methodology and data processing are different in traditional underwriting with AI-driven assessment, and the traditional underwriting is strictly compared by results of insurance policy assessment, and its results are widely different. For instance, the risk of underwriting systems, according to the above theory, utilizes static actuarial models in the process of evaluation of risk, coupled with the evaluation of historical data along with demographic standards such as gender and age as well as occupation (Jaiswal 2023, Boodhun and Jayabalan 2018). Manual underwriting is therefore based on subjectivity and results in longer processing times, different outcomes, and requires human expertise on rule-based methods (Pereira 2024). Big data analytics and automation coupled with AI technology were used to foster the underwriting process with the ease of ML algorithms to adapt in real time to current situations. The actionable, accurate risk profiles are built by AI systems on the basis of human behavioral records and predictive analytical information from analysis of digital traces (Maier et al. 2020, 2019).

In their usage methods, they have the core separation in the data processing technique and the method of data use. Review processes in traditional underwriting are only based on reviewing and underwriting completely constrained structured information using CRUD (Create, Read, Update, and Delete) operations and rule sets that cannot quantify 'huge risk elements' and cannot identify emerging patterns

(Jaiswal 2023). The reason for this is the ongoing development of risk models under AI underwriting using behavioral insights in real time and through integration of advanced data analytics with sensor technologies (Maier et al. 2020, Fung et al. 2021).

Its approach to the comparison is mentioned mostly on the basis of the performance of the automated execution and decision-making capabilities. Manual underwriting is very much human intervention-based, and this leads to longer processing times and higher operational costs. Automated risk assessment, as well as the calculation of premiums in underwriting, is developed and utilized, enabling shorter processing times and more sustainable assessments (Pereira 2024). The use of AI technology in this case enables insurance companies to write policies faster, manage the business at a lower cost, and reduce human errors associated with traditional protocols (Jaiswal 2023).

Finally, AI-based systems provide a boost in predictive accuracy of the underwriting processes by revealing hidden correlations between variables that human underwriters often struggle to identify. Applicants are evaluated in traditional underwriting practices by placing them into broad risk categories based on limited parameter terms. AI models are used by insurers to go through a very detailed risk assessment process so that they can come up with customized coverage plans with suitable price rates, simultaneously increasing cyber insurance customer satisfaction and improving risk assessment (Boodhun and Jayabalan 2018).

As the insurance industry deals with new challenges—such as XAI, regulatory compliance, or bias management—Pereira (2024) and Filabi and Duffy (2021) claim that the introduction of AI underwriting brings its own problems. Transparency in the human process of underwriting is higher because of guidelines that dictate how decisions need to be justified in a familiar regulatory landscape—slower, less adaptable. The explainability frameworks required for insurers to ensure fair and ethical decision-making were demonstrated by Filabi and Duffy (2021), because risk assessment processing is difficult to understand due to its unique and often unexplainable nature for humans. The core differences between traditional underwriting systems and AI-powered underwriting lie in the usage of data, data processing, automation, and predictive capability. Such schemes involving AI-based underwriting solutions provide speedy evaluations and accurate results for tailored policies, while traditional systems remain bound to manual routines and unchanged analytical methods. To achieve faster AI adoption growth, insurers must sustain technological progress, keep methodologies open, and comply with regulatory requirements to ensure fair and accurate risk assessments (Maier et al. 2020, Jaiswal 2023).

DATA SOURCES AND INPUT PARAMETERS

Demographic data, medical records, and historical claims are the basis for underwriting purposes, which traditionally rely on such data sources. Risk assessment has based its foundational standards on describing the risk profiles of applicants and defining the sources referred to above. Bahnhof Life Insurance used to assess mortality risks using underlying health and behavioral patterns for numerous years (Maier et al. 2020). The methods behind the data processing require large time commitments, which slow down underwriting procedures (Bozyiğit et al. 2020).

The use of AI technology to bring in new kinds of data in the underwriting process is an improvement. These are used to merge decisions involving health behavior with lifestyle and environmental details for finer granularity (Jaiswal 2023). Baruah et al. (2023) analyze health insurance risk through underwriting using geographical information systems (GIS) data, including air pollution and living in proximity to industrial areas. However, alternative methods of data collection allow for a very detailed risk perception that is not possible to obtain using traditional methods.

Telematics technology, in itself, has enriched insurers through Internet of Things (IoT), revolutionizing how data is collected, stored, searched, analyzed, and used for more significant insight and transformation. Health and home monitoring IoT devices operate in real time to deliver data to insurance companies to better assess risk. Telematics technology is used by the insurance industry to obtain driver data in order to develop personalized insurance premiums based on risk identity (Agu et al. 2022). Such technologies are utilized by insurance companies to shift from traditional static risk evaluation to dynamic risk evaluation and thereby provide personalized insurance services.

Social media profiles and digital activity trails are big data sets that underwriters are now employing in their assessments. After people showcase their lifestyles and behavioral patterns, these online platforms reveal risk profiles. According to Agu et al. (2022), risk can be determined by using health-related behaviors and financial stability information gathered from social media activity. Due to ethical concerns, privacy issues, and the implications of using this type of data in the underwriting process, it is problematic and requires rigorous data quality and validation diligence.

This very data is key to ensuring quality and validating the information collected with the help of AI-driven underwriting. Hazardous risk assessment errors will senselessly and automatically generate discriminatory practices if poor-quality data are used. Boodhun and Jayabalan (2018) mention that the use of feature selection and dimensionality reduction techniques leads to better data quality, which ultimately results in better model performance. To create a more transparent underwriting process, Shapley Additive Explanation (SHAP), along with other XAI approaches (Nguyen et al. 2023), is used.

Many regulatory issues must be tackled when using new data sources for underwriting. If prohibited characteristics are used in AI decision-making, unfair discrimination may occur, resulting in biased outcomes. This lack of sufficient capacity to address such challenges has given rise to the need for new certification systems and ethical standards to guide the ethical deployment of AI (Filabi and Duffy 2021). In African regions with multiple regulatory frameworks, it is important to ensure compliance with local laws when using AI to support financial inclusion efforts (Agu et al. 2022).

AI is all about advanced risk modeling but such approach to decisions are highly dependent on algorithmic decision making and that is an ethical question. The monitoring of the AI underwriting practices is necessary in order to ensure the fairness in process, since lack of transparency and accountability are sources of bias.

ETHICAL CONSIDERATIONS AND BIAS MANAGEMENT

Bias management is just as important as resolving emerging ethical problems to allow insurers to establish an accountable, fair, and transparent risk assessment system for underwriters. A major ethical issue with AI underwriting is that its algorithms can show discriminatory behavior toward certain populations due to incomplete or inappropriately selected training variables (Filabi and Duffy 2021). Because historical insurance data is used as input into AI systems—and this data contains historical underwriting decision biases (Loi and Christen 2021)—this can result in discriminatory pricing that perpetuates past injustices.

AI underwriting finds its critical problems via the implementation of neutral appearing factors, which include indirect indicators of prohibited elements such as gender, race, and socioeconomic status (SES) (Filabi and Duffy 2021). Without proper monitoring and controls in the operation of AI models, they will make social inequalities worse. However, due to the need for bias detection methods to incorporate adversarial debiasing techniques to train data re-weighting and fairness awareness in the algorithm implementation, these methods must be used for fair risk assessment (Loi and Christen 2021).

The primary issue that needs to be addressed about AI underwriting models is that they cannot produce explainable results. This means that the decision making system of the AI system remains unintelligible to insurers, regulators and consumers alike (Owens et al. 2022). If insurers cannot demonstrate their AI decision process to consumers, their risk score and their premium is not understandable by the consumer, and so AI-driven decisions are not trusted by policyholders. SHAP, and Local Interpretable Model-agnostic Explanations (LIME) approaches offer insurers the ability to provide informative explanations of the risk score that AI has produced for them, as Owens et al. (2022) explain.

An important factor for regulatory compliance in notable deployment of ethical AI solutions is regulatory compliance. Several bodies are in place that rigidly regulate AI discriminatory practices and require explanation of automated decisions to comply with their accountability standards (Du Preez et al. 2024). Insurers' AI-based systems should adhere to existing legal codes such as the European GDPR and newly developing national and international AI laws in order to meet regulatory requirements and protect people's rights (Mullins et al. 2021). Continuous auditing, fairness checks, and human intervention systems must support regulatory standards to prevent unethical AI practice (Filabi and Duffy 2021).

The ethical problem of data privacy protection related to the application of AI systems in underwriting activities is central. To derive accurate outcomes of evaluations,

AI risk assessment systems need large feats of information clusters that include private, sensitive client data. The mismanagement of customer data may breach regulations and jeopardize consumer privacy rights (Agu et al. 2022). When insurers adopt privacy-enhancing technologies such as differential privacy and federated learning, personal data is properly and securely used (Mullins et al. 2021). Without transparency and with embedded biases in AI underwriting, there is a natural increase in ethical risk, regulatory noncompliance, and exceptional data privacy vulnerabilities. These risks can be mitigated through strong regulatory compliance, fairness-aware AI models, and the implementation of explanatory frameworks. The adoption of ethical AI systems ensures that insurance underwriting is carried out according to the necessary criteria of trustworthiness, fairness, and accountability (Filabi and Duffy 2021, Loi and Christen 2021).

CORE AI TECHNOLOGIES IN INSURANCE RISK ASSESSMENT

AI technologies have been adopted by insurers to introduce important changes in how they undertake risk assessment for underwriting purposes. Insurers use AI-driven models to aid in their large data collection processes, discern minute elements of risk, and streamline underwriting workflows (Yang 2021, Boodhun and Jayabalan 2018). Several primary AI technologies help insurance providers make better decisions regarding risk in the insurance sector.

Machine Learning for Risk Prediction

Through ML algorithms, patterns get recognized while risk prediction works by studying historical information alongside behavioral data. Actuarial models with static statistical rules differ from machine-learning models which learn through the continuous processing of new data entry points (Jaiswal 2023). The application of gradient boosting trees and random forests enhances predictive underwriting accuracy, according to research conducted by Yang (2021). The industry utilizes Multiple Linear Regression and REPTree models alongside each other to improve policy price accuracy through better mortality risk prediction techniques (Boodhun and Jayabalan 2018).

Natural Language Processing for Data Extraction

The automation of underwriting processes receives support from NLP, which extracts unstructured information from customer documents, medical records, and claims reports. The implementation of NLP has accelerated insurance document review speeds, boosting efficiency during risk assessment and fraud prevention (Chaubey and Singh 2020). The combination of NLP and AI-powered virtual agents improves customer interactions and claims management processes, reducing administrative workloads (Agu et al. 2022).

Computer Vision for Asset Risk Assessment

Property and casualty insurance companies use computer vision systems to measure risks associated with physical assets. Through AI-driven image analysis, insurers achieve greater accuracy in detecting property damage, verifying claims, and inspecting automobile accident reports (Rehman 2024). Visual recognition technology, alongside video analysis methods, helps reduce deceptive claims and expedite asset damage evaluations, enabling quicker dispute resolution.

Deep Learning for Complex Risk Analysis

Insurers use artificial neural networks and other deep learning algorithms to process extensive risk-related data. These analytical techniques reveal hidden relationships between risks, offering superior underwriting accuracy compared to traditional actuarial practices (Baruah et al. 2023). Deep learning models allow insurers to process electronic health records and deliver individualized life and health insurance underwriting (Boodhun and Jayabalan 2018).

Big Data Analytics for Risk Modeling

Analysis of large volumes of structured and unstructured data through big data analytics reveals hidden risk factors previously inaccessible (Jaiswal 2023). AI predictive analytics systems integrate various risk indicators, enabling insurers to create precise underwriting assessments and develop personalized insurance solutions (Maier et al. 2020).

Risks during underwriting assessment evolve under AI technological advancements, including ML, alongside NLP systems and deep learning capabilities, together with computer vision analytics and big data analytics and analysis systems. Insurance businesses enhance accuracy and automation through these tools while detecting previously undetectable risks (Jaiswal 2023, Yang 2021). Insurers should maintain their focus on model explainability alongside transparency and model compliance because these elements guarantee responsible deployment of AI systems in underwriting activities (Filabi and Duffy 2021).

AI-POWERED RISK MODELING IN INSURANCE

It has the application to be able to better and, in real time, assess the risks of the insurers. This is how real-time data processing can facilitate better use of predictive analytics on an AI-based risk model, enabling it to manage real-time data as opposed to the conventional risk model solely based on fixed data and historical records (Boodhun 2018, Jaiswal 2023).

Predictive modeling systems use ML algorithms to examine past claims, customer behavioral signals, as well as external data to understand future risk metrics. Predictive power of multivariate linear regression, decision trees (REPTree), and artificial neural networks (ANNs) are added to the effect, which means that the insurance company can make better underwriting choices and price better, with less uncertain pricing (Boodhun and Jayabalan 2018, Bhalla 2012). The risk scoring systems are then developed by the AI technology using this to generate numbers that include such things as lifestyle, an individual's behavior, and overall risk standards. Recently, static scoring strategies are approached using models that make individual profiles of risk instead of risk groups, as is practiced widely (Jaiswal 2023). The risk intelligence model (RIM) works on several other factors beyond the conventional actuarial elements to enhance the accuracy and fairness in underwriting (Jaiswal 2023)

Having a dynamic assessment, which may be performed as opposed to a static framework, insurers will have a chance to monitor risk actively and constantly based on data input, since their underwriting capabilities or ability to rely on AI evolve. They enable insurers to not only keep track of gradual patients' health changes, which lead to the creation of a matching modification of the required risk estimate adjustment (Kulinskaya et al. 2021), but also decrease the costs that a disease with cost growth potential entails. As such, this approach leads to increased accuracy and adaptability in the risk assessment. With live data processing that AI systems provide overnight, one other advantage to insurers is that risk can be evaluated at once by risk scoring and policy amendment (Jaiswal 2023). Current provider methods such as mail, voice calls, and online chat will be phased out for this capability, allowing insurers to have instant data insights in a war against fraud and to make better policy products and improvements on new risks (Agu et al. 2022).

Rigorous validation and testing procedures of the models are conducted for both precision and reliability of the models as a basis of the AI risk models. The evaluation's risk models' accuracy, sensitivity and specificity rates, and precision rates make up the insurance performance analytics (Elbhrawy et al. 2023). Then the data balancing techniques that utilize resampling are resampling techniques, as they improve the stability of the predictive model (Elbhrawy et al. 2023).

Applying ML concepts with real-time data makes a big change in the power and effectiveness of AI risk modeling, such as better risk assessment and fraud prevention for insurance underwriting. As noted by Elbhrawy et al. (2023) and Jaiswal (2023), there will continue to be tests on the valuation and fairness assessments alongside compliance for as long as insurers continue to develop these models, which ought to be trusted and dependable in the AI-driven risk evaluation system.

Automated Underwriting Systems – Rule-Based Systems vs. AI Systems

The risk evaluation and decision-making performance was improved and helped in enhancing operational efficiency while transitioning from rule-based to AI-based underwriting systems. Static decision trees and defined criteria in the rules that govern them, rule-based underwriting systems work with principles from logic that are applied to evaluate risk. However, fixed thresholds in these systems are rigid such that they result in effective standardized risk evaluations in the sense that only high-risk factors below some a priori specified threshold are indicated (Pereira 2024, Boodhun and Jayabalan 2018, Jaiswal 2023).

Underwriting with AI technology involves the use of ML and predictive analysis to analyze data in real time to determine the risk. The main difference between the rule-based systems and AI models is the way they update data, where the AI models learn and improve with respect to records from both historical and real-time data, whereas rule-based systems don't have this capability. This helps the insurer deliver customized policy costs and verify more efficiently with trend analysis (Jaiswal 2023).

The rule-based systems have the biggest weakness of their inability to anticipate conditions that occur in nonstandard boundaries and therefore cannot adapt to those conditions. Inaccuracy of these characteristics, in fact, results in misplacement of risk by insurers and lost business opportunities when they place applicants beyond their defined risk profile. To solve this problem, AI underwriting systems combine behavioral data and external market trends with personalized insights to predict more accurate risk and thus provide more targeted policy options (Pereira 2024).

The choice between these models is marked by the difference in the speed at which they make decisions, as well as their level of automation. Delays are caused by policy approval as human beings are required to handle unexpected situation. However, Dubey et al. (2018) discusses how guiding AI underwriting through ML of circumstances is made possible which enables the insurers to get faster speed in issuing policies with higher degrees of accuracy (Dubey et al. 2018). As it scans the document and processes the documents, it further automates customer support (Jaiswal 2023).

Three separate problems exist for insurers in deploying AI underwriting systems because of explainability issues, data management demands, and regulatory compliance obligations. In terms of comparison, although these systems generate a transparent workflow of decision-making, they can be easily readapted and understood by regulators during the justification process. According to Filabi and Duffy (2021), black-box AI systems will require an explainability framework to go through compliance and accountability that the insurers have to design. The reason for this comes in the form of an insurance industry that needs data-powered automated decision processes, and AI underwriting is now the standard. AI underwriting platforms assist in risk assessment, fraud prevention, and in improving operational efficiency, but insurers need to integrate the automated processes with ethical scrutiny and adhere to the regulatory standards of fair underwriting assessment and practices (Jaiswal 2023, Pereira 2024).

SPECIALIZED APPLICATIONS

In many companies that have made strides in predictive analytics and real-time data processing technologies, AI underwriting is a common practice in the world of personal lines insurance. The introduction of the AI-based RIM ushered in the combination of predictive modeling and data analytics with ML capabilities, resulting in a granular view of risk exposure. This allows insurers to assess risk more accurately on their base of insureds, applying many factors beyond the simple characteristics of the insured clients, such as their lifestyle decisions and environmental effects. This allows for customer satisfaction by guaranteeing more accurate insurance product pricing, preventing customers from transferring their insurance providers (Jaiswal 2023).

An implementation where AI is utilized in commercial insurance is in automating the underwriting and reinforcing the accuracy of risk assessment through the use of analytical tools. While AI-driven systems offer affordable insurance products that can be built usefully for individual clients, they strike a good balance. Agu et al. (2022) therefore recommend the use of African markets to implement regulatory management procedures using AI systems that cut down insurance costs to make them affordable and accessible. Predictive analytics tools and ML allow commercial insurers to set up the best risk evaluations, eventually leading to the successful expansion of long-term business.

New ways of being an underwriter emerge, brought to life through AI advances in insurance, which promote processes and increase precision in health and life risk analysis. These models are built using new data sources and historical big datasets, creating life score algorithms to be used in algorithmic underwriting systems. Maier et al. (2020, 2019) also state that both models will offer better accuracy levels and keep operational expenses under control, based on operational improvements. In addition, their use improved the accuracy of forecasting in risk levels by making the algorithms improve user experience through streamlining application processing, as mentioned by Boodhun and Jayabalan (2018), and Bozyiğit et al. (2020).

Along with risk control operations, AI technologies are found useful in the property and casualty insurance industry for better underwriting. The use of the RIM system can benefit some insurance entities by helping them determine risk more effectively in order to manage it efficiently compared to other systems. According to Jaiswal (2023), through this model, insurance companies can use it to prepare business strategies for customers and are capable of choosing the most convenient reinsurance plans to increase risk management as well as to develop premium rates without deviation. The power of AI systems to process real-time data provides the ability to process claims on the fly, thereby strengthening efficiency in property and casualty claims management.

With AI-aided risk evaluations, insurance of specialty lines is becoming data-savvy and providing full protection services to unique, high-risk market segments. In personalized insurance products, multiple insurance variables are used to create market-ready products based on implicit statistical concepts gained using AI-driven underwriting systems to conduct all sums of insurance variable checks. However, there's also a requirement for AI when running risk assessments on specialty lines, as traditional tools generally don't work well in these cases. An AI step-up in the specialty lines insurance branch is affirmed, considering the fact that specialty lines insurance is instrumental in the fight against fraud—especially since AI helps to secure the expensive and risky products being insured (Agu et al. 2022).

RISK FACTORS ANALYSIS IN AI-ENABLED UNDERWRITING

Likewise, before an insurer is willing to provide risk assessment and contract, they apply behavioral analysis of insurance applications for the behaviors and life decisions of the individuals they will potentially insure. Based on the AI-based RIM, traditional risk screening is advanced to analyze multiple non-standard factors such as health behavior trends and lifestyle patterns, to develop complete exposure profiles. Such assessment methods further help insurers look more deeply into moral and morale hazards, allowing them to price their strategies more accurately and assess risk more effectively (Jaiswal 2023). Real-time analysis is performed on large data collections by AI systems to detect behavioral patterns that can signify elevated risk potential (Agu et al. 2022).

As such, critical geodemographic conditions play an important role in risk evaluations because they have significant implications on potential claim events. ML is used in GIS technology, and environmental data about air pollutants and disease statistics is added to the risk evaluation process of insurers. This integration enhances risk prediction accuracy, enabling insurers to develop products that match market segments and population profiles (Baruah et al. 2023). The insurance industry in Africa, through the use of AI technology and geographic analysis, enables service to the African market with price calculation services and financial inclusion, as posited by Agu et al. (2022).

Historical claims data analysis leads to the formulation of risk assessment productivity, where new patterns are revealed to researchers. AI and ML algorithms improve risk model prediction through the evaluation of big data sets using both regression models and decision trees (Bozyiğit et al. 2020, Boodhun and Jayabalan 2018). Boodhun and Jayabalan (2018) state that the combination of historical data on claims with risk factors by insurers improves underwriting practices and reduces the risk of future claims. Maier et al. (2020) develop life score models and mortality and age modeling using historical data and use the results as main components in algorithmic underwriting systems.

Next is the ability to identify new risks that are not spotted by traditional techniques, which can be done using AI technologies. To fairly assess risks, insurers should employ predictive analytics alongside scenario analysis to plan ahead for possible threats. This method is also being used by insurers to gain leadership over emerging threats and create new kinds of insurance products addressing risks from climate change or technological advances (Jaiswal 2023). This ability to detect emerging risks is crucial, as it guarantees both short-term competitive viability of the insurance industry and long-term business sustainability (Agu et al. 2022).

Pattern recognition and trend analysis practices are core features of AI-enabled risk assessment. They use artificial neural networks and clustering techniques to find complex patterns within large organizational datasets. These algorithms allow for the detection of risk associated with such patterns, encouraging insurers to restructure their underwriting procedures. Improved effectiveness of risk models through pattern recognition integration contributes to better risk management and enhanced decision-making, thanks to better accuracy and speed in the underwriting process (Nthenge et al. 2023).

Now, AI technologies offer better processing of behavioral, geographic, demographic, and historical data on risk assessment and underwriting operations of the insurance sector. With better emerging risk detection, risk management is improved while insurers are also able to generate more competitive insurance products based on advance pattern recognition techniques.

FUTURE TRENDS AND INNOVATIONS IN RISK ASSESSMENT AND UNDERWRITING

Among other emerging technologies that made a change, AI remains one of those that created foundational changes within the insurance industry. AI has transformed underwriting processes into innovative systems that develop insurance models based on data and behavior analysis. Insurers use the models for precise risk assessments and personalized coverage design by analyzing extensive data streams, including streaming behavioral data (Van Bekkum et al. 2024). With AI as the basis for conducting ML and geospatial analysis, risk evaluation and premium setting are improved to make insurance more accessible and affordable throughout Africa (Agu et al. 2022).

Advanced analytic systems lead the current innovations in the insurance industry. The use of AI-based predictive analytics alongside ML technologies improves the accuracy of risk evaluation and consumer classifications. High-retention insurance also enables insurers to develop highly detailed pricing plans, where profile-based premium adjustments further improve customer satisfaction and retention (Adeniran et al. 2024). Finally, the AI-based RIM data analytics with predictive modeling provides insurance companies with complete risk information to make better underwriting decisions (Jaiswal 2023).

Today, hybrid AI–human technology systems are being implemented in the operations of the insurance sector. These systems result from combining human underwriters' strategic expertise with AI algorithms' operational precision. Jaiswal (2023) says that AI automation of standard underwriting responsibilities allows human underwriters to allocate time to more difficult strategic work that supports risk management through better decision-making systems. According to Agu et al. (2022), the hybrid system increases underwriting accuracy while also dealing with ethical matters through human supervision of AI processes.

As ML and big data gain recognition, predictive modeling is developing rapidly. These models are essential for insurance companies because they enhance risk evaluation capabilities and enable accurate pricing systems. The use of data-driven systems has also improved the quality of insurance risk evaluation by creating individualized premium rates that are equitable. Supervised learning algorithms are used by life insurance companies to conduct predictive analysis, which has made underwriting faster while enabling better risk analysis (Boodhun and Jayabalan 2018).

The idea of this industry transformation is driven by technology and innovations related to AI technology, and the insurance sector must face this major industry change. Different insurance areas are changed by the redistribution of claims processing, distribution models, and pricing procedures that are carried out by AI. With an algorithm able to rapidly turn real data into a set of patterns, and extensive data set handling capability, insurers now have the power to uncover the best underwriting risk they can price appropriately (Kelley et al. 2018). Tataryntseva and Strokov (2023) state that companies have moved toward a new era of insurance, which will oblige them to solve data privacy problems in conjunction with ethical and regulatory compliance issues. AI is developing and will continue to develop further potential for innovation, driving new growth opportunities and wider socio-economic development of African territories (Agu et al. 2022).

There are three sequential steps to the development of AI-based underwriting that will drive its evolution.

a. IoT devices' integration with policyholder's data that comes from wearables enables policyholder to modify their immediately premium (Van Bekkum et al. 2024).
b. The AI technology of its parametric insurance systems means automatic payout benefits are triggered the moment trigger events like natural disasters or flight delays happen (Adeniran et al. 2024).
c. It is projected that every government around the world will come up with AI certification standards for implementation in ethical underwriting procedures (Mullins et al. 2021).

Implementation Challenges and Solutions

This study identifies the barriers of the AI-based underwriting system for implementation in the insurance industry in four major aspects: technical infrastructure, regulatory compliance and compliance with data privacy standards, workforce adjustments, and impacts on insurance companies' financials. Combining principles of strategic planning, strong validation processes, and common industry standards helps build fair, accurate, and transparent operational decisions in the company, creating efficiency improvements by applying AI to underwriting (Maier et al. 2020, Kharlamova et al. 2024).

Technical Infrastructure Requirements

The power of computing systems, coupled with flexible data storage structures capable of scale and complete system interoperability, are crucial factors for the functioning of the AI underwriting system. Problems arise when attempting to implement AI because most insurers have adopted legacy systems that do not support AI integration. Although AI models can help process current data immediately through predictive patterns that run in cloud systems (Rehman 2024), accurate underwriting delivery still requires it. In order to attain operational stability in the deployment process of their AI, insurance companies must possess and implement Application Programming Interface (API)-driven systems and distributed computing (Maier et al. 2020).

Opt-ins are an important practice, as are cybersecurity requirements in data governance. In the case of heavy processing of sensitive personal information, it's crucial for the AI systems to remain entirely private and to abide by proper regulatory compliance standards. According to Agu et al. (2022), by using secure data pipelines with encryption protocols and relying on federated learning systems that reduce security risks, data integrity is protected. AI model validation operations happen alongside systems monitoring to minimize the amount of bias present, as well as decision-making errors and inconsistencies within the insurance underwriting processes (Filabi and Duffy 2021).

Successful Implementations

AI has been integrated into several insurers' underwriting operations, resulting in positive outcomes with increased accuracy levels, reduced fraud incidents, and shortened policy approval processes. Machines analyze historical records and behavioral parameters along with market trends to build versatile risk assessment patterns (Jaiswal 2023). By leveraging AI-based predictive analytics and fraud detection systems, insurers have successfully addressed claim imprecision and underwriting administrative problems (Maier et al. 2020). AI appears capable of improving the underwriting operation from the standpoint of lowering costs and improving customer satisfaction.

Lessons Learned

Findings from the implementation of AI underwriting systems include fighting bias, adopting transparent processes, and enacting necessary changes in regulations. Without regular supervision through fairness audits, the fairness of AI risk assessment models cannot be assured and may result in discriminatory evaluations of risk (Filabi and Duffy 2021). Since established decision-making is a regulatory requirement, the insurance industry needs explainable XAI frameworks to establish transparent decision-making (Owens et al. 2022). As described in Jaiswal (2023), AI technology should be used in cooperation with human expertise to support underwriters in their work, with humans overseeing the ethical conduct of risk evaluations.

Industry Benchmarks

Regulatory tools are used to review AI performance in underwriting and check compliance with rules and regulations using standard benchmarks. Based on the risk classification accuracy of the AI system, the detection of fraud rates, and underwriting efficiency metrics, insurers can verify the reliability and effectiveness of the system (Pereira 2024). Using industry evaluations, it is found that AI underwriting performs better in terms of policy approval mechanisms and in connection with predictive accuracy and pricing fairness (Maier et al. 2020).

Established benchmarks provide reference points to specify requirements for implemented AI, such as the established standards of desired performance.

Performance Metrics

The performance of AI underwriting consists of model accuracy, sensitivity, specificity, as well as processing speed (Elbhrawy et al. 2023). The predictive capability of AI models needs to be reliable and must also meet ethically defined rules for underwriting. A combination of bias correction algorithms and adversarial testing is used to achieve stable AI risk assessment performance (Jaiswal 2023). The performance monitoring process aims to minimize the incidence rate of false positives in fraud detection and enhance the risk prediction mechanism (Agu et al. 2022).

Return on Investment Analysis

The Return on Investment (ROI) of AI-driven underwriting is generated through three primary factors: efficiency through cost reduction, risk reduction, and revenue stream optimization. The strength of operational processes and the benefits of substantial cost-saving opportunities that arise from automation and fraud detection improvements are gained by decision-makers (Maier et al. 2020). Insurance organizations that utilize AI underwriting systems gain market advantages through the implementation of individualized pricing structures, higher customer satisfaction rates, and quicker claims processing times (Jaiswal 2023). According to Agu et al. (2022), organizations using AI can select better risks at lower underwriting expenses, resulting in greater profit.

The significance of the benefits of AI-driven underwriting—in terms of risk accuracy, fraud prevention, and efficiency improvements—outweighs the challenges of implementing an AI-driven underwriting process, where infrastructure requirements, regulatory standards, and necessary ethical oversight loom large. According to Filabi and Duffy (2021) and Maier et al. (2020), insurers need to develop scalable AI platforms along with thorough regulatory reporting and collaboration with industry-knowledgeable human staff in order to harness the maximum possible AI potential while still ensuring fair underwriting standards.

CONCLUSION

Through the AI migration of companies to get away from the human-led assessment, insurance risk evaluation and policy underwriting are being reformed. In the context of the insurance industry, AI is a boon for better process operations, precision underwriting, and better solutions at a cheaper cost and with a customer-friendly approach. ML with NLP and computer vision is also used by insurers with predictive modeling to make more effective risk assessments and prevent policy delivery and claims fraud. However, there are also barriers from regulation and from the incompatibility of the new or existing systems being used with AI. As a result of constant technological innovation, a dedicated focus on responsible

AI methods, transparency in operations, and mitigation of biased treatment, the maximum results of AI underwriting are achieved.

But insurers must be able to provide strategic models that pull together computational power with human touch and meet the necessary regulatory requirements, and encompass the intricate details of the AI decision protocols to develop the AI technology. A proper implementation of AI technologies on the digital landscape of the insurance industry will allow it to sustainably grow, provide better risk prediction, and ultimately build trust with customers.

In order to maximize AI underwriting benefits and associated risks consideration, insurers must prioritize the following key points.

Interpretability is one part of a suite of benefits that insurance organizations could gain from implementing transparency-based AI frameworks that use XAI models; the others being regulatory compliance and consumer trust. Techniques like SHAP and LIME for understanding models give us helpful knowledge that underwriters and regulators of AI-based risk evaluation can use to interpret a model.

It needs to develop elaborate data protection protocols as an organization, which adhere to the GDPR, CCPA, as well as future AI regulations. To carry out AI systems, data needs to be protected, which can be done using privacy-enhancing protocols such as federated learning and differential privacy.

Each time the AI underwriting models are reviewed, the aim is to look for and remove bias from them in an automated fashion. It is also argued that fairness-aware algorithms, as well as adversarial debate mechanisms, and training systems with diverse training samples are also necessary for fair risk modeling and desegregated pricing in ML systems.

It is recommended that an AI middleware solution and cloud-based architecture, along with API-driven data exchange systems, be adopted to fit the AI-driven, data-driven model as it deploys with the current underwriting framework models. It should also provide training to the organization so that the trained implementers can make the staff skilled enough and also retrain them to interact with AI platforms.

In order to engender and create standard enterprise AI governance standards of ethical and fair AI in underwriting, regulatory partners, insurance organizations and AI ethics experts should come together.

Success Factors for AI in Underwriting

AI implementation success in insurance underwriting requires multiple important technical elements as well as regulatory conditions and organizational needs.

Data Availability and Quality

Underwriting predictions from AI models need structured and unstructured data sets which are also high-quality to achieve accurate results.

Risk-based pricing can transform with the integration of wearables and telematics capabilities while deploying behavioral analytic systems.

AI-Powered Parametric Insurance

Parametric insurance sets up AI technology to automatically make claims payments after a natural disaster or business disruption has occurred once pre-determined triggers have been fired.

The efficiency of fraud detection with claims verification is increased with blockchain technology in AI solutions.

Advanced Predictive Risk Modeling

Instead, climate risk forecasting tools are deployed by AI to inform AI underwriting decisions for insurance via the use of economic trend models and cyber risk intelligence.

To reduce bias in risk estimation and management, AI systems need to incorporate the self-diagnostic checks to decentralize fairness-conscious ML algorithms. These building blocks observe measures of fairness and apply mitigation precautions when the bias is observed.

Human-AI Collaboration

Instead of doing work that is normally done by professionals, AI operates to increase human knowledge.

Underwriters should still own the ability to act autonomously and make decisions in high-risk events where situation-dependent evaluation is required, and can do so with the help of an AI assessment model.

Quantum Computing and AI in Risk Prediction

These are expected to be digital models that will run on quantum computers to increase speed in risk evaluation by rapid processing of massive data collections.

Today's tech capabilities will allow us to advance the predictive models as well as develop better approaches for risk structure.

AI underwriting applications produce substantial opportunities; at the same time, they need proper execution, constant regulatory adherence, and ethical protocols. Insurers can use XAI and robust data governance, together with bias-mitigation techniques, to maximize AI benefits and protect transparency, fairness, and customer trust.

The upcoming era of underwriting AI will bring adaptive learning models that enhance risk precision assessment while creating revolutionary insurance services with personalized real-time solutions. Strategic AI implementation enables insurers to become leaders in their industry during the digital transformation.

REFERENCES

Adeniran, I.A., Efunniyi, C.P., Osundare, O.S., Abhulimen, A.O. and OneAdvanced, U.K. (2024). Advancements in predictive modeling for insurance pricing: Enhancing risk assessment and customer segmentation. *International Journal of Management and Entrepreneurship Research*, 6(8), 2835–2848. *https://doi.org/10.51594/ijmer.v6i8.1469*

Agu, E.E., Abhulimen, A.O., Obiki-Osafiele, A.N., Osundare, O.S., Adeniran, I.A. and Efunniyi, C.P. (2022). Artificial intelligence in African insurance: A review of risk management and fraud prevention. *International Journal of Management and Entrepreneurship Research*, 4(12), 768–794. *https://doi.org/10.51594/ijmer.v4i12.1473*

Baruah, P., Singh, P.P. and Kumar Ojah, S. (2023). A novel framework for risk prediction in the health insurance sector using GIS and machine learning. *International Journal of Advanced Computer Science and Applications*, 14(12), 469–476. *https://doi.org/10.14569/ijacsa.2023.0141249*

Bhalla, A. (2012). Enhancement in predictive model for insurance underwriting. *International Journal of Computer Science and Engineering Technology (IJCSET)*, 3(5), 160–165.

Boodhun, N. and Jayabalan, M. (2018). Risk prediction in life insurance industry using supervised learning algorithms. *Complex and Intelligent Systems*, 4(2), 145–154. *https://doi.org/10.1007/s40747-018-0072-1*

Bozyiğit, F., Şahin, M., Gündüz, T., Işık, C. and Kılınç, D. (2020). Regression based risk analysis in life insurance industry. *International Journal of Engineering and Innovative Research*, 2(3), 178–184. *https://doi.org/10.47933/ijeir.745343*

Chaubey, Arun., and Singh, Sachchidanand. (2020). AI-enabled digital transformation of insurance industry. *Communications on Applied Electronics*, 7(34), 6–9. *https://doi.org/10.5120/cae2020652870*

Du Preez, V., Bennet, S., Byrne, M., Couloumy, A., Das, A., Dessain, J., Galbraith, R., King, P., Mutanga, V., Schiller, F. and Zaaiman, S. (2024). From bias to black boxes: Understanding and managing the risks of AI—an actuarial perspective. *British Actuarial Journal*, 29, e6, 1–52. *https://doi.org/10.1017/s1357321724000060*

Dubey, A., Parida, T., Birajdar, A., Prajapati, A.K. and Rane, S. (2018). Smart underwriting system: An intelligent decision support system for insurance approval and risk assessment. *In: 3rd International Conference for Convergence in Technology (I2CT)*, 1–6. IEEE. *https://doi.org/10.1109/I2CT.2018.8529792*

Elbhrawy, A.S., Belal, M.A. and Hassanein, M.S. (2023). AIRA-ML: Auto Insurance Risk Assessment-Machine Learning model using resampling methods. *International Journal of Advanced Computer Science and Applications*, 14(9), 633–641. *https://doi.org/10.14569/ijacsa.2023.0140966*

Filabi, A. and Duffy, S. (2021). AI-enabled underwriting brings new challenges for life insurance: Policy and regulatory considerations. *Journal of Insurance Regulation*, 40(8), 1. *https://doi.org/10.52227/25114.2021*

Fung, G., Polania, L.F., Choi, S.C.T., Wu, V. and Ma, L. (2021). Artificial intelligence in insurance and finance. *Frontiers in Applied Mathematics and Statistics*, 7, 795207. *https://doi.org/10.3389/fams.2021.795207*

Jaiswal, R. (2023). Impact of AI in the general insurance underwriting factors. *Central European Management Journal*, 31(2), 697–705. *https://doi.org/10.57030/23364890.cemj.31.2.72*

Kelley, K.H., Fontanetta, L.M., Heintzman, M. and Pereira, N. (2018). Artificial intelligence: Implications for social inflation and insurance. *Risk Management and Insurance Review*, 21(3), 373–387.

Kharlamova, A., Kruglov, A. and Succi, G. (2024). State-of-the-art review of life Insurtech: Machine learning for underwriting decisions and a shift toward data-driven, society-oriented environment. *In:* International Congress on Human-Computer Interaction, Optimization and Robotic Applications (HORA), 1–12. IEEE. *https://doi.org/10.1109/HORA61326.2024.10550565*

Kulinskaya, E., Gitsels, L.A., Bakbergenuly, I. and Wright, N.R. (2021). Dynamic hazards modelling for predictive longevity risk assessment. *Insurance: Mathematics and Economics*, 96, 222–231. *https://doi.org/10.1016/j.insmatheco.2020.11.001*

Loi, M., and Christen, M. (2021). Choosing how to discriminate: Navigating ethical trade-offs in fair algorithmic design for the insurance sector. *Philosophy and Technology*, 34(4), 967–992. *https://doi.org/10.1007/s13347-021-00444-9*

Maier, M., Carlotto, H., Sanchez, F., Balogun, S. and Merritt, S. (2019). Transforming underwriting in the life insurance industry. *In:* Proceedings of the AAAI Conference on Artificial Intelligence. 33(1), 9373–9380. *https://doi.org/10.1609/aaai.v33i01.33019373*

Maier, M., Carlotto, H., Saperstein, S., Sanchez, F., Balogun, S. and Merritt, S. (2020). Improving the accuracy and transparency of underwriting with AI to transform the life insurance industry. *AI Magazine*, 41(3), 78–93. *https://doi.org/10.1609/aimag.v41i3.5320*

Mullins, M., Holland, C., and Cunneen, M. (2021). Creating ethics guidelines for artificial intelligence and big data analytics customers: The case of the consumer European insurance market. *Patterns*, 2(10). *https://doi.org/10.1016/j.patter.2021.100362*

Nguyen, K., Islam, M., Huo, H., Tilocca, P., and Xu, G. (2023). Explainable exclusion in the life insurance using multi-label classifier. *In:* International Joint Conference on Neural Networks (IJCNN), 1–8. *https://doi.org/10.1109/IJCNN54540.2023.10191171*

Nthenge, J.K. Musyoka, F.M., and Mugo, D.M. (2023). Implementing a hybrid model using k-means clustering and artificial neural networks for risk prediction in life insurance. *International Journal on Recent and Innovation Trends in Computing and Communication*. 11(9), 3778–3785. *https://doi.org/10.17762/ijritcc.v11i9.9622*

Owens, E., Sheehan, B., Mullins, M., Cunneen, M., Ressel, J. and Castignani, G. (2022). Explainable artificial intelligence (XAI) in insurance. *Risks*, 10(12), Article No. 230. *https://doi.org/10.3390/risks10120230*

Pereira, C. (2024). Impact of automated underwriting systems on insurance risk classification in Singapore. *Journal of Statistics and Actuarial Research*, 8(3), 47–57. *https://doi.org/ 10.47604/jsar.2901*

Rehman, I. (2024). Artificial intelligence (AI) in managing P & C multinational insurance programs. *International Journal of Science and Research (IJSR)*, 13(10), 326–329. *https://doi.org/10.21275/sr241003101503*

Tataryntseva, Y. and Strokov, I. (2023). Modern Information Technologies in Insurance: Analysis of Advantages and Disadvantages. Bulletin of the National Technical University "Kharkiv Polytechnic Institute" (Economic Sciences). *https://doi.org/10.20998/2519-4461.2023.5.80*

Van Bekkum, M.S., Borgesius, F.J.Z. and Heskes, T. (2024). AI, insurance, discrimination and unfair differentiation. An overview and research agenda. arXiv. *https://doi.org/10.48550/arXiv.2401.11892*

Yang, B. (2021). Machine learning in insurance underwriting context. *In:* International Conference on Electronic Information Technology and Smart Agriculture (ICEITSA), Huaihua, China, 478–484. IEEE. *https://doi.org/10.1109/ICEITSA54226.2021.00097*

AI-Driven Diagnostic and Decision Making

3

Adithya Jakkaraju[1], *Nirav Narendrakumar Modh*[2], *Ojasvi Razdan*[3], *and Keshav Kaushik*[4,*]

INTRODUCTION

Artificial intelligence (AI) has enabled the development of AI-driven diagnostics and AI-enabled decision-making, transforming the way we approach problems in diverse domains, analysing large datasets to identify patterns and generate actionable insights. These technologies will improve the efficiency, accuracy, and reliability of decision-making processes that historically depend on human expertise. AI, neural networks, deep learning (DL), and advanced data analytics have allowed AI systems to exceed human performance in individual diagnostic tasks, reduce errors, and make real-time decisions. The confluence of AI and diagnostics is particularly resonant where data complexity and variability, and the pressure to get a rapid but accurate assessment, have their highest stakes.

AI-driven diagnostics has transformed the field of healthcare, one of the most exciting sectors in which this technology is actively being utilised. In medical imaging, AI models that process radiographs, MRIs, and CT scans are helping radiologists detect irregularities such as the presence of tumours, fractures, and infections (Kothinti 2024). For example, the image compression capability of these DL techniques allows researchers to train efficient machine learning (ML) algorithms on large medical datasets, which can help to improve diagnostic accuracy by detecting subtle disease features that human radiologists may overlook, ultimately resulting in earlier diagnoses and improved patient outcomes. AI-based decision-making goes beyond imaging and pathology to predictive analytics, in which algorithms interpret a patient's medical records, genetic data, and lifestyle factors to predict the likelihood of developing certain diseases.

In manufacturing, AI-driven diagnostics have been particularly helpful to equipment monitoring, predicting when a machine may require maintenance before it goes

[1] Technical Architect, HCL America Inc, USA
[2] Consultant, Digital Interactions Professional, Infosys Limited, Chicago, USA
[3] Subject Matter Expert & Researcher, Spark Sleep Solutions, USA
[4] Center for Cyber Security and Cryptology, Sharda School of Computer Science & Engineering, Sharda University, Greater Noida, India
[*] *Corresponding author:* officialkeshavkaushik@gmail.com

DOI: 10.1201/9781003621119-3

down. These are AI-powered systems that keep tabs on machines and production facilities, examining data from sensors and previous maintenance and breakdown records to spot likely failures before they occur. This predictive strategy enables less unplanned downtime, reduced maintenance costs, and improved overall operational efficiency (Gupta 2023). While many companies are using AI to monitor equipment, it is also central to defect detection. The reasons differ, but such systems depend on automated quality control systems reducing human mistakes, confirming adherence to industry standards, and helping to streamline production processes. AI has already shown its worth in the industry with regards to parsing, analysing, and interpreting the massive volume and velocity of sensor information, ensuring the detection of anomalies before they lead to threats—making AI an essential enabler to enhance process reliability and ultimately boost productivity.

The finance sector has meanwhile benefited from AI-powered diagnostics and decision-making that has transformed risk assessment, fraud detection, and investment strategies. Data fed into AI models enables finance companies to analyse transaction trends, detect fraudulent activity, and calculate risks associated with credit far more quickly and accurately than human beings ever could. Traditional fraud detection methods are rule-based, which makes them hard to adjust to new tactics. AI-based models, however, learn from new data easily, constantly improving their ability to detect fraud and block fraudulent sales. Just as analytics is an indispensable aspect of investments, AI uses those analytics alongside market trends, economic indicators, and past performance to derive predictive insights. With real-time data at the forefront, AI-driven algorithmic trading enables rapid decision-making that optimises investment strategies while minimising market risk exposure. By automating complex financial analyses, AI empowers institutions to make more informed, data-driven financial decisions.

AI-powered diagnostics buck the trend beyond healthcare, manufacturing, and finance. AI models in cybersecurity examine network traffic, determine unusual activities, diagnose breach points, and even predict potential cyber threats before they escalate. Such systems enhance threat detection, mitigate risks, and protect proprietary data against potential breaches. In agriculture, AI diagnostics are performing the monitoring when fields are tracked; farmers analyse soil, weed, and pest conditions, and guide irrigation, using laser and data-driven decisions on fertiliser use. Through this precision farming, resources are being used more effectively for a higher yield while also protecting the environment (Tiwari et al. 2022b). AI is also important in environmental monitoring, analysing climate patterns, detecting pollutants, and predicting natural disasters. It can be used for real-time diagnostics and decision-making—supporting governments and organisations to respond better to environmental challenges and take proactive actions to mitigate risks.

A variety of factors have fuelled the advancements in AI that have made these transformative applications possible. DL, and especially convolutional neural network (CNN) and transformer model architectures, has made tremendous strides in enabling AI to process and interpret complex forms of data. CNNs have played a key role in computer vision tasks, allowing machines to learn with high accuracy visual patterns in data. On one side, transformer models have transformed natural language processing (NLP) and allowed AI to handle large amounts of textual information. which is useful for electronic health record (EHR) analysis, legal decision-making, and financial risk assessments.

Access to large-scale datasets and advances in data collection is another crucial development. The Internet of Things (IoT), sensors, and high-resolution imaging technologies have produced exponentially greater data amounts for virtually all industries. These datasets serve as the foundation for AI systems to train their models, enabling them to enhance their accuracy and optimise their decision-making processes. Another significant advancement that has contributed to AI-powered diagnostics is the combination of cloud computing with edge computing, allowing the processing of data with smaller latencies in the moment. Cloud-based AI platforms offer scalable computing resources, enabling organisations to implement AI solutions effectively without heavy investments in infrastructure (Baseer et al. 2024).

Additional areas of exploration have revolved around the explainability and interpretability of AI insights and decision processes, particularly in high-stakes environments including healthcare and finance. Traditional schemes of AI are black-box models; they face transparency challenges and create uncertainty for stakeholders to trust AI-based recommendations. However, with recent advancement in explainable AI (XAI), interpretable models make AI diagnostics and decision-making much more consistent with human expertise and regulatory compliance. Shapley Additive Explanations (SHAP) and Local Interpretable Model-agnostic Explanations (LIME) for AI model interpretability will help to make AI models more transparent and offer insight into what's driving the AI decisions.

The field of AI-driven diagnostics and decision-making also has been shaped by ethical considerations and regulatory frameworks. As AI systems expand and permeate critical sectors, problems of bias, fairness, and accountability have gained attention. Biased training data can lead to discriminatory effects, particularly in areas like healthcare and finance that have direct impacts on people's health and financial well-being. Recent work has therefore been done, in terms of fairness-aware AI models, bias mitigation techniques, regulatory policy, etc., in addressing these problems in order to ensure responsible use of AI. Many organisations and policymakers work on ethical guidelines for developing such systems, providing a framework for the transparent, unbiased, and socially aligned development of AI-based diagnostic technologies.

Emerging technologies, which include but are not limited to federated learning, quantum computing, and neuro-symbolic AI, are thus said to be the future elements fuelling AI-powered diagnostics and decision-making. Federated learning, for example, in healthcare, allows AI models to be trained on multiple decentralised data sources without compromising privacy.

Quantum computing vs. AI will allow for considerably superior processing of vast amounts of information across parallel processes, leading to faster decision-making in AI for solving optimisation problems. This demand requires a platform with human-like reasoning and data-driven learning to support explainable yet generalisable sense-making of complex diagnostic tasks, which can be fulfilled with neuro-symbolic AI, combining symbol-orientated systems working with reasoning supported by DL (Jussupow et al. 2021).

Last but not least, AI-based diagnostics and decision-making is creating a paradigm shift across many sectors, also enabling improved accuracy, efficiency, as well as predictive power. AI has enhanced disease detection and personalised treatment strategies in healthcare; optimised predictive maintenance and quality control in manufacturing; and powered fully autonomous self-driving vehicles. AI is used by the financial sector to assess the risks of investments and identify fraudulent behaviour (Tiwari et al. 2022a), and the trend continues with fields such as cybersecurity, agriculture, and environmental monitoring utilising AI for real-time insights. DL, big data analytics, cloud computing, and XAI are technologies that have greatly supported the evolution of intelligent diagnostic systems. Nonetheless, industrialisation should continue with focus on the challenges of bias, interpretability, and ethical aspects that need to be addressed to build a properly visible execution of a responsible and equitable AI layer. As research progresses and technological advancements unfold, AI-enabled diagnostics, decision support systems, and treatment recommendations will become increasingly sophisticated, enabling smarter, data-driven strategies that augment human decision-making in diverse settings (Bjerring and Busch 2021).

FOUNDATIONS OF AI IN DECISION-MAKING

A dataset is built on powerful processing, utilises massive patterns, and provides high-accuracy output—and this is what the AI decision engine does. In various domains such as healthcare, finance, and manufacturing, traditional decision-making processes tend to depend on human expertise and established guidelines. But the sheer amount, speed, and diversity of data has made it difficult for humans alone to analyse and truly understand information. AI fills this void with a wide range of computational models that can learn from data, reason over knowledge, and make predictions with very few humans in the loop.

AI-aided decision-making has undergone transitions through several paradigms including ML, DL, knowledge-based systems (KBS), and hybrid approaches like neuro-symbolic AI. All these paradigms have their own unique contribution to the ability of AI to assist and augment decision-making across disciplines. KBS implement various mechanisms, utilising human input to draw conclusions based on a set of reasoning rules, while ML and DL models are particularly adept at identifying patterns in data and making predictions based on that. The recent rise of neuro-symbolic AI, leveraging principles from both data-driven learning and symbolic reasoning for improved generalisation and interpretability in decision-making, exemplifies this trend (Mohammed et al. 2024).

In many applications, AI-powered decision support systems are meant to complement human intelligence, not replace it. These systems present recommendations, identify outliers, and surface essential insights to empower specialists in making better decisions. For example, AI can supplement the work of radiologists in medical diagnostics by alerting them about potential abnormalities in imaging scans, or in finance, AI fraud detection systems can monitor transaction patterns to flag suspicious activities. It is no surprise then that AI has not only made processes faster and more accurate—due to its ability to analyse data better than a human ever could—but it also allows organisations to tackle complex problems that exceed human cognitive limitations.

While these are promising advancements, AI-based decision algorithms are not without their challenges. Use of datasets that contain bias, loss of interpretability in DL, regulatory compliance, etc., remain important open problems. As AI models play a decisive role in decision-making, it becomes imperative to maintain not only fairness, but also accountability and interpretability of these models. Developments in XAI and hybrid AI approaches attempt to solve these problems and ensure that decisions made by AI systems are trustworthy and comparable to decisions made by human reasoning (Kumar Mishra et al. 2023).

MACHINE LEARNING AND DEEP LEARNING: ROLE IN DATA-DRIVEN DECISION SUPPORT

ML and DL have emerged as a distinct type of decision-making, allowing AI systems to perform with impressive accuracy by learning from data. In traditional decision-making, rule-based systems were utilised, where you had to explicitly code for every possible scenario. Unlike classic algorithms, which require a lot of feature engineering and fine-tuning, ML/DL models can automatically learn patterns from data, generalise knowledge gained from experience, and get better results over time. In fact, these abilities have rendered them essential across a wide range of fields, such as healthcare, finance, cybersecurity, and manufacturing.

Supervised learning, a widely used ML technique, requires training models using labelled data to predict the results associated with previously unobserved input data. For example, supervised learning models are trained on thousands of patient data points in medical diagnostics to predict the risk of disease (such as diabetes or cancer) (Selvarajan 2021). In the context of financial markets, ML models look at historical stock prices, economic indicators, and even sentiment analysis from news articles to predict the likelihood of positive or negative outcomes. On the other hand, unsupervised learning uncovers hidden relationships in datasets, without any explicit labels. One common approach to unsupervised learning is clustering, and we can see this most often used in fraud detection, where AI groups transaction types and patterns to spot deviations that may indicate fraud.

Although DL is a subfield of ML, it gained prominence when it showed the ability to work well with high-dimensional data and complex decision-making tasks. CNNs are a special type of network that have had tremendous success in image-based diagnosis; for example, identifying tumours in radiology scans. At the same time, recurrent neural networks (RNNs) and transformers revolutionised NLP, allowing

AI to interpret and construct human-like language—a huge boon for use-cases like the automated transcription of medical notes or analysis of legal documents. Another advanced ML technique, known as reinforcement learning (RL), allows AI to analyse how to make decisions in a sequence by seeking to maximise rewards over the long run, making it suitable for applications in robotics and autonomous systems.

Interpretability is one of the main challenges that comes with ML and DL-based decision-making. Though these models can yield very high performance, a lot of the times, they have a "black box" nature, meaning these models are not very interpretable. As constant progress is being made in the AI domain, the cascading behaviour of ML with DL and interpretation methods will result in reliable, robust and trustworthy decision support systems (Selvarajan 2024).

KNOWLEDGE-BASED SYSTEMS: RULE-BASED REASONING AND EXPERT SYSTEMS

KBS are an older approach to decision-making through AI, but they are still in use today. Autonomous systems are defined by rules and explicit knowledge to mimic human domain expertise. Unlike ML and DL models, which learn by exposure to data, KBS have a fixed set of rules, can use logical inferences, and structured representation techniques. Roughly similar to symbolic AI, this sort of thing has been used extensively in specialist systems for medical diagnosis (Haque et al. 2024), legal reasoning, and corporate automation.

The knowledge base is an integral part of the KBS as it encompasses factual information, domain-specific knowledge, and heuristic rules established by experts in the field. For example, in medical diagnosis, a knowledge base might contain rules like "If a patient presents with a persistent cough and a fever, consider pneumonia as a potential diagnosis". An inference engine actually applies these rules and evaluates the logical statements to derive conclusions; thus, it helps ensure the decision-making process is transparent and explainable (Kaur et al. 2024).

KBS are also interpretable, since their reasoning can be traced back to rules defined by humans, which is one of their key advantages. They are especially helpful in regulatory environments where transparency is expected. But, in having been encoded (by humans, no less!), this can be their Achilles' heel. KBS differ from ML models in that ML models have the facility to learn from new data, while KBS need to be updated continually to keep up with the changing domain knowledge. Predictable decisions: data-driven approaches often struggle in complex decision-making scenarios that require flexibility and adaptability to high levels of variability or uncertainty beyond predefined rules.

To overcome these limitations, hybrid systems have been proposed that combine KBS with ML. They can be considered a hybrid of traditional expert systems and ML, leveraging the structured reasoning of expert systems with the adaptability of ML to provide more dynamic and intelligent decision-making support.

NEURO-SYMBOLIC AI: COMBINING REASONING AND LEARNING FOR ROBUST DIAGNOSTICS

Neuro-symbolic approaches represent a new frontier in AI that brings together the best of both worlds, leveraging the power of symbolic reasoning with DL. ML and DL approaches perform better at pattern recognition but are black boxes without interpretability, while symbolic or logic-based AI is more interpretable but does not have a mechanism to scale or learn from raw data. Neuro-symbolic AI aims to combine both paradigms to form intelligent systems that are data-driven yet also logically grounded.

Neuro-symbolic AI bridges the gap between human-like logic and statistical learning, which is one of its main strengths. In these diagnostic use cases, this enables AI-based systems to leverage both data-driven pattern recognition and knowledge represented formally in a structured way to draw more accurate, more interpretable conclusions. Suppose, for instance, that in the domain of medical imaging, a DL model identifies potential anomalies in a chest X-ray; a symbolic reasoning component then cross-checks this with known medical literature to issue an explainable answer (diagnosis) (Zhang et al. 2024)

Combining symbolic logic with neural networks also helps improve the generalisation capabilities of AI systems. Unlike pure DL architectures, which need huge amounts of labelled data, neuro-symbolic systems can leverage core knowledge of how to reason with logic and extend that reasoning to smaller datasets. This is especially advantageous in fields like rare disease diagnosis (Noman et al. 2024), where only a small sample data is available.

Moreover, neuro-symbolic AI enables more effective human-AI collaboration by making sure that decisions made by AI are interpretable and grounded in expert knowledge. For example, in the area of finance, which is intrinsically regulated, neuro-symbolic AI can assist in making decisions on the regulatory floor while ensuring transparency and interpretability of decisions made by models to ensure compliance with regulations. This pioneering research area will open a pathway for neuro-symbolic AI to become more widely used as an important building block for robust and trustworthy decision-making frameworks in numerous domains.

AI-POWERED DIAGNOSTIC SYSTEMS

AI-enabled diagnostic systems have also transformed the decision-making process in multiple industries by allowing for the identification of patterns, anomalies, and risks, thereby increasing the speed, efficiency, and accuracy of detection. Using massive amounts of structured and unstructured data, these systems employ the latest ML, DL, and data analytics technologies to better empower organisations to make more informed decisions. Conventional methods of diagnosis rely on human experience and laborious procedures, whereas AI-based diagnosis automates complex tasks, decreases mistakes, and offers real-time insights.

Recent years have seen AI demonstrate amazing performance, whether in medical diagnostics, industrial fault detection, or financial risk analysis. In the days ahead, with the assistance of radiologists, pathologists, and clinicians who can identify illness at an earlier stage, AI is transforming diagnostics in the field of health. Similarly, AI technology can also be leveraged in industrial environments, where AI-driven predictive maintenance can help maintain operational efficiency by ascertaining failures before they escalate into expensive breakdowns. Risk management involves around-the-clock monitoring of millions of transactions, detecting fraudulent activities and making accurate investment decisions—areas that have been taken on by AI systems, backed up to October 2023 (Joshi et al. 2023).

CNNs populate the first layer at their input end for analysing images, transformer models facilitate NLP, RL addresses decision-making in dynamic environments—and so do diagnostic systems driven by such algorithms that are increasingly able to guide physicians in differentiating diagnostic approaches, planning strategic therapeutic interventions, and regulating disease progression—a powerful weapon of 21st-century clinical practice. In addition, explainability and interpretability are vital elements of the emerging components of AI diagnostics to ensure that AI-based inferences are not only accurate, but interpretable also, in accordance with regulatory requirements. Diagnostic algorithms: AI-powered diagnostic systems encounter data privacy, bias, and ethical issues as well, yet evolve over time and remain favourable means of improving decision-making in critical sectors (Miller 2023).

MEDICAL DIAGNOSTICS: AI IN RADIOLOGY, PATHOLOGY, AND PREDICTIVE HEALTHCARE

The advent of AI in medical diagnostics has revolutionised disease detection, treatment planning, and predictive healthcare. Models fuelled by AI analyse medical images, genetic data, and EHRs to aid healthcare providers in making diagnoses with an accuracy never before possible. AI plays an important role in radiology, pathology, and predictive analytics.

Examples: in radiology, AI computer vision models examine medical images such as X-rays, CT scans, and MRIs to identify abnormalities such as tumours, fractures, and infections. CNNs have been notably successful in pattern recognition tasks within medical imaging, demonstrating greater speed and accuracy than traditional diagnostic modalities (Singh, Sharma, et al. 2024). The large datasets on which the AI models are trained identify early-stage cancers, such as breast cancer in mammograms, and thus reduce the likelihood that a diagnosis will be missed. In addition, AI is also used to assist radiologists in screening cases of high importance, which allows for early treatment and positive patient outcomes.

Pathology is another major field of medicine that has significantly benefited from AI-based diagnostics. Key phrase: AI in Digital Pathology and AI in Histopathology, as DL algorithms are integrated into digital pathology systems to analyse histopathological slides for the presence of cancerous cells, other abnormalities, and even assign grading schemes. And by automating the analysis of biopsy samples,

AI reduces the level of subjectivity involved in manual examination and improves the consistency of diagnosis. Such models, which consume multi-modal data like genomic sequencing results and patient history, can offer a more holistic view for diagnosis (Al-Antari 2023).

Predictive healthcare is an AI-driven tactic which examines patient risk factors and anticipates potential health-related ailments prior to the manifestation of symptoms. ML algorithms trained on these data analyse your medical history; track your weight, blood pressure, and other risk factors over time; and incorporate genetic information to estimate your risk for current diseases such as diabetes, cardiovascular disease, and neurodegeneration. Implementing AI in healthcare solutions can improve patient outcomes and reduce healthcare costs by enabling early diagnosis, customised treatment plans, and specific preventive measures.

But key issues such as data privacy, regulatory compliance, and AI interpretability remain. AI in medical diagnostics has the potential to revolutionise the industry, but it must be ethically aligned and trustworthy to find its place. Each new development in AI represents an opportunity to apply this technology into medical diagnostics as we continue to embrace the fight against regional healthcare and personalised medicine.

INDUSTRIAL DIAGNOSTICS: AI FOR FAULT DETECTION AND PREDICTIVE MAINTENANCE

AI-enabled diagnostics have facilitated a shift away from reactive/scheduled maintenance to predictive/prescriptive maintenance strategies in industrial settings. This includes AI-based fault detection and predictive maintenance, for example, which leverages ML, sensor data, and historical failure patterns to proactively predict issues before they result in expensive equipment failures. These approaches enhance operational performance, reduce downtime, and extend the useful life of critical assets.

Reactive maintenance (fixing equipment after it breaks) and preventive maintenance (performing maintenance at scheduled intervals) often lead to unnecessary expenses and disruption to operations. Predictive maintenance with AI, however, works by using IoT sensors to monitor the performance of a machine, giving real-time updates on devices, vibration analysis, and thermal imaging. Real-time analysis of this data using ML models detects deviations from normal operating conditions to warn operators of failures before they happen.

In manufacturing plants, for instance, AI-powered diagnostic systems evaluate machine sensor data, detecting early indications of component wear and tear. Assets are maintained when they need to be, minimising unplanned outages and allowing maintenance resources to be utilised optimally, by predicting failures before they occur. Similarly, in the energy sector, disseminating AI-driven diagnostics keeps a close watch on turbines, transformers, and pipelines to identify performance anomalies at checkpoints within the cycle to maintain uninterrupted power generation and distribution.

Another industry where AI-based fault detection is critical is, of course, aviation and automotive—where the stakes are high in terms of safety and reliability. AI models can analyse the incredible amounts of data generated by real-time sensors in aircraft engines and automotive systems to identify irregularities. For example, AI-driven diagnostics play a critical role in helping engineers spot possible mechanical failures to minimise the risk of accidents, improve vehicle safety, and keep drivers safe on the road.

Industrial diagnostics is further enhanced by the application of AI with digital twin technology. Digital twins are virtual models of physical assets that constantly receive data in real time from their physical equivalent. Based on this data, AI algorithms contemplate different operating situations, foresee possible problems, and suggest the best maintenance plans. Such a strategy allows industries to optimise functions, enhance efficiency, reduce costly interruptions, and much more.

For all the benefits, we will have to address the challenges—integrating disparate data sources, managing cybersecurity risks, making models interpretable. Creating trust and auditability for AI models is key—especially in sectors where safety and compliance with regulation are paramount. However, the advancement in AI technology will enhance its significance in industrial diagnostics, paving the way for smarter, more effective, and cost-friendly maintenance solutions.

FINANCIAL AND RISK ANALYTICS: AI FOR FRAUD DETECTION AND INVESTMENT DECISIONS

The impact of AI-powered diagnostics on financial risk analysis has been transformative. It is, therefore, not surprising to note that financial institutions utilise AI models to analyse massive amounts of transactions with the ability to identify suspicious patterns and mitigate risks in real time. AI also enables fast and accurate decision-making processes for analysing complex financials, while also improving security and profitability.

One of the most important uses of AI in finance is fraud detection. Most existing fraud detection systems were rule-based and relied on traditional methods, which often failed to keep up with evolving fraud tactics. AI-powered fraud detection, however, uses ML models that learn in real time from incoming data and maximise their accuracy in spotting anomalies and preventing fraudulent actions. These include the use of AI models which assess spending patterns, the geographical location of transactions, and behavioural biometrics to identify suspicious activity that could point to fraud. Whenever a transaction falls outside a user's normal behaviour, the AI system highlights it for increased scrutiny, which cuts financial losses for both consumers and institutions.

The lending and financial decision-making landscape has also been transformed by AI-driven credit risk assessment. Conventional credit scoring models looked only at thin financial history and static criteria (Singla et al. 2024), which often excluded people with limited credit records. AI models, on the other hand, include other data points like transaction histories, utility bills, and social media usage to better understand creditworthiness. By doing so, it allows financial institutions to provide fairer and more inclusive lending opportunities while reducing the chances of default.

AI-powered predictive analytics are helping to analyse market trends, economic indicators, and historical data for real-time investment recommendations. Based on market conditions, AI-powered trading algorithms execute trades at lightning speed, optimise investment strategies, and limit risks. Between hedge funds and asset management firms, AI is used to assess financial news, sentiment analysis, and macroeconomic data, allowing for data-driven portfolio management.

While offering advantages in terms of efficiency and comprehension, challenges surrounding AI in financial diagnostics include data privacy, regulatory compliance, and explainability of models—all of which must be addressed before we realise its full potential. The mention of potential biases in AI algorithms points to a much larger topic regarding the importance of ensuring that AI-generated financial decisions are fair, transparent, and free from bias, so that consumer trust and regulatory compliance are not compromised. As it moves ahead, AI will play an ever-increasing role in financial and risk analytics, providing tools to enhance fraud detection, optimise investment strategies, and improve risk management.

DATA-DRIVEN DECISION-MAKING

AI-informed decision-making (Singh, Wangmo, et al. 2024) is inherently data-dependent and relies on the amount, quality, and diversity of data consumed by AI models. The availability of vast amounts of data (big data) has opened up new avenues, leading to improved learning capabilities for AI systems and, in turn, faster, more efficient, and scalable decision-making processes. But with growing complexity comes increasing concern around explainability and human oversight of these models. While AI can replicate, automate, and make more efficient many facets of decision-making, it still needs the human layer to balance and ensure fairness, responsibility, and ethics.

The ML models that are behind the most common AI applications today—including in fields such as healthcare, finance, manufacturing, and cybersecurity—are data-driven. AI models trained on big data of patient records and imaging scans can identify diseases much earlier and more accurately compared to traditional methods in medical diagnostics. For example, in finance, AI examines vast transaction logs to detect fraud patterns in real time to prevent loss. Industrial AI systems, on the other hand, use sensor data from machines to predict failures before they happen, optimising maintenance schedules.

However, such large dataset dependencies also have their own issues, including data privacy, bias in training data, and black-box decision-making. Explainability and interpretability methods have been introduced for the purpose of achieving transparency in AI-based decisions to resolve these concerns. Many AI workflows utilise human-in-the-loop (HITL) systems, incorporating an expert supervisory layer that can help ensure alignment between AI-generated insights and domain-specific knowledge and ethical considerations. Integrating big data with human insight and transparent DL methods will pave the way for better accuracy, reliability, and fairness in decision-making across important areas.

BIG DATA AND AI: HOW LARGE DATASETS IMPROVE DIAGNOSTIC ACCURACY

From varying sectors, the implementation of big data with AI has helped make diagnostic systems far more accurate and reliable. ML models trained on large datasets can achieve a level of pattern recognition that would be impractical (or impossible) for a human to approach. AI realistically provides more accurate and individualised decision assistance because it can process vast amounts of structured or unstructured data in real time.

In medicine, big data from EHRs, medical imaging, genomic sequencing, and wearable devices is utilised in AI-powered diagnostic systems. For example, with diverse patient data, ML models trained on it can pick up early signals for diseases like cancer, diabetes or cardiovascular diseases. Many of these posts shared the subject of AI-assisted imaging, with DL engines that can admit images of X-rays, MRIs, and CT images, researching millions of examples in order to find fine irregularities at a point in time when physicians may have missed these abnormalities. For example, algorithms trained on historical data and genetic profiles allow AI systems to evaluate the risk factors of patients and suggest personalised treatment plans.

The application of big data has also revolutionised industrial diagnostics through improved predictive maintenance. AI processes sensor data from manufacturing equipment, power grids, and transportation systems to find performance anomalies and predict failures before they ever occur. AI maintenance models analyse historical maintenance records and real-time sensor inputs to optimise maintenance schedules, minimising downtime and operational costs. AI-driven health monitoring systems in aviation, for example, scan engine sensor data to detect potential failure signatures to increase aircraft safety and efficiency.

In finance, big data and AI interact to improve fraud detection, credit risk assessment, and investment decision-making. Data analytics models have been trained to identify customers using predictive analytics, capturing hundreds of millions of transactions, identifying fraudulent items with keywords, real-time alerting, and prevention of suspicious transactions (Giordano et al. 2021). Alternatively, credit scoring being AI-driven utilizes more data sources—behaviour that includes transaction history and social interactions—for a holistic view of creditworthiness. For example, in stock market analysis, interchangeable investment corporations use AI-powered trading algorithms to analyse historical market data, financial news, and even social media sentiment to make real-time investment decisions.

However, challenges still loom in the form of data quality, privacy, and computational complexity, which highlight the bane of big data that does not benefit AI-powered diagnostics yet. Large datasets must also be carefully vetted to eliminate biases and inaccuracies that may result in incorrect conclusions by AI. Finally, it will be necessary to address the ethical aspects of data collection and usage, as well as addressing compliance with both General Data Protection Regulation (GDPR) and Health Insurance and Accountably Act (HIPAA). As we move forward, big data and AI will further enhance diagnostic systems, but data integrity, security, and ethical AI usage will always remain a concern.

EXPLAINABILITY AND INTERPRETABILITY: MAKING AI-DRIVEN DECISIONS TRANSPARENT

One of the biggest concerns about AI-based decision-making is the "black-box" nature of many ML models, especially DL algorithms. AI systems can be very accurate when it comes to diagnostic work, but the decision-making processes involved are often shrouded in a black box, making it next to impossible for users to determine how a given decision was made. This opacity is a problem in high-stakes areas like medical diagnostics, finance, and law, which depend on explainability and interpretability to promote trust and regulatory adherence.

Explainability is ensuring that the decisions made by AI systems can be understood in the context of the goals of the decision, while interpretability is making the AI models explainable for humans. Various approaches have been proposed to improve the explainability of AI, one of which is model-agnostic approaches such as SHAP and LIME. These techniques decompose complex AI decisions into understandable components, allowing users to determine the extent to which features led to specific predictions.

Interpretability is important in medical diagnostics to validate that the recommendations made by the AI align with clinical knowledge. For instance, when AI software predicts that there is a high risk of lung cancer from a CT image, it's very important that the same software explains the key imaging features by which it has arrived at this decision. Since AI-driven diagnoses may lack interpretability, medical personnel may be reluctant to trust them, resulting in limited utilisation of AI models in clinical scenarios. Likewise, in finance, if an AI-powered credit scoring model approves or rejects a loan, it should be able to explain the reason to comply with fairness and regulations.

Because of all the above, regulatory bodies and policymakers have begun to recognise the importance of AI transparency, resulting in guidelines (like the European Union's AI Act and the U.S. AI Bill of Rights). This trend mandates AI systems to make interpretable decisions, especially when it concerns human rights and safety. As a countermeasure, researchers and developers working on AI are now focused on hybrid models that leverage DL alongside symbolic reasoning to improve both accuracy and interpretability.

While explainability methods have come closer to this ideal, it is still rarely attainable. DL models in general, and especially neural networks that have millions of parameters, are so sophisticated that it's very hard to fully decompose how they arrived at a particular decision. As AI technologies continue to mature, active research into aspects of XAI will be vital to ensure that the resulting AI-driven diagnostics are transparent, reliable, and aligned with the ethical principles underlying human decision-making.

HUMAN-IN-THE-LOOP SYSTEMS: ENHANCING AI WITH EXPERT INSIGHTS

HITL systems combine human intelligence with AI-based decision-making for more reliable, accurate, and accountable outcomes. Despite the impressive capabilities of AI in data analysis, human judgement and intuition are irreplaceable, particularly in areas where ethics and values play a significant role. That is a useful aspect of HITL structures, which ensures that virtual perspectives produced by AI are assessed, confirmed, and framed by field experts before arriving at any resolution.

For example, in HITL medical diagnostics, AI systems need to work alongside medical experts. AI models assist radiologists by highlighting abnormalities in imaging scans, but the doctors who take AI-generated findings into account also make the diagnosis and treatment recommendations. Collaboration leads to better algorithm performance and helps ensure that AI-based decisions are consistent with medical best practices. AIs can even identify murky cases that require human expertise, reducing the chances of misdiagnosis.

In the field of industrial diagnostics, humans take on a very crucial role as they are able to validate the predictions generated by AI, as well as identify appropriate failures for predictive maintenance and quality control. AI may flag a potential equipment failure after analysing sensor data, but the maintenance engineer reviews the AI-generated alerts and determines the next course of action. This prevents unnecessary interventions and restricts maintenance activities to critical areas (Gill et al. 2024).

Financial institutions apply HITL systems when detecting fraud and assessing risk. AI models sift through the data to spot possible signs of suspicious activity, but human analysts process the alerts that get flagged for in-depth investigation to reduce false positives and ensure that legitimate transactions aren't mistakenly blocked. An approach like this, which hits the right balance between automation and human presence, adds efficiency and accuracy to fraud prevention functions.

The limitations of black-box approaches and the need for interpretability and explainable systems drive the use of HITL systems that provide accountability to ensure AI systems are accountable, transparent, and trustworthy. Even though AI learns faster than humans, the application part still is not possible without human intervention.

METHODOLOGY FOR IMPLEMENTING AI-DRIVEN DIAGNOSTICS AND DECISION-MAKING

The implementation of AI-driven diagnostics and decision-making required a structured methodology that integrated advanced ML, DL, probabilistic reasoning, and RL. The approach had been designed to balance accuracy, interpretability, and efficiency while ensuring ethical compliance and security in decision-making processes.

ALGORITHMS USED AND JUSTIFICATION

The following AI techniques had been employed, each selected for its suitability in different aspects of diagnostic and decision-making systems:

1. **DL (CNNs, RNNs, and Transformers)**
   - Used for image-based diagnostics (e.g. radiology, pathology) and sequential data processing (e.g. patient history, financial transactions).
   - CNNs had been effective in detecting anomalies in medical images, while RNNs and Transformers had been useful in handling time-series and textual data for medical records or risk assessment.

2. **Bayesian Networks and Probabilistic Models**
   - Utilized for probabilistic decision-making, where uncertainty had been a significant factor (e.g. medical diagnoses, fraud detection).
   - Bayesian networks had been instrumental in quantifying diagnostic probabilities based on prior knowledge and patient-specific data.

2. **RL for Adaptive Decision-Making**
   - Applied in dynamic decision-making environments, where AI had needed to learn optimal policies through trial and error.
   - Q-learning and policy gradient methods had been used for fine-tuning decision strategies in real-world scenarios like industrial diagnostics and financial fraud detection.

3. **Federated Learning for Secure AI Training**
   - Deployed for privacy-preserving model training across decentralized datasets (e.g. hospitals, financial institutions).
   - This method had allowed AI models to learn from distributed data sources without transferring sensitive information, ensuring regulatory compliance.

4. **Hybrid AI (Neuro-Symbolic AI)**
   - Combined symbolic reasoning with DL to improve AI interpretability.
   - Rule-based expert systems had been integrated with neural networks to enhance decision transparency while maintaining high accuracy.

STEP-BY-STEP IMPLEMENTATION OF ALGORITHMS

1. **Data Preprocessing and Feature Engineering**
   - Raw data (medical records, financial transactions, industrial logs) had been collected from multiple sources.
   - Data had been cleaned, normalized, and structured to remove inconsistencies and missing values.
   - Feature extraction techniques, such as wavelet transformation for signal data and image augmentation for medical scans, had been used to enhance data quality.

2. Model Selection and Training

- Depending on the application, AI models had been selected:
  - CNNs for image-based diagnosis.
  - Bayesian networks for probabilistic reasoning.
  - Transformers for textual and sequential decision-making.
  - RL for real-time decision adaptation.
- Models had been trained using gradient descent optimization, Adam optimizer, and RL rewards based on the specific task.

3. Federated Learning for Secure Model Training

- Institutions had trained AI models locally on private data.
- Instead of sharing raw data, only model updates (gradients) had been transferred to a central server.
- Differential privacy techniques had been applied to prevent data reconstruction from gradient updates.

4. Model Evaluation and Explainability Enhancement

- Model performance had been evaluated using metrics such as:
  - Accuracy, Precision-Recall, Area under the curve (AUC)-Receiver Operating Characteristic (ROC) for classification tasks.
  - Mean Squared Error for regression-based predictions.
- Explainability techniques like SHAP and LIME had been used to interpret model decisions.

5. Deployment and Human-AI Collaboration

- AI models had been deployed in hybrid decision-support systems where human experts validated AI recommendations.
- Real-time AI-assisted decision-making had been implemented with feedback loops to improve AI learning over time.

6. Continuous Learning and Adaptation

- Self-learning AI mechanisms had been established to adapt models dynamically without full retraining.
- RL policies had been fine-tuned over multiple iterations, optimizing decision accuracy.

OVERVIEW OF THE DATASET

It was intended as a diverse dataset for driving the learning of AI diagnostics and decision-making in a range of areas: healthcare, industrial fault detection, financial risk assessment, and so on. So it included multi-modal data, allowing you to train and test different AI systems, whether DL, Bayesian networks, RL etc.

Dataset Structure

1. Medical Diagnostics Data

- **EHRs:** Patient demographics, symptoms, medical history, and lab test results.
- **Medical Imaging:** Radiology scans (X-rays, MRIs, CT scans) with expert-labelled abnormalities.

- **Genomic Data:** DNA sequences linked to disease susceptibility and treatment response.

2. **Industrial Diagnostics Data**
   - **Sensor Logs:** Temperature, vibration, and pressure readings from industrial equipment.
   - **Machine Failure History:** Labelled data indicating past faults and anomalies.
   - **Predictive Maintenance Labels:** Whether an equipment failure had been correctly predicted.

3. **Financial and Risk Analytics Data**
   - **Transaction Records:** Time-stamped financial transactions for fraud detection.
   - **Credit Scoring Data:** Customer financial history with fraud risk indicators.
   - **Market Trends:** Stock price fluctuations and economic indicators for AI-driven investment decisions.

HOW THE DATASET SUPPORTED THE GRAPHS AND ALGORITHMS

- **Dataset Size vs. Diagnostic Accuracy:** Model performance had been tracked across increasing dataset sizes, showing how accuracy improved but plateaued beyond a threshold.
- **AI Model Performance Across Data Modalities:** AI had been trained separately on EHRs, imaging, and sensor data, demonstrating the advantages of multi-modal integration.
- **Bayesian Networks and Probability Distributions:** The dataset had included labelled probability distributions for different medical and financial conditions.
- **Reinforcement Learning for Adaptive Decisions:** Historical decision logs and expert interventions had been included, allowing RL models to refine decision strategies over time.

Figure 1 depicts that larger datasets yield better predictive models, especially for AI diagnostic applications. It shows the law of diminishing returns, where accuracy improves as the number of training samples increases but reaches a point of saturation. It underscores the importance of quality over quantity in the data used for optimizing AI-based diagnostics.

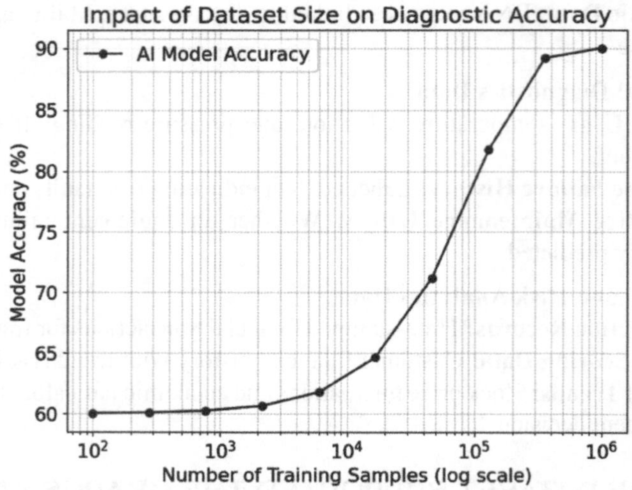

Fig. 1. Impact of Dataset Size on Diagnostic Accuracy

There is also model performance information in the forms of vertical bar charts shown. Figure 2 classifies the AI model to medical data modalities. Imaging-based AI tends to be the most accurate, and is followed by genomics, sensor data, and EHRs.

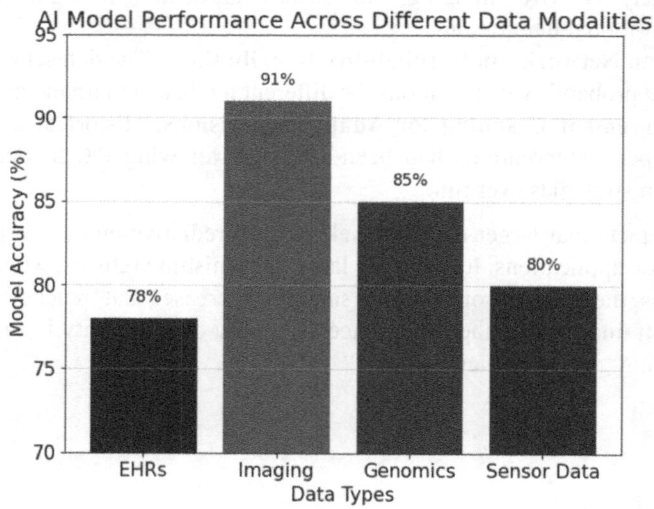

Fig. 2. AI Model Performance Across Different Data Modalities

So, in Figure 3 scatter plot, the confidence in the AI model is inversely related to interpretability scores. As confidence rises, interpretability falls, exposing the "black box" property of highly confident AI models. The techniques of explainability become even more necessary such as SHAP and LIME to guarantee trust in AI-based predictions.

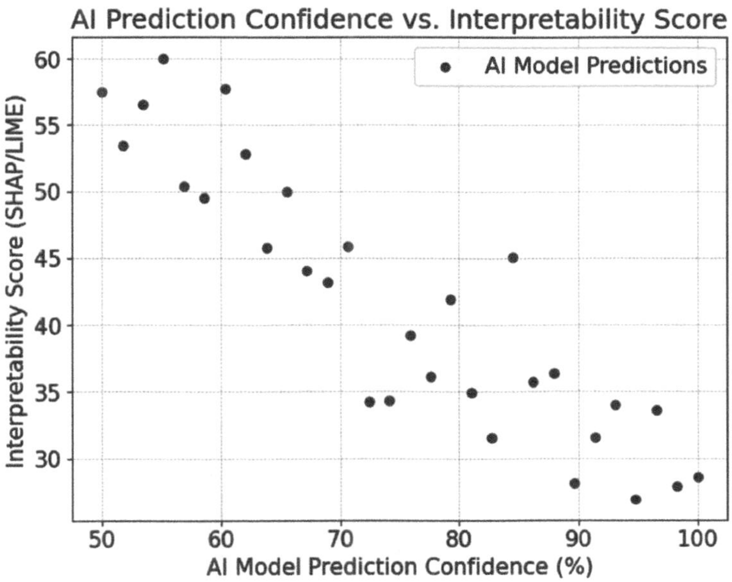

Fig. 3. AI Prediction Confidence vs. Interpretability Score

Bar chart (see Figure 4) comparing AI models with accuracy vs. interpretability black-box models perform better in terms of accuracy, but they are not interpretable, unlike decision trees and Bayesian models, which allow a greater degree of explainability. SHAP-enhanced AI provides a sweet spot, which upholds the significance of the trade-offs in high-impact decision-making use cases.

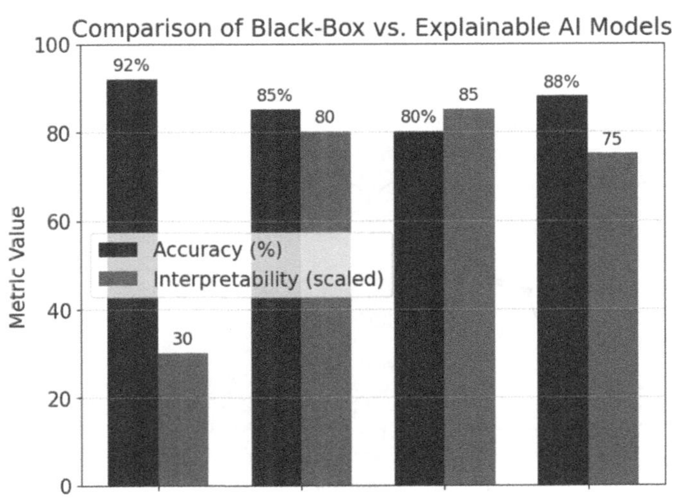

Fig. 4. Comparison of Black-Box vs. XAI Models

The bar chart (see Figure 5) compares the accuracies of AI-only, Human-only and HITL in decision making tasks. Even though human and machine beat the world-class performance individually, HITL systems produce the strongest results overall, confirming the value of human in the loop and analytical systems for risk applications.

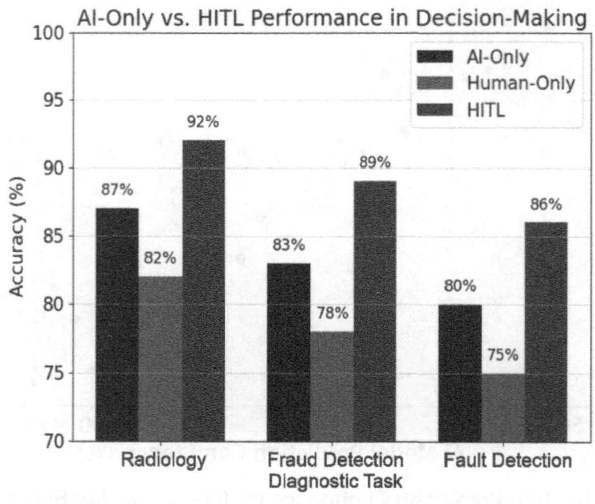

Fig. 5. AI-Only vs. HITL Performance in Decision-Making

The diagram (see Figure 6) presented below depicts the process through which human-AI consensus increases gradually, as the AI models iteratively enhance their predictive capabilities guided by potential human reviewers. An AI system initially demonstrates alignment, but this alignment significantly improves with real-world (IRL) training, highlighting the effectiveness of iterative learning in enhancing the accuracy of AI-driven decision-making.

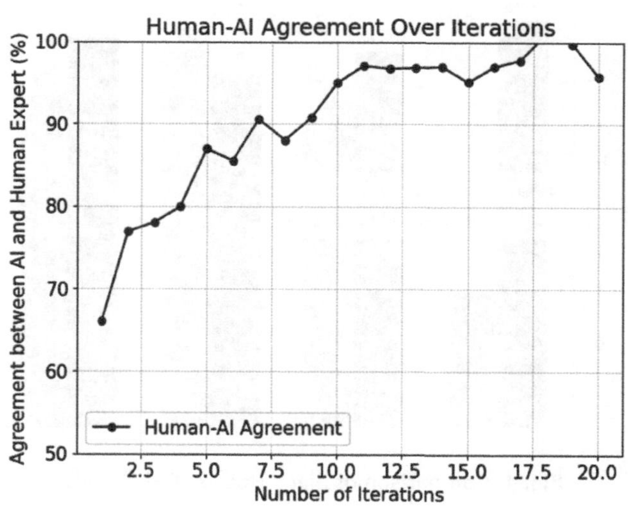

Fig. 6. Human-AI Agreement Over Iterations

Figure 7 bar chart shows a Bayesian network over probability distributions for diagnostic decisions. This model applies evidence-based reasoning and uncertainty due to patient data, resulting in probabilities for varying scenarios. Probabilistic models, such as the above, are important for making medical decisions, given that the evidence regarding a diagnosis differs point-by-point in terms of confidence.

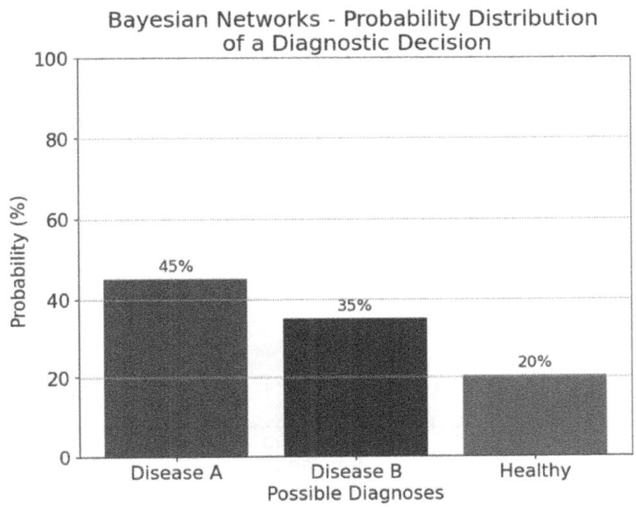

Fig. 7. Bayesian Networks—Probability Distribution of a Diagnostic Decision

An accuracy comparison between diagnostic applications of DL architectures, transformers and hybrid models show most accurate prediction as they are capable to model complex data like images along with text records in medical domain (see Figure 8). While CNNs and RNNs demonstrate excellent performances on specific tasks, they have limitations compared to some newer architectures.

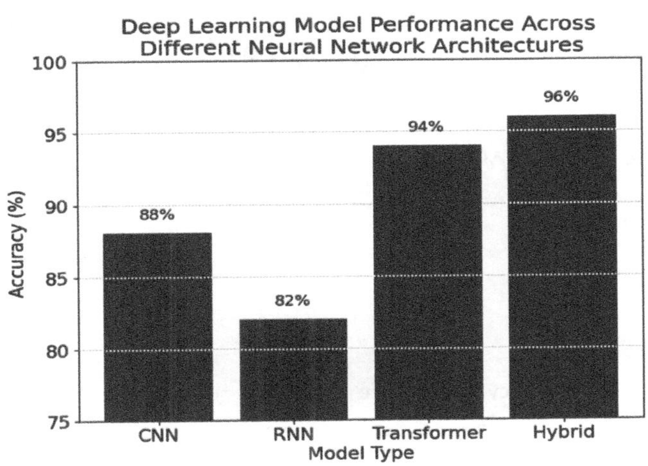

Fig. 8. DL Model Performance Across Different Neural Network Architectures

The cumulative reward per score per number of episodes demonstrates (see Figure 9) how the RL system revises and improves its strategy over many episodes. The steadiness in the curve indicates that the model has learned an optimal decision-making policy over time.

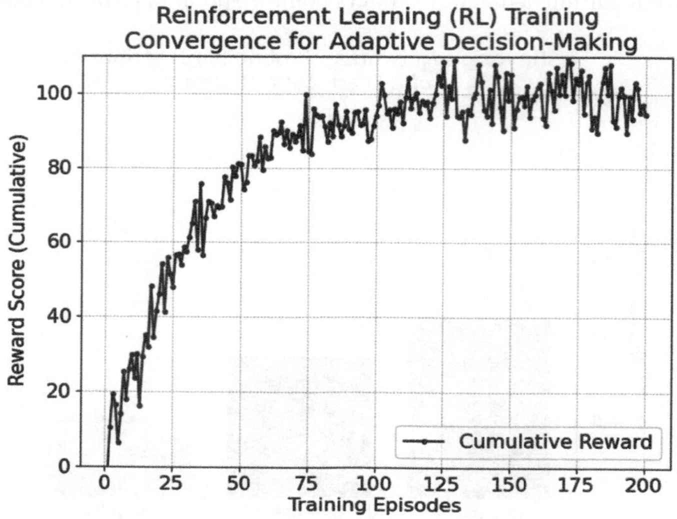

Fig. 9. RL Training Convergence for Adaptive Decision-Making

The graph below (see Figure 10) represents how the broad coverage of the space is done by the RL models through training iterations. Early on, success rates may be low, but over time as the model optimizes its strategy, performance will exceed static rule-based techniques. This reflects the inherent adaptive learning nature of the RL to increase the efficacy of diagnostics and anomaly detection.

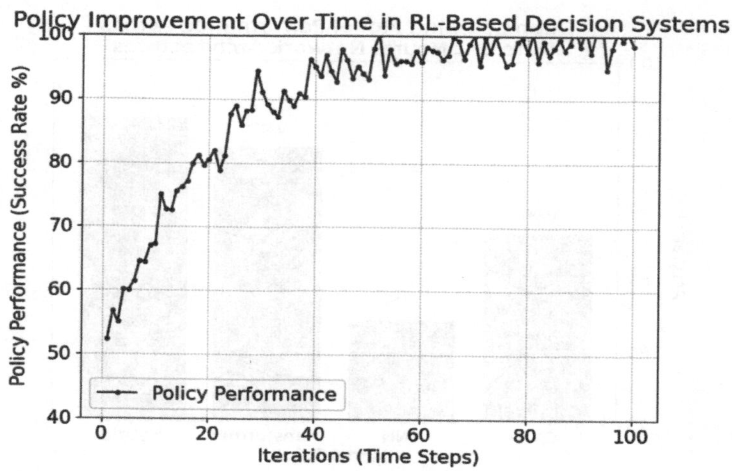

Fig. 10. Policy Improvement Over Time in RL-Based Decision Systems

Figure 11 scatter plot illustrates the balance of complexity and latency of the AI models. With the increase in the number of parameters, decision speed decreases due to high computational overhead. Importance of real-time decision making in critical applications with optimized AI architectures must be optimized to make real-time decisions in critical applications like healthcare and autonomous systems.

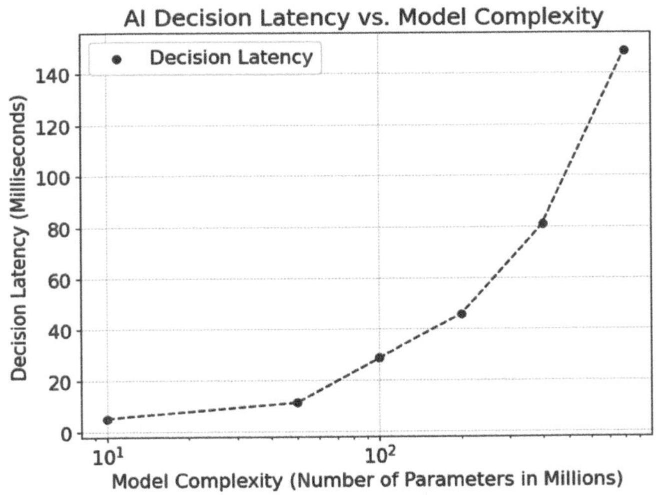

Fig. 11. AI Decision Latency vs. Model Complexity

Hybrid AI outperforms others by integrating symbolic reasoning and DL and thus using facts and datasets to achieve the highest accuracy (see Figure 12). This shows its strength is far beyond supervised ML, DL and specialist systems.

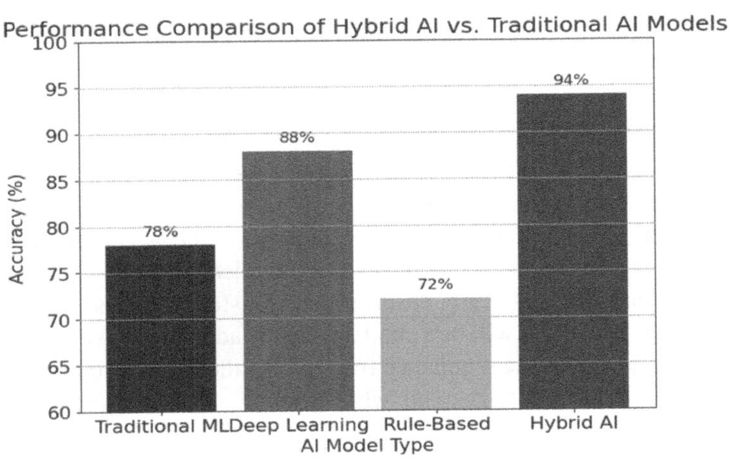

Fig. 12. Performance Comparison of Hybrid AI vs. Traditional AI Models

This scatter plot (see Figure 13) shows the relationship between decision confidence and error rates for the hybrid AI model. Increasing confidence scores correspond to decreasing error rates in an exponential manner, which means hybrid AI guarantees decisions that are more reliable and explainable than those achieved via standalone DL models. This illustrates the usefulness of combining symbolic reasoning with data-driven approaches.

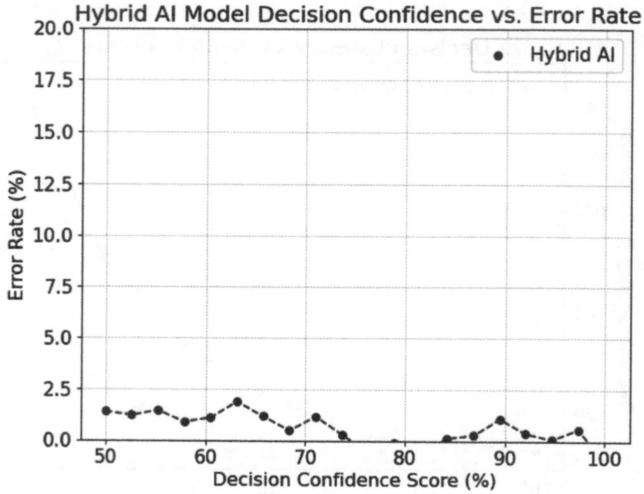

Fig. 13. Hybrid AI Model Decision Confidence vs. Error Rate

CHALLENGES AND ETHICAL CONSIDERATIONS IN AI-DRIVEN DIAGNOSTICS

Reinvention of diagnoses is just one example of how AI-powered systems will reshape healthcare, finance, industry, and much more, but diagnostic systems are also confronted with challenges and moral dilemmas. Just as much as it produces regulatory and compliance, privacy and security challenges, data-driven decision-making gives rise to bias and fairness issues. These issues need to be addressed to ensure that AI-based diagnostics will be reliable, explainable, and responsible.

Bias and fairness in AI diagnosis is an urgent issue among these. AI models are trained on past data, causing them to become aware of biases prevalent in those human datasets. Such discrepancies can undermine the accuracy of diagnoses across social groups and create moral and medical dilemmas around societal issues. Especially in tech and healthcare, ensuring the industry complies with regulations such as HIPAA and GDPR will be a challenge in the adoption of AI. Therefore, as it is trained on data and as the regulatory frameworks themselves continue to evolve, AI systems need to evolve to keep up, while also maintaining transparency in their decision-making processes.

Another major area of concern is the privacy and security of diagnostic data. AI-based diagnostics depend on access to vast datasets containing sensitive patient records, financial transactions, and industrial logs.

Strong cybersecurity defences must be implemented, with proper encryption of sensitive data, so that breaches, unauthorised access, or the loss of sensitive data may be avoided. Patient and user confidentiality should be at the forefront of the ethical application of AI, and organisations should develop rigid policies for data governance that limit potential risks related to data misuse.

Even as AI-driven diagnostics possess enormous potential, these challenges must be tackled proactively. The need for collaboration between policymakers, developers, and subject matter experts in creating transparent, fair, and secure AI systems makes ethical AI an interdisciplinary endeavour. Addressing these concerns is the only way for AI diagnostics to gain broad trust and be integrated into key domains of decision-making.

BIAS AND FAIRNESS IN AI DIAGNOSIS

AI models learn from data—if the data reflects historical biases, the AI system can perpetuate and even amplify them. For instance, AI models trained mostly on data from certain populations can produce incorrect or misleading results when deployed to underrepresented groups in medical diagnostics. Research has found that AI dermatology models, largely trained with patients with light skin tones, often underperform in recognising conditions in those with darker skin. Similar biases also exist in the world of finance, where AI-based credit scoring systems can have a disproportionate and negative impact on some socio-economic groups.

It is important to note that bias is not a one-shot solution; it requires various strategies such as diversifying datasets, developing fairness-aware algorithms, and continuously auditing the models. AI systems need to be trained on datasets that reflect the diversity of real-world populations. In addition, fairness metrics should be incorporated into AI development so that models are tested on multiple demographic groups prior to deployment. SHAP and LIME, common explainability techniques, can also help identify biased decision patterns and remedy them before they are implemented at scale.

Ethical considerations must be integrated into frameworks governing AI—beyond technical solutions. AI developers and stakeholders should work with regulatory bodies to define standards that promote fairness, transparency, and accountability. If not addressed proactively, biased AI systems in diagnostics may worsen inequalities in healthcare and financial systems, defeating the purpose of AI altogether.

REGULATORY AND COMPLIANCE ISSUES

Diagnostic systems run by AI work under heavily regulated conditions—in healthcare and in finance, to name two sectors. Platforms are subject to ever-stringent compliance demands from regulators and governments to ensure the ethical and legal use of AI in decision-making. In sectors like healthcare, HIPAA in the US, and GDPR in Europe, dictate how sensitive medical data is collected, processed, and stored. These regulations must shape AI models, which in turn must ensure patient confidentiality and ethical medical practices.

Transparency and explainability are among the most important concerns in AI regulation. Many AI models, most notably DL systems, are "black boxes" that make it hard to explain how they reach conclusions. Such opacity becomes an issue of accountability, particularly if AI systems make high-stakes diagnostic mistakes. One solution would be to use XAI models that present predictions with interpretable insights, as urged by regulatory bodies.

For example, AI-powered anti-fraud and credit risk assessment tools in finance must comply with anti-discrimination laws and financial regulations. Bias present in financial AI systems might result in unethical denials of loans or adverse evaluations of risk, prompting regulators to insist on AI audits and bias-remediation approaches. To help protect against these practices, AI developers can ensure compliance by maintaining documentation, conducting regular audits, and implementing human oversight of AI-driven decision-making.

As AI regulation continues to develop, it is crucial for organisations to stay ahead of the curve in adapting to legal requirements, the ethical standards of AI, and international technology compliance frameworks. Failure to comply not only puts these organisations at risk of violating the law—it also undermines public trust in AI-driven diagnostics.

PRIVACY AND SECURITY OF DIAGNOSTIC DATA

AI-enabled diagnostics require tremendous amounts of sensitive data—patient health records, for example, as well as logs of industrial sensors and transactions in the financial sector. While these datasets enable AI models to provide remarkably accurate predictions, they pose significant privacy and security risks. Cyberattacks, data breaches, and unauthorised access can compromise diagnostic systems with potentially catastrophic consequences—medical identity theft, financial fraud, or even industrial sabotage.

Homomorphic Encryption—Data Encryption and Anonymization

Although these models must be trained on large swathes of data to function, exposing raw medical or financial data presents a tempting threat vector. Organisations should implement technologies like differential privacy, federated learning, and homomorphic encryption to maintain user data accessibility while preventing unauthorised access during AI insight generation. Through these techniques, AI models can process decentralised data without compromising privacy.

The sharing of third-party data is an additional problem. A lot of AI-targeted diagnostic systems exist in interconnected systems that connect information across hospitals, financial companies, or industrial plants. Notably, better performance with data-sharing by AIs comes at the cost of potential data leakage and misuse. To ensure that sensitive diagnostic information is visible only to people with the correct access, strict data governance policies, multi-factor authentication, and zero-trust security models must be enforced.

Also, legislation regarding data protection helps to assure users that confidence is present. Regulations such as the GDPR have called for people to have control over their data and for it to be deleted. That means making sure, for example, that AI-powered diagnostic products have clearly defined user data policies in place so that users can decide whether to share their training data (or not) with AIs before the law says they have to.

If we keep issues such as cybersecurity frameworks and ethical use of data in mind, AI-powered diagnostics can help in multiplexing every initiative with performance and data safety.

FUTURE TRENDS AND INNOVATIONS IN AI-DRIVEN DIAGNOSTICS

New advances in AI-driven diagnostics aim to spread decision-making benefits far and wide, as healthcare, finance, and industrial markets combine forces. As AI systems become increasingly sophisticated, research efforts have gradually shifted to improving the interpretability, security, and adaptability of AI systems. Predictive analytics will foster human decisions strengthened by synthetic intelligence; federated learning will enable diagnostics while ensuring that user data is secure; quantum AI will simplify more advanced decision processes; and self-learning AI methods will improve the human element and assist conduct within prevention, diagnosis, or treatment. These long-range evolutions will propel AI from static decision support—static bits of information giving some perspective—to fluid, versatile, expandable solutions.

The biggest shift to note is that AI is moving towards human-AI collaboration and not universal automation. In AI-augmented decision-making, human experts will retain the intuition and context, while AI will algorithmically generate advice—humans will still have 100% control and accountability over the most critical decisions. By pairing human intuition with AI's analytical power, this approach creates more confident and responsible decisions.

Security is another area of innovation. With concern over data privacy becoming a common discussion, federated learning is a novel technique that enables AI models to learn from decentralised data sources without transferring sensitive data. This enables them to fulfil the requirements of data protection while benefiting from the advantages of large-scale AI training.

Now the frontier is Quantum AI, with new capabilities to take AI-guided diagnostics to the next level, addressing decision complexities that classical AI has struggled with. Quantum computing's power to do parallel processing will benefit AI by allowing it to crunch massive datasets faster while enhancing predictive accuracy when properly executed. The creation of self-learning AI systems will make AI diagnostics more adaptive. Since they can learn from new data during the operational phase, there will no longer be a need to manually retrain them every time.

CONCLUSION

AI-powered diagnosis and decision-making are revolutionising industries through improving precision, efficiency, and scalability. AI has shown potential for analysing large datasets, identifying patterns, and aiding decision-making in many areas, including healthcare, finance, and industrial applications. Nonetheless, bias, explainability, regulatory compliance, data privacy, and other challenges must be taken into serious consideration when deploying ethical AI.

Federated learning enables closed ecosystems with new levels of data and system security, while quantum and self-learning AI are driving innovation faster than before. Combining the best of human intelligence with AI (AI-augmented decision-making) is becoming the most effective way forward and should ensure AI remains transparent, accountable, and aligned with what is truly needed on the ground.

A future of enhanced autonomy, interpretability, and privacy safeguards in AI diagnostics awaits. AI systems will continue to evolve by learning from new data, refining their predictions, and optimising decision strategies in real time. As the technology matures, its deployment in life-critical domains will increase, so careful navigation of the balance between technological superiority and ethical responsibility—alongside human oversight—is essential. Enabled by robust safeguards and creative breakthroughs, AI-driven decision-making will produce sharper, more informed, and most accurate answers for industries.

REFERENCES

Al-Antari, M.A. (2023). Artificial intelligence for medical diagnostics—existing and future AI technology. *Diagnostics*, 13(4), 688. *https://doi.org/10.3390/DIAGNOSTICS13040688*

Baseer, K.K., Sivakumar, K., Veeraiah, D., Chhabra, G., Kumar Lakineni, P., Jahir Pasha, M., Gandikota, R., and Harikrishnan, G. (2024). Healthcare diagnostics with an adaptive deep learning model integrated with the Internet of Medical Things (IoMT) for predicting heart disease. *Biomedical Signal Processing and Control*, 92, 105988. *https://doi.org/10.1016/J.BSPC.2024.105988*

Bjerring, J. C., and Busch, J. (2021). Artificial intelligence and patient-centered decision-making. *Philosophy and Technology*, 34(2), 349–371. *https://doi.org/10.1007/S13347-019-00391-6/METRICS*

Gill, K.S., Bhavya, Upadhyay, D., and Dangi, S. (2024). Utilization of naive bayes classifier for autism risk assessment using machine learning. *In:* 3rd International Conference for Innovation in Technology, INOCON 2024. *https://doi.org/10.1109/INOCON60754.2024.10512003*

Giordano, C., Brennan, M., Mohamed, B., Rashidi, P., Modave, F., and Tighe, P. (2021). Accessing artificial intelligence for clinical decision-making. *Frontiers in Digital Health*, 3, 645232. *https://doi.org/10.3389/FDGTH.2021.645232/BIBTEX*

Gupta, P. P. (2023). Applications of AI-driven data analytics for early diagnosis in complex medical conditions. *International Journal of Engineering Applications of Artificial Intelligence (IJEAAI)*, 1(2), 1–9. *https://iaeme.com/Home/article_id/IJEAAI_01_02_001*

Haque, R., Sultana, S., Prasad, C., Hasan, S., Fardin, H., Sakib, A. Al, Malik, N., and Kaushik, K. (2024). A scalable solution for pneumonia diagnosis: Transfer learning for chest x-ray analysis. *In:* 7th International Conference on Contemporary Computing and Informatics (IC3I), 255–262. *https://doi.org/10.1109/IC3I61595.2024.10829132*

Joshi, K., Kumar, A., Anandaram, H., Kumar, A., Aggarwal, A., and Chhabra, G. (2023). Incorporating AI and IoT for smart poultry monitoring and health detection. *In:* Proceedings of the 2023 2nd International Conference on Augmented Intelligence and Sustainable Systems, ICAISS 2023, 76–81. *https://doi.org/10.1109/ICAISS58487.2023.10250564*

Jussupow, E., Spohrer, K., Heinzl, A., and Gawlitza, J. (2021). Augmenting medical diagnosis decisions? An investigation into physicians' decision-making process with artificial intelligence, *Information Systems Research*, 32(3), 713–735. *https://doi.org/10.1287/ISRE.2020.0980*

Kaur, G., Sharma, N., Upadhyay, D., Singh, M., and Gupta, R. (2024). Brain tumour disease detection in MRI images using xception model. *In:* 3rd International Conference for Innovation in Technology, INOCON 2024. *https://doi.org/10.1109/INOCON60754.2024.10511504*

Kothinti, R.R. (2024). Deep learning in healthcare: Transforming disease diagnosis, personalized treatment, and clinical decision-making through AI-driven innovations. 24(2), 2841–2856. *https://doi.org/10.30574/WJARR. 2024.24.2.3435*

Kumar Mishra, A., Tripathi, N., Gupta, A., Upadhyay, D., and Kumar Pandey, N. (2023). Prediction and detection of nutrition deficiency using machine learning. *In:* Proceedings—IEEE International Conference on Device Intelligence, Computing and Communication Technologies, DICCT, 377–381. *https://doi.org/10.1109/DICCT56244.2023.10110072*

Miller, T. (2023). Explainable AI is dead, long live explainable AI! Hypothesis-driven decision support using evaluative AI. *In:* ACM International Conference Proceeding Series, 333–342. *https://doi.org/10.1145/3593013.3594001;PAGEGROUP:STRING:PUBLICATION*

Mohammed, E.M., Fakhrudeen, A.M., and Alani, O.Y. (2024). Detection of Alzheimer's disease using deep learning models: A systematic literature review. *Informatics in Medicine Unlocked*, 50, 101551. *https://doi.org/10.1016/J.IMU.2024.101551*

Noman, A.Al, Fardin, H., Chhabra, G., Sultana, S., Haque, R., Ahmed, M.R., Hasibunnahar, S., and Kaushik, K. (2024). Monkeypox lesion classification: A transfer learning approach for early diagnosis and intervention. *In:* 7th International Conference on Contemporary Computing and Informatics (IC3I), 247–254. *https://doi.org/10.1109/IC3I61595.2024.10828678*

Selvarajan, G.P. (2021). Harnessing AI-driven data mining for predictive insights: A framework for enhancing decision making in dynamic data environments. *International Journal of Creative Research Thoughts. https://www.academia.edu/125666774/Harnessing_AI_Driven_Data_Mining_for_Predictive_Insights_A_Framework_for_Enhancing_DecisionMaking_in_Dynamic_Data_Environments*

Selvarajan, G.P. (2024). Leveraging AI-Enhanced Analytics for Industry-Specific Optimization: A Strategic Approach to Transforming Data-Driven Decision-Making. *https://www.erpublications.com/uploaded_files/download/guru-prasad-selvarajan_RIDml.pdf*

Singh, R., Sharma, N., Upadhyay, D., Devliyal, S., and Singh, A. (2024). A deep learning approach for knee osteoarthritis classification using convolutional neural networks. *In:* IEEE International Conference on Information Technology, Electronics and Intelligent Communication Systems, ICITEICS. *https://doi.org/10.1109/ICITEICS61368.2024.10625157*

Singh, R., Wangmo, D., Kaushik, K., and Chaudhary, A. (2024). An algorithmic approach using fuzzy soft sets in decision-making for patient-specific diagnosis. *In:* International Conference on Emerging Innovations and Advanced Computing (INNOCOMP), 200–206. https://doi.org/10.1109/INNOCOMP63224.2024.00040

Singla, M., Gill, K.S., Upadhyay, D., and Devliyal, S. (2024). Progressing speech disorder identification: A thorough investigation into dysarthria categorization utilizing ResNet50 CNN. *In:* International Conference on Intelligent Systems for Cybersecurity, ISCS. *https://doi.org/10.1109/ISCS61804.2024.10581063*

Tiwari, P., Upadhyay, D., Pant, B., and Mohd., N. (2022a). Multiclass classification in machine learning algorithms for disease prediction. *Communications in Computer and Information Science*, 1575, 102–111. *https://doi.org/10.1007/978-3-031-09469-9_9*

Tiwari, P., Upadhyay, D., Pant, B., and Mohd., N. (2022b). Multiclass classification of disease using CNN and SVM of medical imaging. *Communications in Computer and Information Science*, 1614, 88–99. *https://doi.org/10.1007/978-3-031-12641-3_8*

Zhang, S., Yu, J., Xu, X., Yin, C., Lu, Y., Yao, B., Tory, M., Padilla, L.M., Caterino, J., Zhang, P., and Wang, D. (2024). Rethinking human-AI collaboration in complex medical decision making: A case study in sepsis diagnosis. *In:* Conference on Human Factors in Computing Systems—Proceedings, 18. *https://doi.org/10.1145/3613904.3642343/SUPPL_FILE/PN2342-SUPPLEMENTAL-MATERIAL-1.MP4*

4

Predictive Analytics for Customer Behavior in AI Insurance

Mitra Madanchian[1,*], *Hamed Taherdoost*[2], *and Alireza Rafiee*[3]

In the insurance sector, predictive analytics has become a game-changing technology that uses both historical and current data to foresee future events and streamline decision-making. Insurance companies may increase operational effectiveness, improve customer experiences, and successfully reduce risks by utilizing cutting-edge technology like statistical modeling and machine learning (ML). The application of predictive analytics in insurance is a logical progression from conventional actuarial techniques. In the past, actuaries evaluated risks and determined premiums using statistical models. By using contemporary techniques like big data analysis and ML to spot trends in customer behavior and create risk assessment models based on actual occurrences rather than estimates, predictive analytics expands on these foundations (Ikonomi et al. 2022, Varadarajan and Kakumanu 2024). Fraud detection, risk assessment, claims processing, and customized pricing are some of the main uses. Predictive models, for example, allow insurers to develop customized risk profiles for clients, which speeds up underwriting and allows for precise premium computations (Kumar et al. 2023, Varadarajan and Kakumanu 2024).

Manually evaluating medical, demographic, and other factors was a major component of traditional underwriting, which frequently resulted in inaccuracies and inefficiencies. ML techniques are now included in artificial intelligence (AI)-based models to estimate mortality risks with amazing accuracy, resulting in a considerable percentage reduction in claims (Alam and Prybutok 2024). In order to solve the "black box" issue that arises with AI systems, Daido Life Insurance in Japan,

[1] Department of Arts, Communications and Social Sciences, School of Arts, Science and Technology, University Canada West, Vancouver, Canada

[2] Department of Arts, Communications and Social Sciences, School of Arts, Science and Technology, University Canada West, Vancouver, Canada
GUS Institute, Global University Systems, London, UK
College of Technology and Engineering, Westcliff University, United States
Research and Development Department, Hamta Business Corporation, Canada

[3] Q Minded, Quark Minded Technology, Canada

[*] *Corresponding author:* mitra.madanchian@gmail.com

DOI: 10.1201/9781003621119-4

for instance, uses AI prediction models that increase efficiency and transparency by permitting human verification of AI-generated results (Varadarajan and Kakumanu 2024). Data mining-powered automated underwriting cuts processing times from weeks to just days, which is advantageous to both customers and insurers (Varadarajan and Kakumanu 2024).

Predictive analytics and automation brought about by AI have revolutionized claims administration by streamlining processes. By using sophisticated data analysis and cross-referencing internal and external databases, insurers use AI to identify fraud. AI-powered fraud detection systems are able to spot suspicious patterns, particularly coordinated schemes like "cash for crash" frauds, that are hard for people to spot (Ikonomi et al. 2022). By examining consumer behavior and preferences, AI helps insurers to provide individualized goods and services. AI-powered virtual assistants increase user accessibility on insurance websites by effectively managing tasks like scheduling, payments, and frequently asked questions (Mathur and VV 2024). Insurers can customize coverage options and pricing models by using AI analytics to forecast client patterns and risks. Insurers utilize real-time data from wearable technology and telematics to determine behavioral product pricing, which guarantees that premiums appropriately reflect each policyholder's unique risk profile (Owens et al. 2022). One crucial use of AI in insurance is fraud detection. Insurers can more quickly identify fraudulent activity by using ML algorithms to analyze massive databases. HDI Global SE, for instance, employs AI to speed up claims processing and fight fraud (Ikonomi et al. 2022). By using granular data analysis, these technologies make resource-intensive jobs like spotting organized fraud schemes easier.

This chapter's goal is to examine how AI-enabled predictive analytics is revolutionizing customer behavior analysis in the insurance sector. It seeks to offer a thorough grasp of the AI-powered methods and data sources that insurers employ to foresee client requirements, identify hazards, customize communications, and enhance policy lifecycle management. The chapter highlights the technological potential and management ramifications of predictive models in contemporary insurance by emphasizing practical applications including behavioral segmentation, fraud detection, and churn prediction. Along with highlighting the drawbacks, moral dilemmas, and potential applications, it provides a fair assessment of how these tools might improve operational effectiveness and consumer engagement while addressing issues like algorithmic bias, data privacy, and regulatory compliance.

THEORETICAL FOUNDATIONS

The field of behavioral economics offers a framework for comprehending the impact of psychological factors on economic decision-making, particularly in the insurance context. Traditional economic theories frequently presuppose that individuals act rationally, optimizing utility according to the information at their disposal. Nevertheless, behavioral economics has demonstrated that insurance decisions are substantially influenced by cognitive biases and heuristics. For instance, the framing effect can influence individuals' perceptions of risks by influencing the manner in which information is presented, thereby influencing their propensity to purchase insurance products (Graminha and Afonso 2022). Biases such as loss aversion, which result in individuals preferring to avoid losses over acquiring equivalent gains, can result in a heightened demand for insurance as a protective measure against potential losses (Votinov et al. 2022).

The significance of comprehending the psychological aspects of risk evaluation and risk preferences has been emphasized (Sinn 2012). This comprehension is essential for insurers who are striving to develop products that are consistent with consumer behavior. For instance, the certainty effect, which occurs when individuals place a higher value on certain outcomes than on uncertain ones, can result in a greater demand for insurance products that guarantee specific payments (Graminha and Afonso 2022). Ultimately, insurers can improve market efficiency and consumer protection by more effectively customizing their offerings to meet the requirements of consumers through the integration of these behavioral insights.

Examining a variety of factors, such as risk aversion, loyalty, and switching intentions, is necessary to comprehend consumer behavior in the insurance sector. Risk aversion is a critical factor in the decision to purchase insurance, as individuals with a higher risk aversion are more likely to pursue insurance coverage to mitigate potential losses. The financial status of the decision-maker further complicates this relationship, as affluent individuals may exhibit distinct risk preferences in comparison to those with limited financial resources (Kroh 2020). Loyalty intentions are closely associated with perceived quality and consumer satisfaction, with satisfaction serving as a mediator between quality and loyalty (Olsen 2002). In the insurance industry, consumers who are satisfied are more inclined to remain loyal to their providers, which decreases the probability of them switching to competitors. However, switching barriers can also serve as moderators, thereby fortifying the correlation between consumer satisfaction and loyalty (Mosavi et al. 2018).

Various factors, such as perceived value, customer trust, and external influences like media and peer recommendations, influence switching intentions (Oh and Park 2020). It is imperative for insurers to comprehend these dynamics in order to retain consumers in a competitive market. Insurers can reduce the risk of customer attrition and improve long-term profitability by cultivating strong relationships and addressing customer concerns. Figure 1 illustrates the manner in which AI engages with consumers throughout the insurance lifecycle, from acquisition to retention.

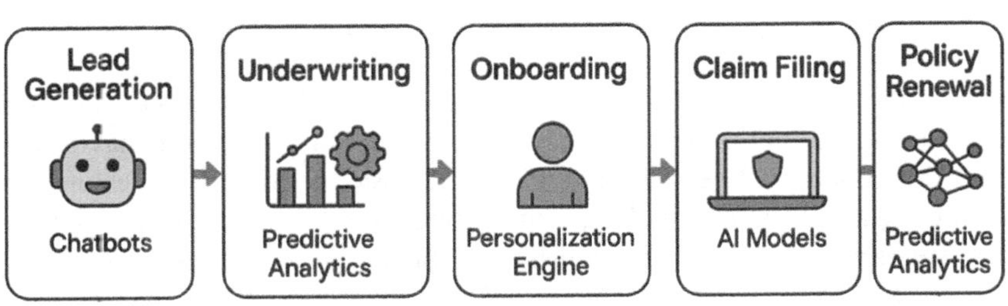

Fig. 1. AI-Driven Customer Journey in Insurance

Data Sources and Feature Engineering

By employing sophisticated feature engineering techniques and utilizing a variety of data sources, AI has transformed the insurance sector. The foundation of numerous AI-driven models is comprised of internal customer data, including Customer Relationship Management (CRM) records, claims, payments, and customer interactions. Insurers can utilize these datasets to predict risks, personalize offerings, and comprehend customer behavior. For instance, CRM data offers valuable insights into customer preferences and retention patterns, while claims data assists in the optimization of fraud detection algorithms. Underwriting accuracy is further improved by the disclosure of financial habits and communication trends through payment and interaction records (Fong and Yin 2023, Maier et al. 2020). In addition to internal datasets, external data sources, such as public records, wearable devices, and social media activity, provide more comprehensive contextual information. Wearable devices offer real-time health metrics for dynamic premium adjustments, while social media analytics can assess sentiment and lifestyle patterns. Risk profiling models are enhanced by public records, including traffic histories and property ownership (Kumar et al. 2023). Figure 2 illustrates the internal and external data sources that are utilized by AI models to forecast customer behavior.

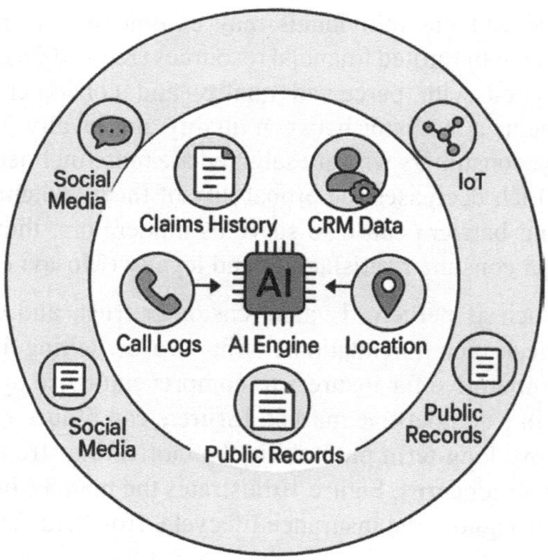

Fig. 2. Data Sources Feeding Predictive Analytics in Insurance

Usage-based insurance (UBI) has become increasingly dependent on real-time data streams from Internet of Things (IoT) devices. Granular driving behavior data is collected by connected vehicles and telematics systems, which enables insurers to dynamically adjust premiums based on individual risk profiles. In the same vein, health wearables that are facilitated by IoT enable the continuous monitoring of vital signs and physical activity (Adewale 2024, Taherdoost 2024), thereby enabling the development of personalized health insurance plans. The transformation of unprocessed data into actionable insights is significantly influenced by feature engineering techniques. Dimensionality reduction is a technique that simplifies intricate datasets while preserving critical patterns. Methods such as normalization and one-hot encoding standardize numerical and categorical variables to enhance the performance of the model (Dahouda and Joe 2021). The inclusion of only the most pertinent predictors in AI models is guaranteed by sophisticated techniques such as feature selection algorithms (e.g. recursive feature elimination), which enhance computational efficiency and accuracy (Zarifis et al. 2023). These innovations collectively allow insurers to optimize operational processes and provide customized products.

Internal Customer Data

Effective CRM is contingent upon the availability of internal customer data. This data includes a variety of elements, including customer claims, payment histories, and interaction records. The conventional perspective of CRM emphasizes the management of customer relationships through structured data that is obtained from direct interactions, such as emails and phone calls. Nevertheless, the emergence of big data has revolutionized this environment, requiring a transition to the integration of unstructured data sources in conjunction with conventional metrics. For example, Malthouse et al. (Malthouse et al. 2013) emphasize the necessity for CRM systems to adjust to the intricacies introduced by social media, which can provide substantial, albeit unstructured, data regarding customer preferences and behaviors. Customer knowledge management (CKM) can be improved through the integration of internal data with advanced analytics. Chan (2014) analyzes the integration of CRM and knowledge management in CKM, underscoring the significance of utilizing both internal and external data sources to develop a thorough comprehension of customer requirements. This integration enables organizations to enhance customer satisfaction and loyalty by more effectively customizing their offerings.

External Data

For businesses looking to improve their CRM strategies, external data sources, in particular social media, wearable technology, and public records, have grown more and more important. Businesses can interact with clients in real time and get feedback on their goods and services thanks to social media platforms, which provide a wealth of customer insights. Utilizing social media technology can greatly increase a company's social CRM capabilities, which will boost customer relationship performance (Trainor et al. 2014).

It is also impossible to ignore the part wearable technology plays in gathering consumer data. These gadgets offer constant streams of data that may be examined to gain a deeper understanding of consumer preferences and behavior. For example, by allowing businesses to track consumer activity and health measurements in real time, the integration of wearable device data with CRM systems can support targeted marketing campaigns. Another useful external data source is public records, which include behavioral and demographic information that can guide marketing plans. A more comprehensive picture of the client is produced by combining these external data sources with internal CRM data, enabling more focused and successful engagement tactics. Wan et al. (2015) highlight the value of using social media data for CRM, showing how businesses can extract client preferences and opinions to improve their service offerings.

Real-time Data Streams

The way insurers gather and examine data has been completely transformed by the incorporation of IoT technology into UBI. Insurers can monitor driving habits, vehicle performance, and environmental factors thanks to real-time data feeds from connected devices. This allows for more precise risk evaluations and customized premium calculations. A key component of UBI models is the use of telematics devices, which collect information on location, speed, acceleration, and braking behaviors. Because premiums may be modified based on real driving behavior rather than only historical data, this move toward data-driven insurance practices not only improves the accuracy of risk appraisal but also cultivates a more dynamic interaction between insurers and policyholders (Chen 2024; Paul 2024). Insurance companies can use predictive analytics, which can detect possible problems before they become real, thanks to their capacity to gather and evaluate enormous volumes of real-time data. For example, insurers can forecast the probability of accidents and modify premiums by examining driving behaviors. In addition to helping insurers by lowering claims, this proactive strategy encourages policyholders to drive more safely, benefiting both parties (Blais et al. 2020, Tanczer et al. 2018).

Feature Selection and Engineering Techniques

The creation of successful ML models for UBI requires careful consideration of feature engineering and selection. The procedure entails selecting the most pertinent characteristics from the enormous volume of data gathered by IoT devices and converting them into an analysis-ready format. By increasing predictive accuracy and lowering computing costs, feature engineering done right can greatly improve model performance. Numerous methods have been put forth to automate feature engineering and selection in order to overcome the difficulties presented by high-dimensional data. For example, by removing redundant and unnecessary features, the Correlation-based Feature Selection (CFS) technique has been effectively used in a variety of fields, including education data mining, to increase forecast accuracy (Doshi 2014). Data scientists may now concentrate on developing models instead of manually extracting features thanks to automated feature engineering techniques that have been developed to expedite the process (Banerjee et al. 2018, Smith et al. 2017).

Techniques for feature selection in the context of UBI must take into consideration the distinctive qualities of driving data. For instance, choosing characteristics like driving speed, how often you brake hard, and the time of day might provide important information on risk assessment. The creation of models for identifying fraudulent insurance claims is one example of how recent research has shown that using sophisticated feature selection techniques can result in notable increases in model accuracy (Kalwihura and Logeswaran 2020, Pushpak and Jain 2022). It has been demonstrated that combining feature engineering and ML methods can improve the effectiveness of UBI models. Deep learning (DL) techniques, for example, have been investigated to automate the feature engineering process, enabling the discovery of intricate patterns in driving behavior that conventional approaches might miss (Liu et al. 2021, Umer et al. 2022). This method increases the overall robustness of predictive models while also cutting down on the amount of time needed for feature selection.

PREDICTIVE ANALYTICS TECHNIQUES

Several AI techniques are used in the insurance industry's predictive analytics to improve client experiences, streamline processes, and reduce risks. As seen in Figure 3, this section lists some popular AI methods for insurance predictive analytics along with examples of their usual applications.

AI Techniques / Use Cases	Churn Prediction	Fraud Detection	Behavior Segmentation
Logistic Regression	✓	✓	–
Decision Trees	✓	✓	✓
Clustering	–	–	✓
Deep Learning	✓	✓	✓
Time-Series Forecasting	✓	–	–

Fig. 3. AI Techniques for Predicting Customer Behavior

Supervised Learning

A popular method in predictive analytics, supervised learning is used to improve decision-making and predict consumer behavior, especially in the insurance industry. Using a labeled dataset, where the input data is coupled with the appropriate output, a model is trained using this technique. By mapping inputs to outputs, the model gains the ability to anticipate new, unseen data. Supervised learning can be used for a number of tasks in the insurance industry, including anticipating payment patterns, risk assessment, and client churn prediction. For example, Bahrami et al. (2020) used logistic regression models to show how well supervised learning techniques can predict client invoice payment behavior, with an accuracy of up to 97%. By predicting payment patterns based on past data and client contacts, this strategy enables insurers to optimize cash flow management and proactively manage customer relationships. Using ML techniques on a dataset of more than 12,000 consumers, Kingawa and Hailu (2022) created a predictive model for customer attrition in the insurance sector. Their research made clear how crucial it is to correctly identify possible churners in order to stay competitive in the market. With a deep neural network, the model's remarkable accuracy of 98.81% demonstrated how supervised learning might improve client retention tactics. Predictive analytics that incorporates supervised learning not only helps to better understand consumer behavior but also makes it easier to create customized insurance plans. Insurers can improve customer happiness and loyalty by customizing their products to match the demands of each individual client by utilizing previous data (Adeoye et al. 2024).

Unsupervised Learning

In the insurance sector, unsupervised learning, in particular clustering techniques, is essential for consumer segmentation. Unsupervised learning, in contrast to supervised learning, finds patterns and groups in the data based on innate similarities rather than labeled data. This method is especially useful for dividing up clients into discrete groups, which enables insurers to successfully customize their product and marketing tactics. One of the most popular unsupervised learning methods for consumer segmentation is K-means clustering. The importance of customer segmentation in comprehending consumer behavior and refining marketing tactics was highlighted by Chellaboina and Gembali (2022). Insurers can use K-means clustering to group clients according to their demographics, buying patterns, and behavioral patterns, allowing for more focused advertising campaigns.

Phyo and Uttama (2023) showed how to use K-means clustering to analyze client behavior at a night market. They were able to divide the customers into five different categories. A deeper comprehension of consumer preferences and trends was made possible by this segmentation, and this knowledge can be used to improve insurance industry marketing tactics. Predictive model accuracy can be increased by using unsupervised learning approaches in consumer segmentation. Adeniran et al.'s (2024) study, for example, emphasized the progress made in predictive modeling for insurance pricing and the importance of consumer segmentation in creating reasonable and customized premiums. Insurers can improve customer satisfaction and pricing strategies by using unsupervised learning to obtain insights into client behavior.

Deep Learning (Artificial Neural Networks for Behavioral Prediction)

A deep increasing-decreasing-linear neural network was proposed by Araújo et al. (2019) in the financial domain with the express purpose of forecasting financial time series. Their model proved to be competitive when compared to more conventional approaches, demonstrating DL's capacity to capture the complexities of financial data. Because artificial neural networks (ANNs) can adjust to the dynamic nature of the data, this fits with the larger trend of using them for behavioral prediction in a variety of disciplines. In order to estimate inter-purchase periods in online retail, Kao et al. (2022) presented a hybrid model that incorporates recurrent neural networks and self-organizing maps. This method highlighted the adaptability of ANNs in behavioral analytics by increasing prediction accuracy while also offering insights into consumer behavior.

Time Series Models (for Lapse Prediction, Renewal Behavior)

In situations like customer lapse prediction and renewal behavior, time series models are crucial for forecasting future events based on existing data. This discipline has been transformed by the use of DL techniques, particularly Long Short-Term Memory (LSTM) networks, which allow for more reliable and accurate predictions. Alboukaey et al. (2020) modeled customer behavior as multivariate time series in order to forecast daily turnover in the telecom industry. The significance of temporal granularity in predictive analytics was highlighted by their findings, which showed that daily models performed better than conventional monthly models. This method emphasizes how time series models must be modified to account for the fluidity of consumer interactions. The adaptability of time series models in a variety of domains was demonstrated by Ma et al.'s (2020) work on ship encounter risk prediction, which used LSTM networks to represent intership behaviors. They were able to anticipate collision risks with great accuracy by converting intricate prediction tasks into time series classification issues. This accuracy can be compared to predictions of customer lapses. The creation of hybrid models, which combine multiple approaches for enhanced prediction performance, is another result of recent developments in DL. A deep gated stacked LSTM model for traffic flow forecasting highlighted the significance of model structure and hyperparameter adjustment in reaching precise time series predictions (Gurusamy and Seenivasan 2024).

AI TOOLS AND PLATFORMS IN INSURANCE TECHNOLOGY

The way insurance businesses function is being revolutionized by the use of AI technologies and platforms in the insurance technology (InsurTech) sector. Insurers can increase productivity, boost customer satisfaction, and simplify operations by utilizing AI. The top AI platforms in InsurTech are examined in this article, along with how they integrate with legacy systems and the function of chatbots and real-time decision engines. A number of AI platforms are leading the charge to change the InsurTech market. These platforms provide insurers cutting-edge solutions through the use of sophisticated ML algorithms, natural language processing (NLP), and data analytics. Platforms such as Guidewire and Salesforce, for example, are being used more and more because of their capabilities in customer relationship management and data management, respectively. These platforms give insurers the ability to improve their decision-making skills, automate procedures, and analyze enormous volumes of data (Adavelli 2022, Reddy 2023).

Predictive analytics is another application of AI-driven platforms that enables insurers to better evaluate risks and customize their products to suit the demands of their clients. AI integration in underwriting procedures has demonstrated great promise, allowing insurers to expedite the evaluation of applications and shorten the time it takes to issue policies (Maple et al. 2023). There are potential as well as obstacles when integrating AI technologies with legacy insurance systems. The use of new technologies may be impeded by the fact that many insurance businesses continue to rely on antiquated IT infrastructures. To improve operational efficiency and guarantee data consistency across platforms, AI must be integrated with these older systems. A thorough grasp of current systems and a methodical approach to data migration are necessary for successful integration. In order to minimize downtime and guarantee data accuracy, Extract, Transform, Load (ETL) procedures, for example, can make it easier to move data from outdated systems to contemporary AI-driven platforms (Hamza et al. 2024). Companies need to spend money on change management and training to make sure that staff members are prepared to use new technology (Muppa 2024).

Chatbots and real-time decision engines are essential elements of InsurTech's AI integration. Particularly, chatbots have become popular because of their capacity to automate consumer interactions and offer immediate assistance. These conversational bots driven by AI are capable of a wide range of duties, including helping with claims processing and responding to consumer inquiries (Kouroupis et al. 2021). NLP and ML techniques are frequently included into the architecture of contemporary chatbots, allowing them to comprehend and efficiently react to user requests (Suhaili et al. 2021). Using up-to-date data, real-time decision engines enable insurers to make well-informed decisions. Incoming data streams are analyzed by these engines to produce actionable insights that can greatly improve risk assessment and underwriting procedures. For instance, real-time AI analysis of consumer behavior and market trends enables insurers to swiftly modify their approaches (Rashidi et al. 2021). By offering individualized services, this capability not only increases operational efficiency but also improves the client experience (Garcia Valencia et al. 2023). Figure 4 shows how AI classifies insurance customers into behavioral segments using predictive analytics models.

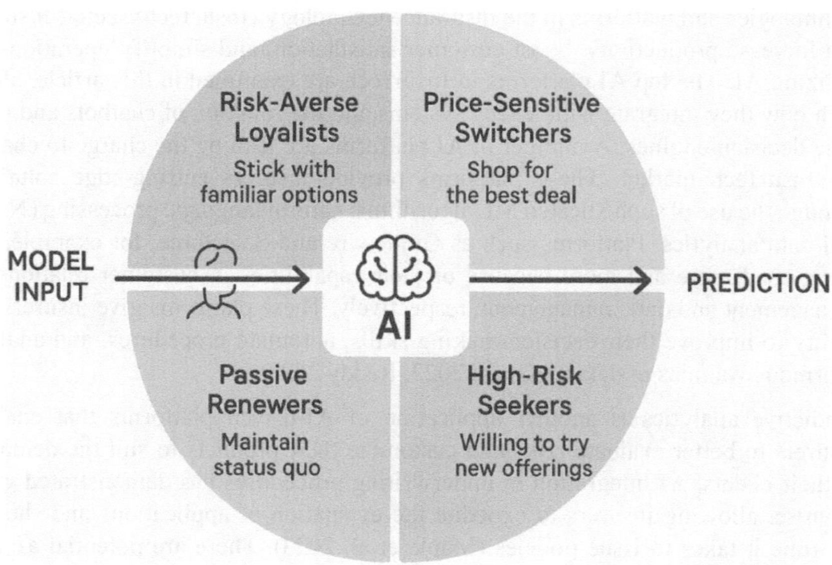

Fig. 4. Customer Segmentation Using Predictive Analytics in AI Insurance

CHALLENGES, LIMITATIONS, AND FUTURE DIRECTIONS

The process is far from smooth, even while the incorporation of predictive analytics into AI-powered insurance systems represents a major advancement in comprehending and reacting to consumer behavior. The complete potential of these technologies is nevertheless hampered by a number of issues and restrictions. Data accessibility and quality are major issues. Large volumes of relevant, clear, and structured data are needed for predictive models to generate insightful results. Numerous factors impact client behavior in the insurance industry, some of which are hard to measure or access, such as behavioral cues from contacts outside of insurance or emotional reactions to life events. While legislative frameworks like the California Consumer Privacy Act (CCPA) and General Data Protection Regulation (GDPR) place stringent limits on the collection, storage, and use of personal data—particularly sensitive data—data fragmentation among departments and systems can further limit the comprehensiveness of input data. These limitations frequently result in inadequate datasets or underutilized data lakes, which lower the accuracy of the models. Algorithmic prejudice is another significant obstacle. Predictive models may perpetuate unfair treatment of particular consumer segments if the previous data used to train them has inherent biases, such as discriminatory underwriting decisions or demographic imbalances. This is especially important in the insurance industry, where compliance, fairness, and openness are closely examined. Insurers cannot overlook the ethical and legal concerns raised by the opacity of complicated models, particularly DL architectures, which makes it more difficult to identify and address such biases.

Neural networks and ensemble models, two of the most accurate predictive analytics tools, function as "black boxes," providing little information about how particular forecasts are generated. This presents challenges for insurers in terms of internal decision-making, customer communication, and regulatory compliance. Consumers anticipate openness, particularly when algorithmic judgments impact their policy statuses, claims, or premiums. Regulators also demand that decisions be justified and explicable, especially when they result in unfavorable consequences. In order to overcome these issues, tools like Shapley Additive Explanations (SHAP) and Local Interpretable Model-agnostic Explanations (LIME) are being used more and more; nevertheless, their use complicates model deployment even further. Additionally, a lot of insurance companies rely too much on outside providers since they lack internal AI competence. This reliance may hinder innovation, restrict customization, and lead to problems with data governance. Additionally, insurers have to deal with model drift, which is the gradual deterioration of prediction models due to shifts in consumer behavior or market conditions. Predictive models, in contrast to static actuarial tables, need constant validation, retraining, and monitoring in order to remain current. This necessitates significant operational resources as well as highly skilled technical supervision.

Many insurers continue to use antiquated IT systems that aren't set up for AI-based automation or real-time data processing. A significant investment in cloud computing, Application Programming Interface (API)-based architectures, and cybersecurity frameworks is frequently necessary to integrate modern predictive technologies; these investments may exceed organizational budgets or encounter opposition from stakeholders used to more conventional approaches. Furthermore, predictive analytics cannot work alone. Within marketing teams, underwriting units, or claims departments, the insights must be operationalized—that is, turned into actions. This calls for a change in the organization's culture toward making decisions based on data. Front-line employees frequently have doubts about AI-generated insights because they see them as challenges to their knowledge or careers. To address this, leadership commitment to creating a cooperative AI-human workflow, training initiatives, and continuous change management are needed.

Predictive analytics in AI insurance has a bright future despite these drawbacks. For example, developments in federated learning provide a way to train reliable models on dispersed datasets without sacrificing privacy. In cross-border insurance contexts or in collaborations between insurers and other industries, like healthcare or the automotive sector, this might be especially revolutionary. In order to provide increasingly more individualized, dynamic, and preventive insurance solutions, real-time data from IoT devices—such as wearable health monitors or telematics in cars—will keep enhancing behavioral datasets. Additionally, predictive analytics can become proactive and adaptable rather than only descriptive and prescriptive. In reaction to real-time customer interactions, future systems might dynamically modify pricing, messaging, and coverage through the use of reinforcement learning and continuous feedback loops. Furthermore, the growing acceptance of moral AI concepts will result in the creation of algorithms that are more open, equitable, and responsible. To strike a balance between innovation and consumer protection, regulatory sandboxes—controlled settings where new AI models can be tested under supervision—will be crucial.

Predictive analytics combined with cutting-edge technologies like augmented reality, blockchain, and digital twins may open up new risk models and customer experiences. For example, policyholders' digital twins could mimic behavioral shifts in reaction to life events or new policy offerings, providing insurers with a virtual environment for policy testing. Blockchain could improve trust and traceability in analytics pipelines by offering immutable and verifiable behavioral data logs. Augmented reality, on the other hand, might be utilized for immersive customer onboarding or claims processing, where predictive systems leverage user behavior to capture needs or pre-load probable requests. In order to strike a compromise between interpretability and performance, insurers are also anticipated to invest in hybrid AI frameworks that integrate ML and symbolic reasoning, or rules-based logic. These hybrid systems offer insurers strong data-driven insights and the ability to stay compliant.

CONCLUSION

The way insurers comprehend, interact with, and serve their clients has been completely transformed by the incorporation of predictive analytics into AI-powered insurance networks. Insurance companies may predict client demands, spot trends in behavior, spot fraud, streamline claims processing, and customize experiences with previously unheard-of precision by utilizing sophisticated data modeling approaches. A proactive, customer-centric insurance strategy driven by real-time behavioral intelligence has increasingly replaced the conventional reactive model, which was only concerned with risk pooling and post-incident compensation. This change not only improves operational effectiveness but also increases client retention and happiness, both of which are critical in the cutthroat insurance market of today.

There are challenges along the way, though. The full potential of predictive analytics is currently hampered by a number of issues, such as data silos, algorithmic bias, regulatory limitations, and legacy infrastructure. These problems necessitate deliberate expenditures in interdisciplinary cooperation, data governance, and AI ethics. The human element is equally crucial: building confidence in AI-driven decision-making among internal stakeholders and policyholders. Strong ethical foundations, explainable models, and transparent communication are essential for reducing resistance and guaranteeing equity for all client segments. In order to facilitate the cultural transition toward data-driven operations, insurers also need to give organizational change management and ongoing training top priority.

Predictive analytics in insurance has a very bright future. Real-time adaptive modeling, deep personalization, and federated learning innovations have the potential to revolutionize the sector. In order to provide a more comprehensive picture of customer context, external data sources including social media, IoT devices, and geolocation data will progressively supplement internal data repositories. In order to co-create hyper-personalized, preventive, and digitally enhanced insurance services, insurers are likely to establish strategic partnerships with internet companies, healthcare providers, automakers, and other entities as industry boundaries become increasingly hazy. In order to guarantee that innovation is directed by accountability and openness, ethical AI and regulatory sandboxes will continue to develop concurrently.

REFERENCES

Adavelli, S.R. (2022). Digital transformation in insurance: How guidewire, AWS, and snowflake converge for future-ready solutions. *International Journal of Computer Science and Information Technology Research*, 3(1), 95–114.

Adeniran, I.A., Efunniyi, C.P., Osundare, O.S., and Abhulimen, A.O.(2024). Advancements in predictive modeling for insurance pricing: Enhancing risk assessment and customer segmentation. *International Journal of Management and Entrepreneurship Research*, 6(8), 2835–2848.

Adeoye, O.B., Okoye, C.C., Ofodile, O.C., Odeyemi, O., Addy, W. A., and Ajayi-Nifise, A.O. (2024). Integrating artificial intelligence in personalized insurance products: A pathway to enhanced customer engagement. *International Journal of Management and Entrepreneurship Research*, 6(3), 502–511.

Adewale, T. (2024). Cloud Computing for Real-Time Health Monitoring and Wearable Devices.

Alam, A., and Prybutok, V.R. (2024). Use of responsible artificial intelligence to predict health insurance claims in the USA using machine learning algorithms. *Exploration of Digital Health Technologies*, 2(1), 30–45.

Alboukaey, N., Joukhadar, A., and Ghneim, N. (2020). Dynamic behavior based churn prediction in mobile telecom. *Expert Systems with Applications*, 162, 113779.

Araújo, R.d.A., Nedjah, N., Oliveira, A.L., and Meira, S.R.d.L. (2019). A deep increasing-decreasing—linear neural network for financial time series prediction. *Neurocomputing*, 347, 59–81.

Bahrami, M., Bozkaya, B., and Balcisoy, S. (2020). Using behavioral analytics to predict customer invoice payment. *Big Data*, 8(1), 25–37.

Banerjee, S., Chattopadhyay, T., Pal, A., and Garain, U. (2018). Automation of feature engineering for IoT analytics. *ACM Sigbed Review*, 15(2), 24–30.

Blais, P., Badard, T., Duchesne, T., and Côté, M. P. (2020). From massive trajectory data to traffic modeling for better behavior prediction in a usage-based insurance context. *ISPRS International Journal of Geo-Information*, 9(12), 722.

Chan, J.O. (2014). Big data customer knowledge management. *Communications of the IIMA*, 14(3), 5.

Chellaboina, S., and Gembali, M. (2022). Product recommendation based on customer segmentation engine. *In:* 2nd International Conference on Intelligent Technologies (CONIT), 1–7.

Chen, X. (2024) Transforming Auto Insurance: The Impact of Telematics and Real-Time Data on Pricing and Risk Assessment, *Regent Journal of Business and Technology*, 1(1), 36–43.

Dahouda, M.K., and Joe, I. (2021). A deep-learned embedding technique for categorical features encoding. *IEEE Access*, 9, 114381–114391.

Doshi, M. (2014). Correlation based feature selection (CFS) technique to predict student Perfromance. *International Journal of Computer Networks and Communications*, 6(3), 197.

Fong, P.H.Y. and Yin, P.H. (2023). Feasibility of artificial intelligence in improving sales and service of insurance agents in the life insurance industry of Malaysia, UTAR, 291.

Garcia Valencia, O.A., Thongprayoon, C., Jadlowiec, C.C., Mao, S.A., Miao, J., and Cheungpasitporn, W. (2023). Enhancing Kidney Transplant Care through the Integration of Chatbot. Healthcare.

Graminha, P.B., and Afonso, L.E. (2022). Behavioral economics and auto insurance: The role of biases and heuristics. *Revista de Administração Contemporânea*, 26, e200421.

Gurusamy, R., and Seenivasan, S.R. (2024). DGSLSTM: Deep gated stacked long short-term memory neural network for traffic flow forecasting of transportation networks on big data environment. *Big Data*, 12(6), 504–517.

Hamza, O., Collins, A., Eweje, A., and Babatunde, G.O. (2024). Advancing data migration and virtualization techniques: ETL-driven strategies for oracle BI and salesforce integration in agile environments. *International Journal of Multidisciplinary Research and Growth Evaluation*, 5(1), 1100–1118.

Ikonomi, A., Nast, B., Shi, L., Levrault, L., Purcell, T.M., and Skordi, P. (2022). Artificial Intelligence in Insurance.

Kalwihura, J., and Logeswaran, R. (2020). Auto-insurance fraud detection: A behavioral feature engineering approach. *Journal of Critical Reviews*, 7(3), 125–129.

Kao, L.J., Chiu, C.C., Lin, Y.F., and Weng, H.K. (2022). Inter-purchase time prediction based on deep learning. *Comput. Syst. Sci. Eng.*, 42(2), 493–508.

Kingawa, E.D., and Hailu, T.T. (2022). Customer churn prediction using machine learning techniques: The case of lion insurance. *Asian Journal of Basic Science and Research*, 4(4), 60–73.

Kouroupis, K., Vagianos, D., and Totka, A. (2021). Artificial intelligence and customer relationship management: The case of chatbots and their legality framework. *E. Eur. YB on Hum. Rts.*, 5, 5–10.

Kroh, C. (2020). Essays on Optimal Insurance Demand. Dissertation, Duisburg, Essen, Universität Duisburg-Essen.

Kumar, P., Taneja, S., Özen, E., and Singh, S. (2023). Artificial intelligence and machine learning in insurance: A bibliometric analysis. *In:* Smart Analytics, Artificial Intelligence and Sustainable Performance Management in a Global Digitalised Economy, 191–202. Emerald Publishing Limited.

Liu, Y., Li, A., Zhao, X.M., and Wang, M. (2021). DeepTL-Ubi: A novel deep transfer learning method for effectively predicting ubiquitination sites of multiple species. *Methods*, 192, 103–111.

Ma, J., Li, W., Jia, C., Zhang, C., and Zhang, Y. (2020). Risk prediction for ship encounter situation awareness using long short-term memory based deep learning on intership behaviors. *Journal of Advanced Transportation*, 2020(1), 8897700.

Maier, M., Carlotto, H., Saperstein, S., Sanchez, F., Balogun, S., and Merritt, S. (2020). Improving the accuracy and transparency of underwriting with AI to transform the life insurance industry. *Ai Magazine*, 41(3), 78–93.

Malthouse, E.C., Haenlein, M., Skiera, B., Wege, E., and Zhang, M. (2013). Managing customer relationships in the social media era: Introducing the social CRM house. *Journal of Interactive Marketing*, 27(4), 270–280.

Maple, C., Szpruch, L., Epiphaniou, G., Staykova, K., Singh, S., Penwarden, W., Avramovic, P. (2023). The AI revolution: Opportunities and challenges for the finance sector. arXiv. *arXiv:2308.16538*.

Mathur, T., and VV, R.K. (2024). AI-powered chatbots in health insurance: assessing their effectiveness in consumer search processes. *In:* 11th International Conference on Electrical Engineering, Computer Science and Informatics (EECSI), IEEE, 579–582.

Mosavi, S.M., Sangari, M.S., and Keramati, A. (2018). An integrative framework for customer switching behavior. *The Service Industries Journal*, 38(15–16), 1067–1094.

Muppa, K.R. (2024). Enhanced identity and access management with artificial intelligence: A strategic overview. *International Journal of Information Security and Cybercrime (IJISC)*, 13(2), 9–17.

Oh, C.G., and Park, J. (2020). Insights for sustainability of smartphone business: Understanding customer switching behavior in smartphone services. *Sustainability*, 12(3), 1082.

Olsen, S.O. (2002). Comparative evaluation and the relationship between quality, satisfaction, and repurchase loyalty. *Journal of the Academy of Marketing Science*, 30(3), 240–249.

Owens, E., Sheehan, B., Mullins, M., Cunneen, M., Ressel, J., and Castignani, G. (2022). Explainable artificial intelligence (XAI) in insurance. *Risks*, 10(12), 230.

Paul, J. (2024). AI-Powered Data Analytics: Shaping the Future of Auto Insurance Pricing and Claims Processing.

Phyo, T., and Uttama, S. (2023). Unveiling patterns in the night market: A machine learning approach to customer segmentation and market basket analysis. *In:* 7th International Conference on Information Technology (InCIT), 514–519.

Pushpak, S.N., and Jain, S. (2022). An implementation of quantum machine learning technique to determine insurance claim fraud. *In:* 10th International Conference on Reliability, Infocom Technologies and Optimization (Trends and Future Directions)(ICRITO), 1–5.

Rashidi, H.H., Tran, N., Albahra, S., and Dang, L.T. (2021). Machine learning in health care and laboratory medicine: General overview of supervised learning and auto-ML. *International Journal of Laboratory Hematology*, 43, 15–22.

Reddy, A.S. (2023). Future Proofing Insurance Operations: A Guidewire-Centric Approach to Cloud, Cybersecurity, and Generative AI. PhilArchive.

Sinn, H.W. (2012). Economic Decisions Under Uncertainty. Springer Science and Business Media. Physica-Verlag Heidelberg.

Smith, M.J., Wedge, R., and Veeramachaneni, K. (2017). FeatureHub: Towards collaborative data science. *In:* IEEE International Conference on Data Science and Advanced Analytics (DSAA), 590–600.

Suhaili, S.M., Salim, N., and Jambli, M.N. (2021). Service chatbots: A systematic review. *Expert Systems with Applications*, 184, 115461.

Taherdoost, H. (2024). Wearable healthcare and continuous vital sign monitoring with IoT integration. *Computers, Materials and Continua*, 81(1), 79.

Tanczer, L., Steenmans, I., Brass, I., and Carr, M. (2018). Networked World: Risks and Opportunities in the Internet of Things, 1–72.

Trainor, K.J., Andzulis, J.M., Rapp, A., and Agnihotri, R. (2014). Social media technology usage and customer relationship performance: A capabilities-based examination of social CRM. *Journal of Business Research*, 67(6), 1201–1208.

Umer, M., Sadiq, S., Karamti, H., Karamti, W., Majeed, R., and Nappi, M. (2022). IoT based smart monitoring of patients' with acute heart failure. *Sensors*, 22(7), 2431.

Varadarajan, V., and Kakumanu, V. K. (2024). Evaluation of risk level assessment strategies in life Insurance: A review of the literature. *Journal of Autonomous Intelligence*, 7(5), 1–19.

Votinov, M., Knyazeva, I., Habel, U., Konrad, K., and Puiu, A.A. (2022). A bayesian modeling approach to examine the role of testosterone administration on the endowment effect and risk-taking. *Frontiers in Neuroscience*, 16, 858168.

Wan, S., Paris, C., and Georgakopoulos, D. (2015). Social media data aggregation and mining for internet-scale customer relationship management. *In:* IEEE International Conference on Information Reuse and Integration, 39–48.

Zarifis, A., Holland, C.P., and Milne, A. (2023). Evaluating the impact of AI on insurance: The four emerging AI-and data-driven business models. *Emerald Open Research*, 1(1).

5

AI in Property and Casualty Insurance

Hamed Taherdoost[1,*], *and Alireza Rafiee*[2]

INTRODUCTION

Property, liability, and damages from accidents and natural catastrophes are covered by property and casualty (P&C) insurance. This financing technique reduces property loss risk and liability. P&C insurers set premiums based on charging client risk, including claim likelihood and severity (Zhao 2019). Auto, workers' compensation, liability, cyber liability, and event liability insurance are provided by the industry. Regulations, financial cycles, and organizational structures influence P&C insurance economics. Regulatory processes, including automobile insurance rate regulation, impact industry practices (Klein 2012).

Insurance Technology (InsurTech) and machine learning (ML) are revolutionizing P&C insurance. Technology improves risk assessment, pricing, and policyholder service. Technological advances drive improvements in industry efficiency, while empirical research identifies, measures, and validates these effects (Liu et al. 2023). By analyzing big consumer behavior and claims history databases, ML is improving premium calculations (Blier-Wong et al. 2020). Economic, societal, and climate risks like convective storms face the industry. These phenomena raise insurance costs and reduce market capacity. Reinsurance rate hikes harm personal and commercial profitability. New product innovation in risk management and aggressive pricing models need to be introduced to negate these issues. Customer awareness significantly influences the take-up of P&C insurance. A systematic review of literature suggests that effective marketing approaches entail insight into client attitudes and behaviors (Ismail et al. 2018). Awareness campaigns can bridge knowledge gaps concerning coverage options and benefits.

[1] Department of Arts, Communications and Social Sciences, School of Arts, Science and Technology, University Canada West, Vancouver, Canada
GUS Institute, Global University Systems, London, UK
College of Technology and Engineering, Westcliff University, United States
Gisma University of Applied Sciences, Germany
Research and Development Department, Hamta Business Corporation, Canada
[2] Q Minded, Quark Minded Technology, Canada
[*] *Corresponding author:* hamed.taherdoost@gmail.com

DOI: 10.1201/9781003621119-5

Artificial intelligence (AI) technologies like ML, predictive analytics, and automation are helping insurers automate claims, enhance underwriting, and detect fraud. These technologies are changing insurance into a data-driven and customer-centric industry. AI has improved P&C insurance customer experience by providing customized services and faster response times. AI-powered chatbots help policyholders with premium payments and policy details in real time. Real-time claims management using AI reduces delays and improves client satisfaction. Predictive analytics enables insurers to tailor policies to individual risk profiles for fair pricing and higher coverage (Gupta et al. 2022, Kumar et al. 2019).

AI has a strong impact on P&C insurance through automation. Insurers use AI to automate data entry, document checks, and claim routing. There is less human intervention, and hence time is saved and errors are minimized. Telematics and usage-based insurance (UBI) make efficiency optimal by using real-time data in pricing (Eling et al. 2022, Erem Ceylan 2022). Real-time claims fraud detection can be achieved through ML algorithms detecting suspicious patterns. Data source cross-checking can assist insurers in reducing fraud risk. This is a win for insurers and confidence-building for policyholders. Strategic implementation of AI in P&C insurance is unavoidable. Insurance companies need effective data science expertise in order to gain valuable insights from vast datasets. Technology companies dealing with AI must collaborate to remain competitive. Compliance with rules ensures ethical use and consumer trustworthiness (Aldboush and Ferdous 2023, Du and Xie 2021). Figure 1 shows how technology advances, operational efficiency, customer-centric innovations, market dynamics, strategic planning, and their interconnected subtopics drive AI adoption in P&C insurance.

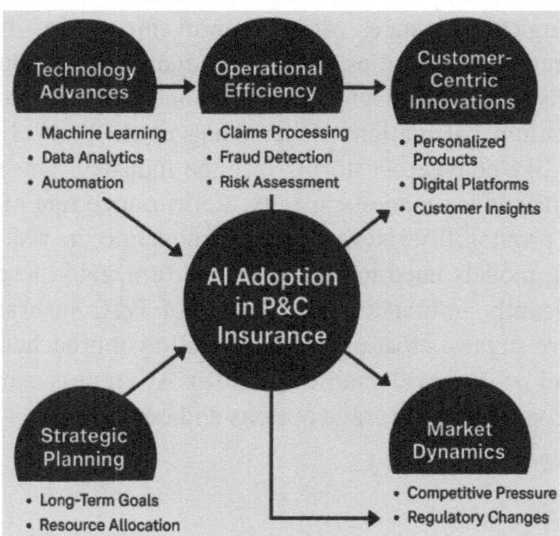

Fig. 1. Key Drivers of AI Adoption in P&C Insurance

AI technologies are making data processing more efficient and redefining important processes in P&C insurance, which is rapidly changing. AI for underwriting, claims adjusting, customer service, pricing, and catastrophe response is essential to insurers' competitiveness. The developments raise data privacy, ethical, and regulatory compliance issues. This chapter examines AI's revolutionary role in P&C insurance, its promise and drawbacks, and directions for the future and potential AI implementation avenues.

AI-POWERED UNDERWRITING AND RISK ASSESSMENT

Underwriting has traditionally been a manually intensive and subjectively judgment-based process. Underwriters assess risks by considering a list of criteria, which includes claims history, health, and demographic information. Although relatively effective, the process tends to be time-consuming and prone to human errors. Underwriters are also challenged by the increasing complexity of the data, including unstructured data from various sources (Dubey et al. 2018). The constraints of legacy systems, which often struggle to accommodate new sources of data and types of analysis, also hinder the conventional underwriting process. It is challenging to estimate the systematic risk of different insurance lines, e.g. transportation, using traditional approaches (Lai 2008).

Automation powered by AI presents a hopeful answer to the issues of conventional underwriting. Insurers are able to improve decision-making, improve accuracy, and accelerate the underwriting process via the utilization of sophisticated algorithms as well as ML models. For instance, Kitchens (2009) illustrates the use of artificial neural networks for automating underwriting in automobile insurance through handling high volumes of data more effectively compared to human underwriters. According to Turner and Agarwal (2008), the incorporation of alternative data sources improves underwriting even more. Insurers can develop a more holistic view of risk profiles, especially for thin-file borrowers, by leveraging data from social media, transaction history, and other alternative data sources. Besides placing risk evaluation on a sounder basis, the strategy improves the accessibility of insurance products to disadvantaged groups. ML models are leading the way in transforming underwriting operations (see Figure 2).

These algorithms are able to analyze intricate datasets to find patterns and relationships that might be missed by conventional approaches. As an example, Maier et al. (2019) discuss how a life score built using rich history data can outperform conventional underwriting approaches, resulting in better risk assessment and improved operational efficiency. Life insurance is not the only underwriting application of ML. For underwriting health insurance, where medical information complexity can outstrip conventional procedures, Dubey et al. (2018) stress the need to automate information collection and processing. By using ML classifiers and natural language processing (NLP), insurers can extract pertinent features from unstructured information to improve underwriting decision quality.

CLAIMS PROCESSING AND FRAUD DETECTION

AI in Claims Automation and Efficiency

Claims processing in healthcare has been transformed through AI, which enhances operational effectiveness and streamlines day-to-day functions. AI technologies like Robotic Process Automation (RPA) greatly reduce human error within the insurance industry by automating mundane tasks like data entry and document verification. Sophisticated data analysis allows real-time fraud detection through monitoring questionable trends that might be missed by human adjusters. Through quicker response, these features increase customer satisfaction while enhancing the accuracy and efficiency of claims processing. By answering questions in real time and making it easier to process claims, AI chatbots also increase efficiency (Gagan and Srinivasagopalan 2021, Machireddy 2022). While these advantages are present, some of the disadvantages—like data silos and legacy systems—are inhibiting the integration of AI into insurance (Ali Albasheir 2023, Tavares et al. 2025).

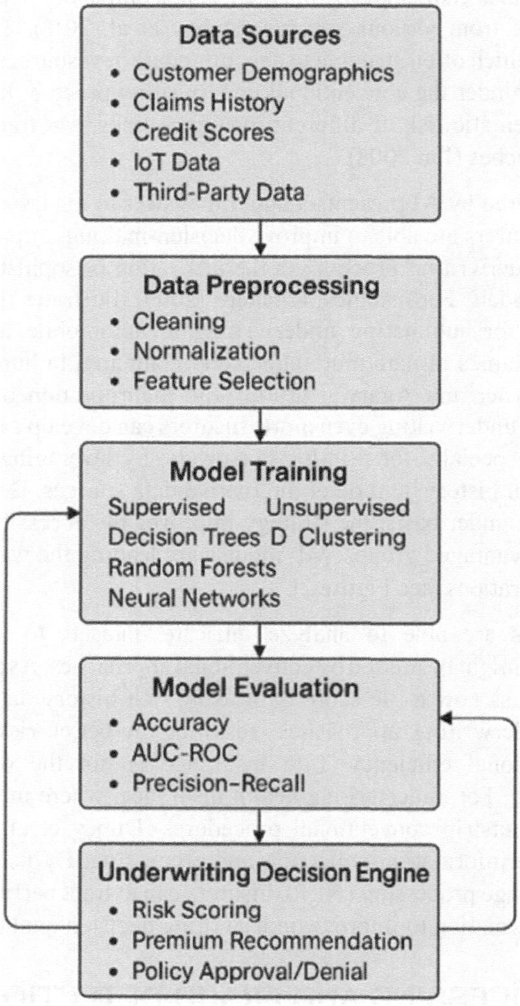

Fig. 2. Machine Learning Models for Underwriting

In industries, AI-powered solutions have seen tremendous gains in efficiency. Automatons and ML techniques minimized inefficiencies involved in data-centric work in processing healthcare claims (Danda et al. 2024). During registration of claims, for example, NLP minimizes errors and improves the process's speed by taking pertinent information out of documents (Bauer et al. 2023).

Computer Vision and Natural Language Processing in Claims Processing

Deep learning (DL) methods have greatly improved computer vision and NLP, enabling new opportunities in numerous industries. Multimodal learning has been made easier through the blending of these modalities, which combine text-based information processing with visual data interpretation. In claims processing, where document analysis, fraud detection, and decision-making involve both language thinking and visual comprehension, this combination is especially applicable. Recent developments include the use of NLP models for named entity recognition and sentiment analysis with convolutional neural networks (CNNs) for image classification and object detection. These technologies are being used more and more to automate processes that include textual claims and visual evidence, improving decision-making precision and efficiency (Kafle et al. 2019, Wiriyathammabhum et al. 2016).

In the insurance industry, claims processing tends to include the review of records such as invoices, damage photos, and medical records. Computer vision algorithms facilitate automatic viszual feature extraction from images, e.g., identifying damaged areas on vehicles or homes. In contrast, NLP models review text descriptions to extract relevant information, e.g., claim summaries or policy details. For example, natural language reasoning systems check for textual coherence against visual evidence, and visual question answering systems can respond to questions about images held in claims (Kafle et al. 2019, Sampat 2024). By maintaining consistency and minimizing labor, these solutions increase operational efficiency. Despite the progress made, integrating NLP and computer vision remains challenging.

When techniques rely on inaccurate correlations rather than actual multimodal input comprehension, dataset bias can result in misleading predictions. For instance, due to dataset limitations, visual models can misread images, and NLP models can fail to read advanced claim descriptions. To provide consistent performance, research emphasizes the need for strong benchmarks that examine multimodal ability in isolation (Liang et al. 2021, Sharma and Giannakos 2020). For claim processing systems, semantic reasoning is an important challenge requiring enhancements in the modeling and learning of context as well as representation (Bettini et al. 2010, Chaccour et al. 2024).

AI-Powered Fraud Detection Techniques

Across many industries, AI has become a game-changing weapon in the fight against fraud. Conventional rule-based systems have not been able to keep up with the increasing complexity of fraudulent operations since they rely on predetermined criteria. ML and DL algorithms are used by AI-powered systems to find hidden patterns, spot irregularities, and make remarkably accurate predictions about possible fraud. By continuously learning from both previous and current data, these systems are able to adapt to changing fraud strategies and guarantee strong detection capabilities (Btoush et al. 2023). AI-powered fraud detection employs several advanced techniques as shown in Table 1.

Table 1. AI Techniques and Models for Fraud Detection

Category	Models/Techniques	Application/Effectiveness	Reference
ML Models	Random Forest (RF), Extreme Gradient Boosting (XGB)	High accuracy in detecting fraud, especially in credit card transactions	(Btoush et al. 2023)
	Restricted Boltzmann Machines (RBM)	Effective in scenarios with data imbalance or inadequate annotation	(Btoush et al. 2023)
DL Architectures	Deep Belief Networks (DBN)	Integrates feature engineering and behavioral analysis, identifying nuanced fraudulent behaviors	(Btoush et al. 2023)
Explainable AI (XAI)	XAI frameworks	Provides transparency in decision-making, enabling interpretability and trust in AI-driven fraud detection outcomes	(Nobel et al. 2024)

Blockchain and AI Integration for Fraud Prevention

The intersection of blockchain and AI has been touted as a game-changing solution to misconduct prevention in financial systems. The decentralized and immutable ledger of blockchain technology guarantees data integrity and transparency, while the predictive analytics of AI facilitate identification of fraudulent activities in real-time. This intersection resolves core issues of conventional fraud detection methods, including operational efficiency, flexibility, and scalability (Masud et al. 2024, Rane et al. 2023).

Blockchain technology provides a secure, immutable ledger that captures transactions in a transparent way, in such a manner that unauthorized changes are thwarted. It provides strong data security via the removal of single points of failure, possible because of its decentralized operation. Smart contracts, a feature of blockchain, automate fraud prevention mechanisms by initiating actions when suspicious activity is detected. For instance, blockchain technology can enhance the integrity of financial transactions by auditing the data of transactions in real time and preserving it securely (Kumar 2022). AI algorithms are particularly amenable to detecting anomalies that indicate deception by analyzing large amounts of data.

Unsupervised techniques, such as clustering, reveal new patterns of fraud when there is no labeled data, while supervised learning models, such as logistic regression and neural networks, successfully predict fraudulent transactions. By automating

Know Your Customer (KYC) and Anti-Money Laundering (AML) processes and facilitating adaptive smart contracts, the integration of AI in blockchain systems further reinforces fraud prevention (Rane et al. 2023). By proactively mitigating risks beforehand, this synergy guarantees adherence to regulatory policies.

CUSTOMER EXPERIENCE AND PERSONALIZATION

AI Chatbots and Virtual Assistants in Customer Support

AI chatbots and virtual assistants have transformed customer service (Harbola 2021). Real-time individualized communication automates mundane tasks and provides high-quality service (Vashishth et al. 2024). Chatbots are improving efficiency and user experience in customer service, healthcare, education, and e-commerce. Chatbots process high-volume inquiries, solve issues, and provide personalized service 24/7, freeing human agents to perform more complex tasks (Kyrylenko 2024). NLP enables chatbots to understand and respond to client queries in natural language, gaining contextual meaning and accuracy (Udeh et al. 2024). With the use of ML, they can learn from past experiences and enhance future responses, becoming better and more efficient (Soori et al. 2023). AI-based customer service is estimated to grow, highlighting its relevance in current business (Inavolu 2024). Chatbots require serious consideration of ethical issues like data safety and openness (Ghosh et al. 2024).

AI is applied in insurance to personalize policy recommendations and provide proactive support. AI programs personalize insurance and risk management packages according to user data. Analytical prediction helps the insurer provide timely and relevant services that increase customer satisfaction and loyalty. Proactive development of the insurer-customer relationship creates long-lasting relationships (Adeoye et al. 2024).

AI-Driven Personalized Policy Recommendations

AI-based personalized product recommendation is transforming online purchasing. AI-based solutions make time-saving recommendations based on browsing and purchase history. Personalization boosts consumer interaction, satisfaction, loyalty, and sales (Raji et al. 2024). Personalization extends beyond recommendation since AI can forecast user behavior and apply personalized information strategically. AI in Customer Relationship Management (CRM) tools promotes personalization, personalizing marketing and improving support (Boppana 2023). Personalized marketing works best when directed towards specific consumer segments based on their behavior and interests. It maximizes conversions and brand loyalty (Babatunde et al. 2024). There has to be a balance between personalization and data privacy. AI is applied to hyper-personalize Fast-Moving Consumer Goods (FMCG) marketing. It is more than just personalization and utilizes real-time data along with behavior analysis to personalize customer experiences during the buying process. AI-driven chatbots and virtual assistants increase client interaction and revenues in extremely personalized marketing methods. AI-driven consumer sentiment surveys lead to brands improving their offers and customer satisfaction (Wagh and Ramesh 2024).

AI has an impact on customer experience differently in every sector. AI virtual try-on technology can be leveraged by retailers to support more informed decision-making and reduced returns (Boppana 2023). In tourism and hospitality, smartphone apps, AI chatbots, VR, and Internet of Things (IoT) drive customer convenience and interaction. Through automation and robots, AI facilitates enhanced hospitality efficiency as well as personnel focusing on more personalized interactions with guests (Roy and Pagaldiviti 2023). AI-based fintech communication utilizes chatbots and NLP to increase banking support and offer customized and targeted offerings (Udeh et al. 2024). AI-based CRM takes this further, delivering a seamless and customized customer experience. This is via customized information, product recommendation, and proactive customer care (Boppana 2023).

AI's Impact on Customer Retention Strategies

Predictive analytics through AI is revolutionizing client retention strategies. Organizations can preemptively intervene and create customized retention strategies from examining previous records and detecting patterns that correlate with client attrition (Chinta and Renuka 2023). Increased client loyalty and lower turnover rates are the outcomes of this preemptive intervention, enabling customized interventions (Brynjolfsson et al. 2025). In order to achieve greater accuracy and provide more precise recommendations, companies can now design very personalized experiences along the entire customer journey because of AI. Customer satisfaction and relationships are strengthened by personalization through AI—from personalized product suggestions and segmented marketing to real-time customer service through chatbots (Bawa 2022). A good customer retention strategy is greatly based on this improved interaction, raising Customer Lifetime Value (CLV). AI is transforming prediction and optimization of CLV, the most critical driver of business success. Highly accurate CLV forecasts that adjust dynamically to shifts in customer behavior and the market are produced by AI-based forecasting models, in which ML algorithms process ginormous amounts of data. AI-supported CLV knowledge facilitates improved client segmentation, improved resource allocation, and improved retention strategies (Egorenkov 2024).

AI IN PRICING AND POLICY OPTIMIZATION

AI-driven pricing models utilize vast data sets to develop real-time risk-based pricing strategies. The move away from fixed pricing towards adaptive models helps insurers align rates with risk profiles, improve profitability and customer satisfaction. Insurers can examine past data, forecast future claims, and adjust pricing through ML algorithms, resulting in more accurate and fair premium estimates (Adeniran et al. 2024). Figure 3 shows how AI powers pricing and automation in P&C insurance.

Telematics and IoT are crucial to automobile insurance pricing. Insurers can create UBI models that offer customized premiums based on driving behavior, vehicle usage, and environmental factors. Telematics data allow insurers to classify drivers into risk profiles based on their behavior, improving risk assessment and pricing. A study concluded that velocity- and acceleration-classified driving profiles can maximize premium pricing through the adjustment of rebates or surcharges (Weidner et al. 2017). Telematics and big data analytics have made it possible for insurers to refine pricing strategies. Insurers can use vast IoT datasets to identify patterns and correlations that drive their pricing models, making them more competitive (Niyato et al. 2016). Data-driven risk assessments improve accuracy and transparency between insurers and policyholders. Big data assists insurance companies in tailoring policies according to customer requirements.

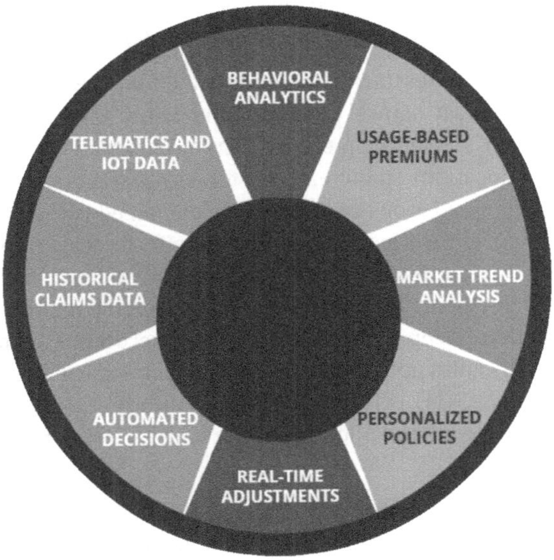

Fig. 3. The Role of AI in Pricing and Automation within P&C Insurance

The capacity to analyze vast volumes of data enables insurers to segment their customers and create customized pricing plans that consider the risk level of each policyholder (Adeniran et al. 2024). Advanced analytics can help insurers identify low-risk customers who are likely overpaying under standard pricing models, enabling insurers to offer more competitive prices that attract them (Cather 2018). Big data allows insurers to create customized insurance products to address emerging market requirements. By observing customer behavior and preferences, insurers are able to tailor plans to changing client demands, improving customer satisfaction and loyalty (Ye et al. 2021).

Through offering customers additional choices and fair pricing, data-driven policy tailoring serves the interests of insurers and engages customers. AI-based insurance pricing has various benefits but also raises ethical concerns. AI and big data analysis may result in privacy intrusions, discrimination, and adverse selection.

Telematics data can place drivers who lack the technology at a disadvantage relative to UBI schemes (Mullins et al. 2021). The risk of "cream skimming", or insurers skimming off low-risk clients at the cost of insuring high-risk clients, destroys insurance market fairness and inclusion (Cather 2018). These ethical issues call for regulatory frameworks and guidelines. The EU has actively promoted ethical AI principles for insurance, emphasizing transparency, accountability, and justice in AI-driven pricing models (Mullins et al. 2021).

CATASTROPHE MODELING AND DISASTER RESPONSE

AI helps insurers screen vast amounts of climate, weather, and socioeconomic information. More accurate data-driven risk assessment and modeling are facilitated. AI detects climate change risks like flooding and hurricanes and helps insurers modify their policies. AI-enabled geospatial intelligence offers insurers rapid access to risk assessment details, allowing them to react to climate change (Haleem et al. 2023).

AI excels at climate risk assessment, as demonstrated in recent studies. For instance, ML methods can forecast natural disasters and allow insurers to foresee claims (Linardos et al. 2022). AI can help create custom-designed climate-risk insurance policies for diverse locations to increase customer satisfaction and retention. ML's risk avoidance recommendations can be greatly enhanced by disaster management. ML algorithms can use historical and current data to forecast floods, earthquakes, and hurricanes to facilitate an early response (Atmaja and Fukushi 2022, Linardos et al. 2022). New developments in ML like DL and ensemble methods have improved catastrophe prediction. Deep neural networks can scrutinize complicated data to recognize patterns of catastrophes, which improves early warning systems (Linardos et al. 2022, Olier et al. 2021). AI and Geographic Information Systems (GIS) make risk analysis more in-depth and allocation of resources in the face of disaster more effective (Li et al. 2022).

Quality and quantity of data impact the performance of ML models. Model training and validation would need to be ongoing to maintain accuracy (Atmaja and Fukushi 2022). More robust models capable of adapting to changes in environmental conditions and eliciting varied data sources for better prediction are what need to be developed in future research. Catastrophe claims management is transforming the insurance sector using AI by streamlining processes and improving customer service. AI technologies like NLP and ML allow insurers to automate claims handling, saving time and cost. Automated claims handling with AI-driven automation speeds up claims handling, improves damage assessments, and improves customer service. AI can detect patterns and trigger alarms for fraudulent claims in claims data, lowering insurer losses. AI-driven chatbots and virtual assistants can improve policyholder communication and satisfaction in the claims process (Chinta and Renuka 2023).

REGULATORY AND ETHICAL CONSIDERATIONS

To enable effective AI use in underwriting, claims handling, pricing, and fraud detection, there should be an effective regulatory environment and attention to ethical concerns. AI technologies can transform insurers but present challenges regarding governance, bias, data security, privacy, and fairness. All these need to be addressed to comply with regulations and make AI use in P&C insurance beneficial to policyholders, insurers, and regulators. Insurers must develop transparent governance frameworks to ensure ethical application of AI processes. This includes specifying accountability for AI results, transparency for AI systems, and protocols for monitoring and auditing AI-based decisions. AI systems must explain and justify their decisions due to the complexity and lack of transparency of the majority of ML algorithms. Without transparency, policyholders are likely to mistrust the insurance process, especially if computer software makes decisions behind the scenes without intervention or consciousness. Computers in underwriting can directly affect an individual's finances by making risk and premium determinations, so this is a very sensitive function. Transparent AI governance standards will continue equitable and accountable use and limit the risks of unguided automation.

P&C insurers are already regulated on fairness, transparency, and consumer protection. As AI becomes more central to claims handling and pricing, regulators will need to ensure that companies comply with these legislations. AI models must comply with anti-discrimination laws so that they do not discriminate against particular groups on the basis of age, gender, color, or socioeconomic status. Insurers are not allowed to discriminate when determining premiums or denying coverage under the Fair Lending Act. AI systems should be designed and implemented in accordance with such rules to safeguard customers and avoid legal issues. With the onset of big data, insurers have to face threats of data security and privacy breaches.

In order to perform risk assessment during underwriting, settle claims, and personalize offers, P&C insurance AI systems need vast amounts of personal and sensitive data. This raises very serious issues related to collecting, storing, and using data. Insurers must guard sensitive consumer data to avoid reputational loss, regulatory penalties, and consumer distrust. This also means insurers must disclose their data collection habits to customers so customers know what information is being collected and why. Insurers must also strike a balance between data usage for AI efficiency and consumer privacy. If their training data has biases from the past, AI models will generate decisions that reflect such biases. An AI underwriting system with inherent societal biases against some demographic segments based on historical data can then reflect these biases in its risk assessments or prices.

Based on skewed historical data, AI-driven claims processing systems can discriminate unfairly between policyholder segments. The dilemma is to render AI models fair and equitable to all customers. Insurers need to invest in trustworthy, impartial algorithms to counter such fears and not unfairly disfavor any group. As technology improves, so does the fear of how much AI ought to be making decisions without human intervention. Ought AI systems be responsible for ultimate claims decisions, or must human adjusters always be involved? AI improves efficiency and speed of processing, but not every decision is data-driven. AI is unable to replace subtle human factors like empathy and understanding. Insurers must balance AI's capabilities with human judgment in sensitive issues like claims controversies and policy cancellations. AI allows insurers to create highly personalized pricing models from vast quantities of data from telemetry devices, social media, and web usage. This can lead to more personalized rules, but at the expense of fairness in pricing models.

AI systems can generate pricing structures that unfairly penalize low-income or technology-illiterate people.

Insurance companies must make AI-based pricing transparent and nondiscriminatory. AI pricing algorithms should not take advantage of vulnerable consumers or unfairly influence consumer behavior. Insurers should follow AI development and deployment ethics. Make AI systems explainable, transparent, and auditable. Insurers can establish trust among consumers, regulators, and other stakeholders by being proactive about AI ethics and using AI technology ethically and with social responsibility.

CHALLENGES AND FUTURE DIRECTIONS

AI has the potential to transform insurance but is hindered. Implementation of AI within legacy systems is a major impediment to P&C insurance AI adoption. Many insurance companies formed years ago operate outdated technology that is not compatible with AI products. With substantial cost and time required to recreate these systems, insurers might hesitate to make investments without immediate returns. Staff training to work with new AI-driven technologies and reengineering workflows to automated processes can lead to resistance within organizations.

AI is capable of processing huge amounts of data, but the data must be clean, structured, and high-quality. Incomplete or fragmented data makes it hard to draw conclusions from P&C insurance data. Insurance firms may struggle to merge data from client contacts, claims history, and risk assessments, which typically come from siloed departments and structures. This data requires sophisticated data handling technologies and experienced data scientists to structure and prepare it for AI processing to generate meaningful insights.

Data breaches and abuse increase with AI-driven systems processing sensitive client information like personal information, claims history, and monetary details.

The General Data Protection Regulation (GDPR) in the European Union (EU) and analogous models in other countries place strict data privacy mandates on insurers. To protect client and company data, insurance companies must invest heavily in cybersecurity to comply with these demands while using AI solutions for data analysis. Clients may also be concerned about the use of their information, especially when they suspect it is being misused. Misgivings about AI-based solutions can undermine trust in them, which will cancel out the benefit of using AI. If AI programs are trained using historical data with prejudices like racial, gender, or socioeconomic prejudices, their output can perpetuate them. A biased data set can cause an AI underwriting system to discriminate against some demographic groups or advantage others.

Insurers must use explainable and transparent AI models and audit their algorithms to spot and eliminate biases in order to reduce this threat. This requires constant collaboration with ethicists, regulators, and technical experts to create AI deployment best practices. AI-powered claims handling technology is currently efficient, but computer vision and NLP can automate it further. AI can analyze images of car or property damage to assess damage and construct claims settlements automatically. This would reduce processing time and human error, improving operational efficiency and customer satisfaction.

As more decisions are made by AI, insurers will need to balance human oversight with automation to guarantee fairness and accuracy, especially in complex or high-value claims where human instinct is vital. More and more insurers will use real-time data and predictive analytics to refine pricing and underwriting models using AI. Telematics are already widely used in motor insurance, and as IoT devices become more commonplace, insurers will be able to learn more about customers' driving behavior and property status. This can result in more tailored policies, charging premiums according to individual behavior and situations rather than risk classes. But the action morally falls short from the point of view of justice because poor people may be given higher premiums due to factors outside their control.

Insurers must ensure their AI models consider these variations and do not discriminate. Blockchain technology and advanced ML algorithms to predict calamities suggest that AI in P&C insurance will be innovative. Blockchain and AI can improve the claims process, while ML can predict natural disasters and reduce their cost. These trends are promising, but they require robust infrastructure, widespread acceptance, and regulatory and ethical resolution.

CONCLUSION

In short, AI has transformed P&C insurance. AI technology is helping insurers improve operations and customize services through automating the handling of claims, underwriting, and interactions with customers. AI is helping insurers make faster, fact-based decisions at lower costs by leveraging ML, NLP, and data analytics. This digital change is transforming models of insurance and opening up new markets for growth and innovation.

AI integration into P&C insurance is difficult. Legacy infrastructure, data quality, and the technical intricacies of applying new AI technology present challenges and require substantial investment. Insurers must also address AI ethics issues like algorithmic bias and underwriting and pricing discrimination. With growing cyberthreats, data security and privacy are key concerns. The benefits of automation must be balanced against the pitfalls of AI adoption, as these challenges exemplify.

Despite these challenges, AI for P&C insurance has vast potential. Offering more customized pricing options, accelerating claims payments, and estimating future risk accurately can increase the insurer's bottom line and customer satisfaction. AI also enables new business models like UBI that have the potential to revolutionize policy arrangements. Insurers leveraging AI technologies will be better positioned to react to a changed market and meet customer needs for quicker, more consistent services.

The role of AI in P&C insurance will grow, affecting the business in the long term. AI will fuel innovation in disaster response and customer service as new technologies emerge. Successful adoption of AI will involve balancing the advantages of automation with human monitoring and ethical deployment of AI. Managed effectively, AI can help insurers overcome current challenges and thrive in the future, allowing them to become digital leaders.

REFERENCE

Adeniran, I.A., Efunniyi, C.P., Osundare, O.S., Abhulimen, A.O., and OneAdvanced, U. (2024). Advancements in predictive modeling for insurance pricing: Enhancing risk assessment and customer segmentation. *International Journal of Management and Entrepreneurship Research*, 6(8), 2835–2848.

Adeoye, O.B., Okoye, C.C., Ofodile, O.C., Odeyemi, O., Addy, W. A., and Ajayi-Nifise, A.O. (2024). Integrating artificial intelligence in personalized insurance products: A pathway to enhanced customer engagement. *International Journal of Management and Entrepreneurship Research*, 6(3), 502–511.

Aldboush, H.H., and Ferdous, M. (2023). Building trust in fintech: An analysis of ethical and privacy considerations in the intersection of big data, AI, and customer trust. *International Journal of Financial Studies*, 11(3), 90.

Ali Albasheir, K.A.M. (2023). The impact of IT on insurance of the technological industry. *Journal of Advanced Zoology*, 44.

Atmaja, T., and Fukushi, K. (2022). Empowering geo-based ai algorithm to aid coastal flood risk analysis: A review and framework development. *ISPRS Annals of the Photogrammetry, Remote Sensing and Spatial Information Sciences*, 3, 517–523.

Babatunde, S.O., Odejide, O.A., Edunjobi, T.E., and Ogundipe, D.O. (2024). The role of AI in marketing personalization: A theoretical exploration of consumer engagement strategies. *International Journal of Management and Entrepreneurship Research*, 6(3), 936–949.

Bauer, E., Greisel, M., Kuznetsov, I., Berndt, M., Kollar, I., Dresel, M., and Fischer, F. (2023). Using natural language processing to support peer-feedback in the age of artificial intelligence: A cross-disciplinary framework and a research agenda. *British Journal of Educational Technology*, 54(5), 1222–1245.

Bawa, V. (2022). Framework to understand and deploy AI-based smart CRM in the airline industry. *In:* Adoption and Implementation of AI in Customer Relationship Management, 154–165. IGI Global Scientific Publishing.

Bettini, C., Brdiczka, O., Henricksen, K., Indulska, J., Nicklas, D., Ranganathan, A., and Riboni, D. (2010). A survey of context modelling and reasoning techniques. *Pervasive and Mobile Computing*, 6(2), 161–180.

Blier-Wong, C., Cossette, H., Lamontagne, L., and Marceau, E. (2020). Machine learning in P & C insurance: A review for pricing and reserving. *Risks*, 9(1), 4.

Boppana, V.R. (2023). AI Integration in CRM Systems for Personalized Customer Experiences. Available at SSRN 4987149.

Brynjolfsson, E., Li, D., and Raymond, L. (2025). Generative AI at work. *The Quarterly Journal of Economics*, qjae044.

Btoush, E.A.L.M., Zhou, X., Gururajan, R., Chan, K.C., Genrich, R., and Sankaran, P. (2023). A systematic review of literature on credit card cyber fraud detection using machine and deep learning. *PeerJ Computer Science*, 9, e1278.

Cather, D.A. (2018). Cream skimming: Innovations in insurance risk classification and adverse selection. *Risk Management and Insurance Review*, 21(2), 335–366.

Chaccour, C., Saad, W., Debbah, M., Han, Z., and Poor, H.V. (2024). Less data, more knowledge: Building next generation semantic communication networks. *IEEE Communications Surveys and Tutorials*, 27(1), 37–76.

Chinta, U., and Renuka, A. (2023). Leveraging AI and Machine Learning in Salesforce for Predictive Analytics and Customer Insights. Universal Research Reports.

Danda, R.R., Yasmeen, Z., and Maguluri, K.K. (2024) AI-Driven Healthcare Transformation: Machine Learning, Deep Learning, and Neural Networks in Insurance and Wellness Programs. JEC Publication.

Du, S., and Xie, C. (2021). Paradoxes of artificial intelligence in consumer markets: Ethical challenges and opportunities. *Journal of Business Research*, 129, 961–974.

Dubey, A., Parida, T., Birajdar, A., Prajapati, A.K., and Rane, S. (2018). Smart underwriting system: An intelligent decision support system for insurance approval and risk assessment. *In:* 3rd International Conference for Convergence in Technology (I2CT), 1–6.

Egorenkov, D. (2024). AI-powered predictive customer lifetime value: Maximizing long-term profits. *Valley International Journal Digital Library*, 12, 7339–7354.

Eling, M., Nuessle, D., and Staubli, J. (2022). The impact of artificial intelligence along the insurance value chain and on the insurability of risks. *The Geneva Papers on Risk and Insurance-Issues and Practice*, 47(2), 205–241.

Erem Ceylan, I. (2022). The effects of artificial intelligence on the insurance sector: Emergence, applications, challenges, and opportunities. *The Impact of Artificial Intelligence on Governance, Economics and Finance,* 2, 225–241.

Gagan, P.S.S.M., and Srinivasagopalan, L.N. (2021). Advanced artificial intelligence algorithms for streamlining claims processing and decision-making in healthcare insurance systems. *Journal ID*, 2(1), 1–12.

Ghosh, S., Ness, S., and Salunkhe, S. (2024). The role of AI enabled chatbots in omnichannel customer service. *Journal of Engineering Research and Reports*, 26(6), 327–345.

Gupta, S., Ghardallou, W., Pandey, D.K., and Sahu, G.P. (2022). Artificial intelligence adoption in the insurance industry: Evidence using the technology-organization-environment framework. *Research in International Business and Finance*, 63, 101757.

Haleem, A., Javaid, M., Khan, I.H., and Mohan, S. (2023). Significant applications of artificial intelligence towards attaining sustainability. *Journal of Industrial Integration and Management*, 8(4), 489–520.

Harbola, A. (2021). Design and implementation of an AI chatbot for customer service. *The Philippine Statistician,* 70(2), 1295–1303.

Inavolu, S.M. (2024). Exploring AI-driven customer service: Evolution, architectures, opportunities, challenges and future directions. *International Journal of Engineering and Advanced Technology*, 13(3), 156–163.

Ismail, N., Husin, M.M.M., Ishak, I., and Manaf, N.A. (2018). Insurance awareness: A literature review. *Int. J. Asian Soc. Sci*, 8, 28–33.

Kafle, K., Shrestha, R., and Kanan, C. (2019). Challenges and prospects in vision and language research. *Frontiers in Artificial Intelligence*, 2, 28.

Kitchens, F. (2009). Underwriting automobile insurance using artificial neural networks. *In:* Encyclopedia of Information Science and Technology, Second Edition, 3865–3870. IGI Global Scientific Publishing.

Klein, R.W. (2012). Principles for insurance regulation: An evaluation of current practices and potential reforms. *The Geneva Papers on Risk and Insurance-Issues and Practice*, 37, 175–199.

Kumar, N., Srivastava, J. D., and Bisht, H. (2019). Artificial intelligence in insurance sector. *Journal of the Gujarat Research Society*, 21(7), 79–91.

Kumar, Y. (2022). AI techniques in blockchain technology for fraud detection and prevention. *In:* Security Engineering for Embedded and Cyber-Physical Systems, 207–224. CRC Press.

Kyrylenko, Y. (2024). Chatbots and Virtual Assistants vs. Human Agents in IT Customer Support. University of Lapland.

Lai, L.H. (2008). An evaluation of fuzzy transportation underwriting systematic risk. *Transportation Research Part A: Policy and Practice*, 42(9), 1231–1237.

Li, C., Sun, N., Lu, Y., Guo, B., Wang, Y., Sun, X., and Yao, Y. (2022). Review on urban flood risk assessment. *Sustainability*, 15(1), 765.

Liang, P.P., Lyu, Y., Fan, X., Wu, Z., Cheng, Y., Wu, J., and Zhu, Y. (2021). Multibench: Multiscale benchmarks for multimodal representation learning. *Advances in Neural Information Processing Systems*, 2021, 1.

Linardos, V., Drakaki, M., Tzionas, P., and Karnavas, Y. L. (2022). Machine learning in disaster management: Recent developments in methods and applications. *Machine Learning and Knowledge Extraction*, 4(2), 446–473.

Liu, J., Ye, S., Zhang, Y., and Zhang, L. (2023). Research on InsurTech and the technology innovation level of insurance enterprises. *Sustainability*, 15(11), 8617.

Machireddy, J.R. (2022). Revolutionizing claims processing in the healthcare industry: The expanding role of automation and AI. *Hong Kong Journal of AI and Medicine*, 2(1), 10–36.

Maier, M., Carlotto, H., Sanchez, F., Balogun, S., and Merritt, S. (2019). Transforming underwriting in the life insurance industry. *In:* Proceedings of the AAAI Conference on Artificial Intelligence, 33(1), 9373–9380.

Masud, S.B., Rana, M.M., Sohag, H.J., Shikder, F., Faraji, M.R., and Hasan, M.M. (2024). Understanding the Financial Transaction Security through Blockchain and Machine Learning for Fraud Detection in Data Privacy and Security. Available at SSRN 5164958.

Mullins, M., Holland, C.P., and Cunneen, M. (2021). Creating ethics guidelines for artificial intelligence and big data analytics customers: The case of the consumer European insurance market. *Patterns*, 2(10).

Niyato, D., Alsheikh, M.A., Wang, P., Kim, D.I., and Han, Z. (2016). Market model and optimal pricing scheme of big data and Internet of Things (IoT). *In:* IEEE International Conference on Communications (ICC), 1–6.

Nobel, S.N., Sultana, S., Singha, S.P., Chaki, S., Mahi, M.J.N., Jan, T., and Whaiduzzaman, M. (2024). Unmasking banking fraud: Unleashing the power of machine learning and explainable AI (XAI) on imbalanced data. *Information*, 15(6), 298.

Olier, I., Ortega-Martorell, S., Pieroni, M., and Lip, G.Y. (2021). How machine learning is impacting research in atrial fibrillation: Implications for risk prediction and future management. *Cardiovascular Research*, 117(7), 1700–1717.

Raji, M.A., Olodo, H.B., Oke, T.T., Addy, W.A., Ofodile, O.C., and Oyewole, A.T. (2024). E-commerce and consumer behavior: A review of AI-powered personalization and market trends. *GSC Advanced Research and Reviews*, 18(3), 066–077.

Rane, N., Choudhary, S., and Rane, J. (2023). Blockchain and Artificial Intelligence (AI) Integration for Revolutionizing Security and Transparency in Finance. Available at SSRN 4644253.

Roy, B., and Pagaldiviti, S. (2023). Advancements in arena technology: Enhancing customer experience and employee adaptation in the tourism and hospitality industry. *Smart Tourism*, 4(1), 2330.

Sampat, S.K. (2024). Reasoning and question answering about image-text multi-modal contexts. Thesis, Arizona State University.

Sharma, K., and Giannakos, M. (2020). Multimodal data capabilities for learning: What can multimodal data tell us about learning? *British Journal of Educational Technology*, 51(5), 1450–1484.

Soori, M., Arezoo, B., and Dastres, R. (2023). Artificial intelligence, machine learning and deep learning in advanced robotics, a review. *Cognitive Robotics*, 3, 54–70.

Tavares, E.d.S., Leardini, M., and Pessoa, M.S.d.P. (2025). How do the barriers that prevent or hinder the applicability of artificial intelligence impact its use in an insurance company. *Innovation and Management Review*, 22(1), 13–46.

Turner, M.A., and Agarwal, A. (2008). Using non-traditional data for underwriting loans to thin-file borrowers: Evidence, tips and precautions. *Journal of Risk Management in Financial Institutions*, 1(2), 165–180.

Udeh, E.O., Amajuoyi, P., Adeusi, K.B., and Scott, A.O. (2024). AI-enhanced fintech communication: Leveraging chatbots and NLP for efficient banking support. *International Journal of Management and Entrepreneurship Research*, 6(6), 1768–1786.

Vashishth, T.K., Sharma, V., Sharma, K.K., Kumar, B., Kumar, A., and Panwar, R. (2024). Artificial intelligence (AI)–powered chatbots: Providing instant support and personalized recommendations to guests 24/7. *In:* Technology and Luxury Hospitality, 211–236. Routledge.

Wagh, V., and Ramesh, G. (2024). A study on the role of AI in hyper-personalization marketing of FMCG products. *Economic Sciences*, 20(2), 267–278.

Weidner, W., Transchel, F.W., and Weidner, R. (2017). Telematic driving profile classification in car insurance pricing. *Annals of Actuarial Science*, 11(2), 213–236.

Wiriyathammabhum, P., Summers-Stay, D., Fermüller, C., and Aloimonos, Y. (2016). Computer vision and natural language processing: recent approaches in multimedia and robotics. *ACM Computing Surveys (CSUR)*, 49(4), 1–44.

Ye, X., Weng, D., Sha, Y., Zhang, H., Ya, L., Xiao, J., and Qu, W. (2021). Analysis on pricing model of UBI auto insurance in China from the perspective of big data. *International Journal of Frontiers in Sociology*, 3(2), 79-86.

Zhao, Y. (2019). Valuation and Risk Management of Some Longevity and P&C Insurance Products. PhD Thesis, The University of Western Ontario (Canada).

6

Navigating Obstacles in AI Integration: Challenges Facing the Insurance Sector

*Sara Ramzani**, *Peter Konhaeusner, Ahmad Abu-Alkheil, Phungmayo Horam, Vahab Esfandani, and Mohammad Amin Borghei*

OVERVIEW OF AI'S POTENTIAL IN INSURANCE

Growth in productivity for businesses, reduction in costs, and improved customer satisfaction—these are all the benefits artificial intelligence (AI) is bringing to the insurance sector. It even has the power to transform methods of detection, risk evaluation, and underwriting operations entirely through technologies like predictive analytics, machine learning (ML), and other algorithmic methods. Accurate assessments using these technologies provide insurers with a way to determine and calculate precise prices for the packages they offer based on their uniqueness. The accessibility and affordability of insurance have become much easier, making it attractive to penetrate the populace as a means of enhancing financial inclusion (Agu et al. 2022). The use of AI in the health insurance industry can improve customer satisfaction and operational efficiency in risk evaluations, preference determination, fraud detection, and claims acceleration (Dutt 2020).

Nevertheless, the insurance sector has not yet fully embraced the potential of AI, and there are still many hurdles to its widespread adoption. In their study, Lopez and Rojas (2024) identified high costs, skill shortages, and technological uncertainties as the main obstacles to AI adoption in insurance across Organisation for Economic Co-operation and Development (OECD) industries. A number of challenges also affect the adoption of AI solutions in the Zimbabwean insurance market, including lack of funds, insufficient knowledge of AI, and high costs associated with these solutions (Moyo et al. 2022). The use of AI in the African insurance market is also limited due to varying regulatory standards and inconsistent digital infrastructure (Agu et al. 2022).

AI solutions in the Indian insurance industry are seen as strategies for market expansion and improving customer satisfaction. Nevertheless, the sector faces organizational problems due to the need to be technologically prepared (Pradeep and Patil 2022). Legal concerns, mandatory human oversight, and data problems still need to be addressed before this is widely adopted, although there are some

Gisma University of Applied Sciences, Berlin, Germany
* *Corresponding author:* sara.ramzani@gisma.com

DOI: 10.1201/9781003621119-6

insurance companies in Egypt moving towards using AI systems for integration (Ismail and Mohammad, 2023).

Using AI, the insurance market can be transformed in a way that enhances productivity and reduces the cost of operations while achieving high levels of customer satisfaction. At present, several barriers surround the complete adoption of AI. Therefore, in order to overcome the existing challenges and allow AI to reach its full potential in the insurance industry, deliberate investment in resources, training, and the development of a conducive regulatory framework is necessary.

SUCCESSFUL AI IMPLEMENTATION IN INSURANCE

The insurance sector has benefited from improvements in accuracy, efficiency, and customer satisfaction brought by AI. AI-powered systems for fraud detection and risk assessment are excellent examples of how AI can be adopted in real-world insurance applications. These transformations reduced errors and minimized staff intervention, changing previously tedious insurance procedures (Dhieb et al. 2020). The following section explains key elements of AI systems in this business.

Important uses of AI technology in insurance include fraud detection and risk measurement. One of them is ML, named XGBoost, and demonstrated to be an effective successor of the previous approach to the fraudulent claims detection.When applied on vehicle insurance data, XGBoost was 7% worse than decision tree models (Dhieb et al. 2020).

AI systems are now being combined with blockchain technologies in such a way that all transactions and data sharing is safe. In addition, smooth communication between different agents in the insurance network has been achieved facilitating insurance operations. The use of AI systems with online learning helps meet the demand for instant adaptation in the insurance network. This feature allows the system to surpass the behavior of other advanced algorithms by adapting to new data and improving its performance continuously (Dhieb et al. 2020).

TECHNOLOGICAL CHALLENGES

As such, the development of specific technological solutions is needed to make this technology widely used in this industry. The main challenge with adopting AI in this industry is that current data infrastructure has problems with getting systems to communicate well enough with each other while standardizing data formats and avoiding integration issues.

Data Infrastructure Limitations

One major technological problem of adopting AI in insurance industry is that it is not compatible with legacy systems. However, a significant number of insurance companies still rely on the old technologies that do not work well with the most recent modern AI technology. The difficulty for an insurer to fully leverage AI is that these legacy systems cannot be easily adapted to accommodate AI-driven procedures. These systems may be inflexible and limit the implementation of AI models, as they are not easily modified to integrate new technology (Leff and Lim 2021). The situation is aggravated when insurers are unwilling to update current systems because of the high costs and risks involved (López and Rojas 2024).

Successful implementation of AI applications in insurance companies requires standardizing procedures as well as high-quality data. In order to operate an AI system, high-quality standardized data is essential. As many insurance organizations face operational bottlenecks in dealing with separated data sources, they tend to rely on unpredictable and imprecise AI outputs (Leff and Lim 2021). And because various departments and systems have not set consistent data formats, the implementation of AI technology becomes harder. To move forward with underwriting and claims management, Rehman (2024) says that international insurance programs must merge multiple datasets from various partners. Agu et al. (2022) indicate the negative effects on operational efficiency due to the quality of insurance sector data used in AI-based risk assessment and fraud detection systems. Combining AI technology with existing insurance operational methods is a complex challenge as it must overcome several technical problems. To ensure successful integration of AI technology in insurance operations, one needs not only to understand AI technology systems but also to have complete comprehension of insurance sector operations. Numerous insurers find it difficult to integrate AI into existing insurance systems, as there are time delays and increased costs involved (Rehman 2024). When insurance companies need to follow different regulatory requirements within various markets and locations, basic integration becomes complicated (Agu et al. 2022). As this change brings significant disruption, organizations will need to implement substantial innovations in their current operational flows when integrating AI systems, which will require extensive training combined with change management programs (Nair et al. 2024).

The implementation of AI in insurance has been restricted by outdated infrastructure, poor data quality, and integration issues. Modernizing old technology, streamlining data management, and enhancing integration processes are necessary to overcome these problems. Addressing these concerns can fulfill AI's potential in terms of efficiency, better risk management, and delivering an improved customer experience.

Technical Complexity

AI has been adopted on a wide scale for insurance operations; however, technical obstacles have prevented its broader application. Not surprisingly, there is a lack of robust learning systems, complex algorithms, and sufficient computing resources required to implement AI in insurance practice. Advanced AI technologies produce both productive and disruptive operational consequences in this domain. Adversarial learning and federated learning, combined with deep learning (DL) methods, can work with complex data structures and offer better results in advisory services. These algorithms allow for the replication of human skills and reasoning abilities to reduce assessment errors and improve detection accuracy (Śmietanka et al. 2021). Moreover, current challenges are also related to the sophistication and complexity of existing algorithm systems. These systems come with complex algorithms that require advanced knowledge to implement—knowledge that some insurance companies do not currently have in-house. Moyo et al. (2022) further note that a lack of skilled staff is one of the challenges faced by Zimbabwean insurance companies in employing AI technology.

The problem that AI systems had to solve was created with large amounts of computing power. Conversely, there is still a need for processing power and hardware infrastructure—especially in relation to AI systems that are performing ML and DL. High-performance computing equipment capable of storing large datasets and running sophisticated algorithms is required (Śmietanka et al. 2021). There are considerable challenges in building technology frameworks that meet the computational needs of AI in the insurance industry. As indicated by Agu et al. (2022), African insurance operations are characterized by different digital infrastructure setups that make successful adoption of AI difficult. This is further hindered by the high cost of acquiring and maintaining the necessary computational resources—resources that many insurance companies cannot afford (Moyo et al. 2022, López and Rojas 2024).

Moreover, limitations in ML models may prevent their full implementation in this sector. Generalization errors represent a major drawback. These trained AI systems may fail when working with data different from what they were trained on. If generalization fails, predictions may be inaccurate, leading to poor decisions—particularly concerning in a precision-driven industry like insurance. ML programs that yield unjustified outputs are often the result of unintentional bias in training data. Since decisions in insurance often concern people's financial stability, errors can be significant. As per Kelly et al. (2019), the ability of AI models to generalize, and for their results to remain unbiased and equitable, must be thoroughly reviewed and validated.

To actually work in insurance operations, the benefits of experts, infrastructure deployment and ethical model evaluations will be needed by the AI technologies. The implementation of this system in insurance industries gives the AI technology a high level that has many advantages such as offering risk evaluation, fraud detection and operation efficiency, despite the usual roadblocks associated with the implementation.

Technological Security Concerns

Several technological barriers are preventing the wider spread of AI across the insurance sector. Most of these problems are associated with system compromises, personal data privacy, and cybersecurity vulnerabilities. As the insurance sector increasingly depends on AI technologies, there is an urgent need for robust cybersecurity frameworks. AI systems, once integrated into insurance companies, introduce new cyber threats. Cybercriminals are drawn to AI systems due to their massive data requirements, and the system designs make them highly vulnerable. System dependencies and algorithms are often difficult to identify and correct. There is a real possibility that threats may alter data inputs or outputs, negatively impacting

AI-driven risk assessments or claims fraud detection in insurance (Agu et al. 2022, López and Rojas 2024). Therefore, it is critical to implement strong cybersecurity defenses to safeguard AI systems and sensitive data, while maintaining the integrity of AI operations.

The second is the problem of data privacy, which makes it hard to implement AI. However, when you use AI, you also have to obtain and process a lot of people's data, which presents issues regarding how that data will be shared, used, and stored. Customers are increasingly conscious and concerned about privacy, particularly with sensitive data like health records. A negative tendency in customers' relationship with AI-powered insurance solutions is their concern about privacy protection. While privacy concerns tend to expand in the case of AI within health insurance, the effect of these concerns is statistically different in strength (Dutt 2020, Zarifis et al. 2021). In order to tackle complex data protection laws and maintain customer confidence, insurers must ensure that their AI systems comply with regulatory standards.

When insurers use AI, there is significant concern about the risk of system breaches. Data loss, manipulation, or theft can occur when unauthorized individuals gain access and compromise AI systems. Such infractions may lead to financial losses, reputational damage, and legal liability. It would therefore require stringent safety precautions and regular monitoring of AI systems to detect and respond to potential breaches quickly. However, due to the complexity of AI systems and the volatility of cyber threats, complete security cannot always be guaranteed (Agu et al. 2022, López and Rojas 2024). For this reason, to avoid large damages that can occur due to breaches, which if occur, the losses can be huge, insurers need to make strategic investments in the advanced security systems and develop and follow a comprehensive incident response strategy.

EXAMPLES OF SUCCESSFUL MODERNIZATION

Legacy systems pose significant challenges for insurance organizations in adapting to new technologies and undergoing market transformation. System modernization achieved by some insurance companies has improved customer experience and brought productivity gains. One example is the implementation of Microservice Architecture, where an insurance firm migrated from a mainframe legacy system to microservices. This method helped solve the complex problem of data synchronization across services, ensuring both data security and consistency (Koschel et al. 2019).

Indian Insurers and Industry 4.0: Indian insurance companies are actively seeking modernization to comply with Industry 4.0 standards, as maintaining outdated technological environments has become unsustainable. This process involves revisiting conventional IT-driven approaches and exploring multiple alternatives for timely and effective transformation (Singh 2018).

Progressive adoption of cloud based technologies by insurance companies: Insurance companies are increasingly realizing that the utilization of AI is only possible by changing traditional on-premise IT infrastructure to cloud-based technologies. Work demonstrates the need for such a system in practice to increase scalability, flexibility and cost efficacy, all of which are often limited in conventional systems (Martins N.M.R. 2023). Cloud computing offers the infrastructure necessary for high complex information processing and storage for AI and helps underwriters manage very large amounts of data (Mateen et al. 2023, Martins N.M.R. 2023). Cloud-based AI technologies offer multiple benefits for the insurance industry. These solutions simplify AI integration, enabling institutions to strengthen cybersecurity, comply with regulations, and standardize data processing (Rehman 2024). AI solutions support native integration with existing business systems for key functions such as claims management and underwriting (Rehman 2024, Kumar 2024). Additionally, cloud-based AI systems enhance risk assessment and fraud detection, reducing human error and improving the accuracy of identifying false claims (Dhieb et al. 2020).

However, cloud-based AI comes with disadvantages, mainly around data security and privacy. According to Kumar (2024), insurance companies are implementing AI governance frameworks to ensure regulatory compliance and address these challenges. Maintaining business continuity during the transition is crucial, as organizations must align their trained IT staff with hybrid cloud systems and undertake extensive execution planning (Martins N.M.R. 2023).

Emerging technologies such as serverless computing and 5G are expected to significantly enhance AI applications, making the future of cloud-based AI in the insurance sector promising (Martins N.M.R. 2023). When AI is combined with other technologies like blockchain and the Internet of Things, insurance services can become more innovative and efficient (Mateen et al. 2023, van der Vlist et al. 2024). These innovations can also help insurers increase customer engagement, deliver personalized solutions, and stay ahead in an increasingly digital and dynamic market (Adeoye et al. 2024).

ORGANIZATIONAL BARRIERS

Cloud-based AI solutions present disadvantages that primarily concern data security and privacy. The AI governance frameworks adopted by insurance companies help ensure regulatory compliance while addressing identified issues (Kumar 2024). Maintaining business continuity during the transition requires organizations to coordinate trained IT staff with hybrid cloud environments and conduct detailed planning (Martins N.M.R. 2023).

Cultural Resistance

One major organizational issue in the implementation of AI in the insurance sector is cultural resistance. This opposition often manifests as organizational inertia, a traditional mindset, and fear of job displacement. Like many other industries, the insurance sector is frequently characterized by a conservative culture that can be resistant to change. Introducing new technologies such as AI may face pushback due to this deeply embedded mindset. Employees and management might question the benefits of AI, especially if they are comfortable with existing procedures. A lack of knowledge about AI technologies and how they can support productivity and improve decision-making may fuel such skepticism (López and Rojas 2024, Cubric 2020). At the same time, traditional mindset could lead to a preference for keeping things as they are rather than being aligned with the innovative alternatives that AI offers.

The fear of employment displacement is another essential aspect of cultural resistance. Routine tasks might get automated by AI technology, which may cause employees to feel concerned about their job security. AI can replace some jobs, especially those that involve repetitive tasks, so this concern is not unreasonable. Research evidence indicates that when people use AI technology, they can direct their efforts toward critical and advanced duties (Booyse and Scheepers 2024). Staff members fail to adopt AI because they expect job reductions and regard technology as hazardous rather than developmental for their careers, according to Cubric (2020) and Booyse and Scheepers (2024).

Organizational inertia causes most companies to maintain their current infrastructure patterns and operational processes in opposition to change. Organizations that avoid technological investment and maintain operational stability display two major obstacles that stop them from adopting AI systems. Organizations in the insurance sector confront risks of resistance to change because of established practices combined with regulatory requirements. A strategic approach that incorporates changes in organizational culture and mindset, in addition to technology investment, is required to address such a challenge (Raftopoulos 2024). To successfully integrate AI technologies, organizations need to foster a climate that values innovation and flexibility (López and Rojas 2024, Raftopoulos 2024).

To conclude, cultural resistance is one of the organizational challenges limiting the insurance industry's adoption of AI. The resistance comes from three causes: organizational traits, maintenance of the status quo, and anxiety about job security. Overcoming employee resistance requires a diverse plan that educates workforce members about AI benefits, showcases future employment possibilities, and creates an environment welcoming to creative thinking and innovation. AI technology enables full utilization across the insurance sector for enhanced performance, decision quality, and productivity when these challenges are addressed.

Skill Gap and Talent Acquisition

Adequate knowledge of AI solutions proves to be a significant obstacle to its adoption in insurance processes. The number of qualified professionals who can develop, implement, and manage AI technology falls far short of market demand. This deficiency creates a major problem because it hinders insurance companies from achieving the maximum potential from AI applications. López and Rojas (2024) conducted a study that shows a shortage of AI specialists across all business sectors, including finance and insurance (López and Rojas

2024). Business organizations face dual challenges in finding personnel with both AI expertise and the technological experience to drive their AI projects. Training current employees and building their skills represent dual challenges due to the general lack of AI expertise. Many insurance companies recognize the need to fund employee training programs to build AI proficiency among staff. The development of such programs faces two difficulties: maintaining effectiveness while adapting to the fast-moving dynamics of AI technology. Research by Kajwang (2022) on the challenges and prospects of the insurance industry in AI societies identifies employee training fund deficiencies as a critical element for skill development (Kajwang 2022). The rapid evolution of AI technology demands that businesses allocate significant resources to continually update existing programs to maintain their relevance.

Insurance companies must develop diverse capabilities to fully exploit the advantages offered by AI technologies. In-demand professionals combine AI solution integration expertise with knowledge of AI ethics and regulatory matters. These roles are even more sought after than purely technical AI specialists. This calls for a blend of corporate strategy, data science, and compliance expertise. Insurance companies need professionals who can bridge the gap between technology and business operations, given that AI projects are inherently multidisciplinary. Research into barriers to AI adoption shows that insurance industry managers require a diverse range of skills to navigate AI integration complexities (López and Rojas 2024). The lack of AI experts, along with uncertainty about skill development, creates significant obstacles. Workforce acquisition becomes difficult because companies need employees with hybrid competencies. A financial investment strategy is necessary in the insurance sector to build a workforce capable of fully deploying AI technology and tackling current operational challenges.

Investment and Resource Allocation

The substantial upfront costs of implementing AI often discourage the insurance industry from considering its adoption. These costs include the purchase of AI technologies, system integration, and required infrastructure modifications. For example, the high cost of AI-compliant products in Zimbabwe limits the ability of companies to invest in these technologies, creating considerable financial barriers for the insurance sector (Moyo et al. 2022).

AI implementation expenses are even higher for insurance companies operating in African nations, which exhibit varying digital infrastructure and differing legal systems (Agu et al. 2022). Companies face financial hurdles in acquiring technology, training staff, and upgrading systems to be AI-compatible (Moyo et al. 2022).

The sector must overcome undefined Return on Investment (ROI) challenges that hinder AI adoption. Insurance organizations often delay substantial investments in AI technologies, waiting for clear evidence of profitability. Business uncertainty regarding the organizational effects of AI is heightened by the lack of reliable performance evaluation techniques and insufficient data. Pradeep and Patil (2022) explain that Indian insurance companies remain skeptical about the financial impact of AI implementation because the relationship between AI and profitability has not been sufficiently demonstrated. The financial outcomes of AI applications in underwriting, claims processing, and fraud detection remain unclear, complicating companies' decisions to allocate resources toward deployment (Ismail and Mohammad 2023).

The insurance industry also faces widespread budgetary constraints that limit the ability of companies to provide adequate resources for AI deployment. Narrow profit margins prevent insurance entities from investing heavily in new technological development. These financial limitations create significant technological roadblocks and stall progress in both the finance and insurance sectors, according to López and Rojas (2024). The demand for investment in AI platforms—driven by competition and the need for technological advancement—intensifies this issue. The financial constraints of underdeveloped countries, which face economic hardship and limited access to capital, further clarify why AI adoption remains out of reach for many businesses (Moyo et al. 2022, Agu et al. 2022).

Regulatory and Ethical Challenges

Specifically, the regulations on the application of AI technology in insurance operations lead to many intricate difficulties in terms of compliance. The implementation of telehealth solutions must follow existing insurance regulations so that they will be properly run or operated to protect the customers. Moreover, as AI systems work on unknown methodologies, it implies that human operators cannot satisfy the transparency requirements (Angenent 2022, Anang et al. 2024). Since organizations are not able to access the internal processing of AI models, they are unable to meet the underwriting and claims processing standards, as stated by Agu et al. (2022) and Uzougbo et al. (2024).

During the deployment of AI tools in an organization, there are big data security risks that organizations have to face; hence, utilizing data sets from an insurance company's databases is required to accomplish this activity. Since the General Data Protection Regulation (GDPR) (2024) in Europe and other data protection rules make it compulsory to follow strict standards while collecting, processing, and storing personal data (Uzougbo et al. 2024, Wang 2024), it has become necessary to provide clear and logical reasons for accessing personal data. While it is difficult to execute AI systems that require extensive training data, insurers' AI systems are regulated by law and, therefore, must meet compliance requirements. Customer data privacy and information security will be protected through the implementation of robust data governance policies (Eghaghe et al. 2024, Agu et al. 2022).

As such, AI governance frameworks are required elements for the responsible and ethical deployment of AI technologies in this domain. In turn, these frameworks manage the creation, deployment, and monitoring of AI technologies from start to finish and cover issues such as unfairness, bias, and accountability (Ridzuan et al. 2024, Anang et al. 2024). Therefore, AI governance organizations must develop specific policies that encompass procedures for AI use and periodic evaluation approaches to ensure adherence to ethical standards and regulatory mandates (Angenent 2022, Eghaghe et al. 2024). One effective development in Explainable AI (XAI) systems is increasing AI accountability through full explanations of every part of the AI decision-making process (Anang et al. 2024, Angenent 2022).

It must be ensured that AI systems follow governance structures and comply with industry regulations and data security laws. Insurance organizations must have strong governance systems with explainable AI technology that enhances accountability and increases transparency. In doing so, the insurance industry will be able to enjoy the benefits of AI by resolving ethical and regulatory challenges such as consumer trust and legal compliance.

ETHICAL CONSIDERATIONS

Many ethical challenges of responsible AI are yet to be resolved to achieve equitable AI use, which insurance companies are striving for. The three main problems to be solved within AI-powered insurance solutions are fair underwriting and pricing practices, improvement of explainability techniques, and the development of unbiased algorithms. Some of the challenges with algorithmic bias in risk assessment systems and underwriting solutions based on AI are unique. Large datasets have to be used to train AI to make predictions. This increases the risk that previous biases in the datasets will be perpetuated, leading to unfair discrimination. Furthermore, unfair discrimination can occur when facially neutral features in AI systems reflect prohibited characteristics (Filabi and Duffy 2021). Societal biases also creep into systems and new sources of data used in life insurance in unintentional ways, often with worse outcomes (Filabi and Duffy 2021). The application of algorithmic audits and transparency methods aims to detect and correct biases found in AI systems, helping to reduce these risks (Agu et al. 2024).

In the insurance industry, particularly for healthcare service providers, AI systems are required to act transparently and explainably to build trust with users. The processes of claims management and underwriting within the "black box" framework of various AI-driven algorithms are poorly explained. The lack of transparency causes users to lose trust, which is critical in the insurance industry (Dexe et al. 2021). As a result, XAI frameworks serve two functions: removing biased decisions from algorithms and facilitating transparency (Matai 2024). AI technologies will likely be handled by organizations with a legal obligation to integrate transparency protocols as a standard ethical practice. When underwriting operations are conducted, it must be recognized that AI provides extremely accurate, individualized assessments, changing how insurance premiums are calculated. This raises questions about how insurance rates can be fairly distributed. Despite being two key methods of AI-driven underwriting—personalized and efficient delivery of insurance solutions—ML and predictive analytics require active management to prevent discriminatory pricing (Agu et al. 2022). Thus, Qureshi et al. (2024) indicate that to ensure fair treatment of policyholders, ethical guidelines for managing AI in underwriting and premium decisions should be put in place. These AI systems will also need regulatory frameworks and ethical guidelines to prevent discriminatory policies from influencing pricing and underwriting decisions (Uzougbo et al. 2024). The main problem companies face is the need to examine various ethical aspects of AI adoption in insurance. If insurance companies responsibly adopt AI and implement responsible AI practices, the industry can overcome current challenges through governance, auditing, and transparency.

EXPLAINABLE AI IN INSURANCE REGULATION

Insurance industries require transparency and trust, making it crucial to begin adopting Explainable Artificial Intelligence (XAI). Due to their responsibility for handling large volumes of data from essential societal areas, insurance companies find that adopting XAI presents an exceptional opportunity to improve decision-making processes that comply with existing regulations. Beyond actuarial use, XAI also brings value to other parts of the insurance value chain, such as claims administration and underwriting. According to Owens et al. (2022), knowledge distillation and rule extraction methods assist in making complex models more understandable for stakeholders. Although scaling these solutions remains difficult for complex data and regulatory compliance, XAI-based decision explanations can improve trust formation in health insurance underwriting (Vel 2023).

Given the regulatory demands of the insurance sector, integrating XAI into compliance processes is imperative to ensure accountability and fairness. The European Union (EU) AI Act and Pavlidis (2024) equally emphasize the importance of XAI by defining oversight procedures and guidelines to uphold these principles. Applying XAI facilitates regulatory enforcement and supports clear, justifiable decision-making, which is essential for realizing the legal and ethical objectives of the insurance industry (Sewada et al. 2023).

Two main barriers in the application of XAI are identified in obtaining adequate solutions for complex data sets and balancing predictive accuracy and knowledge transparency (Vel 2023, Sewada et al. 2023). Further research is needed for the development of XAI frameworks in order to create models that meet all necessary requirements to integrate smoothly into existing regulatory frameworks without a decrease in precision or effectiveness standards (Saeed and Omlin 2023, Longo et al. 2024). According to Longo et al. (2024), full insurance regulatory benefits from XAI depend on active collaboration between different fields of expertise.

OPERATIONAL CHALLENGES

Performance and Reliability

In the implementation of AI solutions, organizations need AI model accuracy to be a top priority. Its operations make use of predictive models for two main functions of the insurance business: risk assessment in underwriting and fraud detection. However, the inaccurate performance of predictive models is unacceptable in the business context, as it affects financial budgets and operational execution decisions.

Two AI-driven methods of risk and rate assessment in African insurance markets that replace the underwriting and risk assessment processes are ML and predictive analytics. These models often face issues related to the complex characteristics of various regulatory backgrounds and data quality, which result in doubts about their reliability (Agu et al. 2022). Accurate predictive models are needed for organizational success in the deployment of AI in the Indian insurance sector to escalate market penetration and customer satisfaction.

The problem with deploying AI is the fact that edge cases—i.e., unpredictable situations—are hard to manage. An AI model may face an edge case situation when it encounters data outside the usual training distribution. In the insurance sector, accuracy is of utmost importance, and wrong forecasts under such circumstances could be harmful. Any robust technology infrastructure that can successfully handle edge cases in Zimbabwe's insurance sector should be based on research findings. Moyo et al. (2022) state that limited knowledge and scarce resources lead to operational failures in dealing with special situations. The Egyptian insurance sector also struggles with outlier cases that affect the reliability of AI systems used in claims processing and underwriting (Ismail and Mohammad 2023).

As AI systems require maintenance, model drift also occurs, impacting system reliability. A fundamental decrease in model accuracy is caused by model drift, which results from changes in the statistical profile of the target variable during the monitoring period. Given the fast-changing market conditions and customer behavior in the insurance industry, this issue is particularly significant. In both the insurance and banking sectors, continuous model maintenance is essential to sustain model performance and manage drift, as stated by López and Rojas (2024). Agu et al. (2022) add that organizations need constant human oversight and periodic model updates to avoid drift and maintain reliability.

To achieve AI technology efficiency, model drift must be managed, edge case handling must be improved, and predictive model accuracy must be ensured. To enhance the effectiveness and reliability of AI systems in the insurance industry, technological advancements are necessary, alongside proper resource allocation and skilled personnel.

Integration with Existing Processes

The main barrier in integrating AI technology into current insurance procedures is workflow disruption. These integrations often cause short-term operational inefficiencies and employee confusion, requiring significant adjustments to existing operations. AI implementation disrupts traditional functions such as underwriting, claims processing, and customer service. Organizations must reorganize task execution and information flow (López and Rojas 2024, Pradeep and Patil 2022). As a result, even minor changes in mature insurance processes become complex. Additionally, because employees must be trained on new AI-based procedures and adapt to changes, implementation may slow down (Ismail and Mohammad, 2023).

To resolve the barriers to AI adoption in insurance companies, effective change management strategies must be implemented. Change management relates to the process of preparing individuals and groups and providing them with assistance while undergoing organizational transformation. It is important to understand that implementation of AI requires cultural adjustment throughout the business organization since all employees are required to adapt to the new operational technologies and systems. The problem arises because the transition requires the solutions to worker opposition and doubts, because personnel are concerned about job security and perceive the AI innovations with fear (López and Rojas 2024, Pradeep and Patil 2022). Training employees to explain the benefits of revolutionizing AI across the organization and enabling people to improve effectiveness through training; involving employees in the implementation phase to foster levels of acceptance. (Agu et al. 2022).

However, many organizations find it challenging to adapt and implement AI solutions within their operations. Incorporating new AI technologies requires adjustments to existing processes, internal culture, and organizational structure. Pradeep and Patil (2022), and Ismail and Mohammad (2023) state that insurance companies must create new departments for data analytics and AI and establish new roles. Companies that historically relied on human expertise may struggle with transitioning to data-driven decision-making (Agu et al. 2022). According to López and Rojas (2024), the adaptation process must ensure accessibility to the fundamental infrastructure and resources necessary to support AI, including effective data management and cybersecurity safeguards.

Insurance firms can fully utilize AI to improve customer satisfaction, reduce costs, and enhance process efficiency by overcoming these implementation hurdles.

CUSTOMER-RELATED CHALLENGES

Trust and Acceptance

The insurance business has faced major obstacles to AI adoption because customers often view AI unfavorably. The public generally approaches AI with skepticism due to concerns about privacy and the misuse of personal data. Privacy and trust are essential in health insurance systems. Research indicates that using AI explicitly can reduce trust levels, even when consumers are already familiar with technological solutions that replace human contact. Zarifis et al. (2021) found that trust levels decrease when customers can clearly see AI interfaces and recognize their role in decision-making. Health insurance is not alone in its struggle to gain customer trust—many insurance sectors face similar issues when customers do not understand how AI reaches decisions (Dexe et al. 2021).

Customers develop confidence primarily through transparent operations. The lack of transparency in many AI-based algorithms makes it difficult for insurance companies to implement AI in an industry that relies heavily on trust. People struggle to understand how AI systems make decisions—this is known as the "black box" problem. In Sweden, each insurer has concerns about transparency levels due to the risk of revealing proprietary decision algorithms (Dexe et al. 2021). Customers who lack clarity about decision-making processes will exhibit dissatisfaction and show resistance to adopt insurance solutions powered by AI technology.

For years, insurance companies operated as relationship-oriented organizations where face-to-face interactions complemented human assessment throughout all operations. The adoption of AI technologies poses an obstacle to traditional human-managed processes such as insurance claims assessment and underwriting operations. A perceived loss of personal customer care touches emerges as the change happens in the industry, where this aspect formed the core basis for insurance service delivery. AI systems generate an impersonal atmosphere, which drives customers toward dissatisfaction and hesitation toward AI technology usage (Ismail and Mohammad 2023). Insurers must handle the challenging task of achieving technology efficiency alongside maintaining human-level customer relationships very carefully. Improved transparency and data privacy protection measures and established automation–personal interaction ratios will enable the insurance sector to resolve these obstacles and execute successful AI implementations.

Data Privacy Concerns

The introduction of AI to the insurance field brings numerous difficulties, with data protection as its main challenge. The implementation of AI makes data management a core focus point for proper insurance data practices. This section explains data privacy matters that affect how insurance companies manage and secure client data when obtaining customer consent and utilizing collected information. The natural operation of AI systems in insurance demands a significant volume of customer-related information. Multiple uses of the gathered information involve fraud detection while also assisting in premium calculations and risk assessments. Public privacy stands in danger because of customer data collection processes in contemporary information systems. Insurance organizations must handle data utilization for AI applications while protecting client confidentiality. The increasing customer comfort with technology stands in opposition to their concern over AI detection, which causes privacy issues, according to Zarifis et al. (2021). The ethical use of data, along with keeping information private, presents the greatest challenge among all issues.

People must provide explicit approval before anyone can access their personal data while retaining autonomy regarding their information control. Insurance companies need to obtain explicit consumer permission before they can use data in their AI integration process. Every consumer must learn which entities plan to access their information, along with the purposes of use and related activities. Insurance adoption rates may decrease when companies fail to establish transparent consent processes that build trust with their customers. Research shows that insurance companies must base their activities on patient consent approaches that ensure exclusive control of customer data and total transparency about usage actions (Murdoch 2021). The implementation should focus on building robust consent systems with built-in options for customers to decline or modify their data-sharing consent permissions.

Protecting personal data represents a major issue that arises when insurance uses AI technology. As AI technologies are deployed more often, the risks of data breaches and unauthorized access to private data increase. Insurance organizations must build robust data protection methods for their practices to safeguard client information. Insurance companies must implement contemporary encryption algorithms, conduct frequent security audits, and follow all national privacy laws.

ML models that rediscover anonymized information compound the information security obstacles and lead to greater privacy risks (Murdoch 2021). The industry will gain leadership and decrease privacy breaches only through embracing innovative data protection approaches and anonymization methods.

The insurance industry implements different methods for showing transparency to customers while building their confidence in service clarity. Insurance organizations carry out this mission through several methods, as illustrated below.

- Insurance companies make policy terms, pricing, and benefits easily comprehensible as they work toward openness. This approach, which aligns with community values, creates positive effects on customer loyalty and trust (Pertiwi 2024). The Croatian insurance market requires insurers to explain insurance contract terms and conditions to their policyholders to achieve better transparency (Belanić and Jurić 2019).
- Blockchain technology applies secure real-time data technologies to make insurance more transparent while operating more efficiently to improve customer experiences (Guruprakash et al. 2024). Employing transparent algorithms in decision-making addresses the "black box" characteristic of AI and boosts customer trust, as noted by Dexe et al. (2021).
- The transparency standards of insurance contracts in England and Germany under European legislation work to enhance security for customers and establish trust-based business relationships. The Solvency II Directive of the EU enhances transparency requirements for insurers to deliver specific information to policyholders before and during their insurance period (Belanić and Jurić 2019).
- Insurance companies should maintain regular contact with their customers to help consumers better grasp financial services and understand the importance of insurance in risk mitigation (Ćirić 2024). The preservation of consumer empowerment, together with brand integrity, requires transparent marketing communications because of their influence on behavioral intentions and brand trust (Cambier and Poncin 2020).

RISK MANAGEMENT CHALLENGES

Several important risk management issues exist when AI systems are used in insurance applications. AI systems perform insurance operations with greater reliability and effectiveness when these critical issues are properly addressed.

Model Risk

The damage to insurance companies would be significant if AI models generated inaccurate outputs that led to model risk. Black swan events, scenario uncertainty, and flawed predictive modeling all increase model risk.

Prevention is possible through predictive AI models that analyze historical data and predict future incidents. However, these systems naturally have constraints. The quality of data fed into the system is the primary factor influencing accuracy, and flawed data can lead to incorrect outcomes. In addition, a lack of proper assessments and premium evaluations may result in issues such as overcharging some customers or financial losses (Moyo et al. 2022, Ismail and Mohammad 2023, Pradeep and Patil 2022). It is difficult to understand how the AI model predicts outcomes when dealing with complex model structures, and this must be addressed correctly (Angenent 2022).

Here, the uncertainty is scenario uncertainty because an AI model is not aware of all the possible futures. Risk management is everything in insurance, and it is impossible to take the risk while there are inordinate numbers of guesses over many outcomes that can occur. This is because the implementation of AI models in the insurance company will bear extreme risks because AI models are not capable of responding swiftly to new cases of unexpected situations, including changes in the market conditions and the regulatory structure (Agu et al. 2022, López and Rojas 2024). In fact, the real issue begins once an AI model is used under unstable conditions because the AI cannot handle an unexpected change it was unaware of (Caporuscio et al. 2021).

Black swan events are a form of unforeseen situation in the insurance industry that cannot be predicted yet have a strong effect. For example, these deviations from historical data reveal several critical operational challenges when training the AI models, due to the availability of such historical data, but they are not ready to handle those deviations. As well illustrated above, current AI systems do not predict the insurance market and cannot cope well with crises (Śmietanka et al. 2021, Caporuscio et al. 2021). Black swan incidents that were not identifiable have caused vast financial and operational risks to insurance businesses.

In order to cope with the present problems faced by AI applications, a unified design system of data benchmarking, model interpretability, and adapting the algorithm in response to unexpected events is proposed. The AI system resolution will enable the insurance sector to better manage risk with the help of efficient innovation.

Systemic Risk

The implementation of AI systems in insurance operations can trigger multiple breakdowns which propagate from one process element to another. The interconnected organization of AI systems creates a situation that is highly dangerous. The breakthrough advances in AI-based underwriting methods must be properly managed because poor supervision leads to systemic failures. The breakdown of any of these operational procedures leads to comprehensive errors in risk evaluation and premium calculation, causing instability throughout the insurance system (Agu et al. 2022, López and Rojas 2024). The real-time data processing responsibilities of AI have made it vital for both fraud detection and claims processing systems in insurance service operations (Ismail and Mohammad 2023, Maple et al. 2023).

Any system failures or errors would quickly affect multiple insurance service components.

Multiple insurance operations and all insurance functions—like underwriting, claims processing, and customer support—share information through integrated AI systems. These connected systems combine multiple benefits but present substantial hazards for operational security. System corruption that begins with a single AI system creates further damage that results in an organization-wide risk. Regulatory compliance alongside fraud detection tasks within the African insurance market make use of AI systems, which expose the market to broad damaging consequences, including impaired profitability when system failures occur (Agu et al. 2022). System breakdowns can be prevented through attentive supervision combined with management strategies for complex interrelating systems (López and Rojas 2024, Cubric 2020).

AI systems display unexpected behavior patterns when they are engineered as data-driven entities that use learning algorithms. These patterns generate unpredictable outcomes that diverge from the stated insurance company objectives. Pradeep and Patil (2022), alongside Maple et al. (2023), establish that training data biases lead to unfair discrimination in insurance operations controlled by AI systems. Insurers find it difficult to understand AI-based decision processes because of their unclear nature, which leads to systemic problems becoming more likely (Cubric 2020). AI system development leads to unexpected behavior which requires complex design methods together with monitoring protocols, according to López and Rojas (2024).

CASE STUDIES ON AI FAILURES IN INSURANCE AND LESSONS LEARNED

The research by Trout (2024) examines system failures from advanced autonomous AI systems by comparing them to nuclear power industry operations. The research demonstrates how nuclear power operations serve as a reference point to support limited liability measures, which should be applied to AI model developers whose Critical AI Occurrences (CAIO) result in adverse effects. The occurrence of these events may cause catastrophic losses or demonstrate the potential to create such devastating outcomes. The study recommends that developers should have to buy CAIO liability insurance, which solves their judgment-proof nature while reducing winner's curse incidents and allowing financial companies to serve as regulatory entities. Following the payment of premiums, insurers need to carry out risk modeling while simultaneously conducting monitoring activities, advocating for stronger regulation standards, and delivering loss prevention recommendations. The strategy enables improved resource funding toward risk modeling and safe design without replacing regulatory requirements (Trout 2024).

Luciano et al. (2023) reviews how adversarial AI affects broad areas while examining AI and ML applications that boost insurance resilience. The acceptance of adversarial attacks by AI systems becomes an enormous challenge because such attacks transform input data to achieve wrong system responses. Throughout the article, the author demonstrates defense strategies for AI applications in insurance by analyzing real-life cases with prevention methods against each classification. The article emphasizes better defensive measures against adversarial attacks and shows verification procedures for systems which utilize AI and ML technology (Luciano et al. 2023).

The insurance systems with their liabilities achieve complete results in managing AI risks throughout the entire insurance operational lifecycle. mysqli provides essential guidance to financial institutions about constructing protection systems which sustain insurance operational dependability and security against adversarial threats.

SUGGESTING MITIGATION STRATEGIES

For effective deployment of AI to be possible, strong governance structures will be needed, as this ensures responsible, efficient system operation. A regulatory framework that is defined and precise in terms of standards and guidelines for the use of AI should be built. According to Agu et al. (2022), Roski et al. (2021), and Lee et al. (2021), data privacy and transparency with an ethical component of fixing bias need to be part of the framework for improving stakeholder trust. Such an industry self-governing framework is more comprehensive since it could serve as a governance framework for AI rather than an additional layer on the existing regulatory frameworks. However, in order to come up with guidelines and procedures that will maintain that confidence and keep it away from the disaster called "another 'AI Winter' owing to disillusion," collaboration between the AI developers, users, and—most importantly—the regulators is needed (Roski et al. 2021).

To ensure accuracy, reliability, and conformity to legal standards of AI models, they have to be continuously monitored. It also involves real-time iteration of model performance monitoring to identify any deviation and bias that might happen (Rehman 2024). In this respect, AI-driven solutions can automate monitoring and regulatory compliance and optimize the process for this purpose, reducing the pressure on human resources and increasing the efficiency of operations (Agu et al. 2022, Rehman 2024). Continuous monitoring, which allows scalability and interoperability of AI systems, ensures the systems can handle increasing data and transaction volumes without fail (Rehman 2021).

However, the AI system still carries a high degree of risk; therefore, it is imperative to put in place security protocols to protect the AI systems from cyberattacks and data breaches. AI cybersecurity solutions are used to protect sensitive information as well as to keep insurance operations secure by detecting threats in real-time. These protocols should be exceptionally secured through strong encryption and access limitations and regularly audited for security to find and eliminate any vulnerabilities (Rehman 2024). Insurers can do the same, and at the same time, trust can develop among their clients and stakeholders provided data privacy and security—which are essential for AI technology adoption—are consistently ensured (Agu et al. 2022, Rehman 2024).

Being in line with the fast-paced growth of AI technology, continual learning is a key necessity. The insurer is first required to invest significantly in constant development and training programs to advance the skill set of their employees. Preparation of an enabling environment to support learning and the ability to adapt to new AI methodologies and tools, as well as technical training, is covered in this process (Moyo et al. 2022). Organizations continue to learn from their staff members to minimize resistance and increase the probability of successful adoption. The organization needs to bring in multiple players who collaborate with it as it moves through the AI development adoption process. The idea is to share valuable assets and also to create partnerships between organizations engaged in the process. In the current issues that the insurance sector has to deal with—such as data protection and project expectations with misaligned interests—this is useful. Combining resources and expertise from organizations can strengthen efforts to create more reliable and effective AI solutions. It is easier to collaborate with others, making it possible to gain several viewpoints that will eventually lead to more creative and complete AI applications (Campion et al. 2022).

In addition to enhancing operational efficiency and the reliability of AI systems, this enables stakeholders to trust the AI system, which is crucial for the successful integration of AI in the insurance sector.

FUTURE OUTLOOK OF AI ADOPTION

The technological revolution approaching the insurance industry involves the use of strong AI systems. Now, these technologies begin with ML, predictive, and geospatial analysis that give today's underwriters the ability to run risk assessments. Real-time big data processing by AI is available, and thus insurance services with real-time processing that are more accurate and accessible are made available to clients (Agu et al. 2022). As in the case of other technologies, blockchain and IoT are used to integrate AI (Śmietanka et al. 2021) to allow for automated insurance markets. Insurers can achieve better operational effectiveness and customer satisfaction by providing technologically competitive and personalized products (Pradeep and Patil 2022). Insurance sector innovations through DL, Adversarial Learning, and Federated Learning represent emerging models and algorithms in AL. With the improvement of computing power and accessibility of data, new applications of this modeling approach are born (Śmietanka et al. 2021). Generative Adversarial Networks and Long Short-Term Memory networks will be implemented—technologies that will change the way insurers receive, process, and act on data based on prediction. This amplifies risk mitigation approaches through fraud detection technology, enabling better loss prevention routines and higher profits in the insurance industry (Agu et al. 2022, Śmietanka et al. 2021).

Basically, this means that organizations can create new business products while also increasing service offerings using AI technologies. As per Lamberton et al. (2017) and Ismail and Mohammad (2023), AI-powered automation is now used for effective and affordable claims processing and customer services. As part of regulatory compliance, automated systems are implemented in monitoring and reporting for legal requirements with the help of AI technologies. Such processes can be applied to areas with complex regulatory needs (Agu et al. 2022). As a result of a successful implementation of the AI system, there will be better opportunities for the organization, and future competition within the insurance sector will be transformed (Kajwang 2022, Pradeep and Patil 2022).

At this rate, the adoption of AI in the insurance sector has become the order of the day, as the market quickly evolves with emerging advanced AI technologies that will enhance operations and improve the market. These new developments are driven by efforts to improve operational efficiency and maintain high-quality service to the customer. However, poor data quality standards, inability to meet regulatory requirements, and the challenge of hiring the required expert staff make accessing the benefits of AI a difficult challenge for the insurance sector. AI has the power to transform the insurance sector into a highly resilient, operationally advanced, and personalized customer-focused system.

RECOMMENDATIONS AND CONCLUSION

In order to become successful in AI, in the coming years insurance companies will have to replace their old IT systems with cloud-based solutions and adopt flexible AI-powered platforms. Key basic requirements are related to data quality enhancement and standardization. Companies need to implement a complete data governance framework along with blockchain solutions for protected data exchange. Monetary support and collaboration with academic institutions will be required to develop AI talent to address skill deficits, with ongoing training programs to complement this effort.

To create effective AI governance guidelines, organizations must work with policymakers to establish transparency, accountability, and fairness. Data security professionals must encrypt sensitive data using industry-standard encryption, supported by real-time threat detection systems and regular security audits. For insurers, it is not enough to conduct routine audits; additional datasets are required to assess the fairness of their underwriting and claims processing activities.

To achieve customer trust, AI processes should be transparent, AI systems should be understandable, and users should have the ability to control access to their data. Thus, it can be stated that successful AI planning within an organization enables an AI-centered work environment that supports the development of human skills. The acceleration of industry-wide challenges and fintech innovation will be driven by collaboration between insurers, financial technology corporations, AI startups, and governmental regulatory entities.

Continuous monitoring of AI model performance helps prevent model drift and ensures accuracy. Organizational reliability requires real-time monitoring tools for system maintenance and updates using new information. AI has the potential to achieve greater efficiency, enhanced risk monitoring, and improved customer experience. However, for this to be realized, insurers must commit to innovation and fully exploit AI's potential, including the ethical deployment of AI technologies.

CONCLUSION

With the improvements that AI brings in productivity, risk assessment, fraud detection, and improving customer experience, insurance organizations have a full set of transformative opportunities. This chapter outlines the key barriers in the AI adoption process, including organizational resistance, ethical issues and cybersecurity threats, legislative hurdles, and technological constraints.

Insurers need to modernize outdated technology systems, improve data management, and train employees to enhance the effectiveness of AI solutions. Regulatory compliance must be upheld in ways that both support innovation and align with strategic regulatory objectives. The development of AI systems involves collaboration among stakeholders to operationalize AI processes, maintain user trust through transparency, and ensure accountability to meet regulatory expectations. Insurers place a high priority on protecting both data privacy and cybersecurity, as these allow them to safeguard customer information and prevent data breaches.

A proven investment strategy and collaborative approach, as well as standardized ethical practices for the use of AI systems, will extend company-wide AI roll-out into future operating periods. Barrier elimination and responsible technology deployment provides the insurance industry opportunity to achieve its best possible customer oriented resilient business model as an efficient operation.

REFERENCES

Adeoye, O.B., Okoye, C.C., Ofodile, O.C., Odeyemi, O., Addy, W.A. and Ajayi-Nifise, A.O. (2024). Integrating artificial intelligence in personalized insurance products: A pathway to enhanced customer engagement. *International Journal of Management and Entrepreneurship Research*, 6(3), 502–511. *https://doi.org/10.51594/ijmer.v6i3.840*

Agu, E., Abhulimen, A., Obiki-Osafiele, A., Osundare, O., Adeniran, I., and Efunniyi, C. (2022). Artificial intelligence in African insurance: A review of risk management and fraud prevention. *International Journal of Management and Entrepreneurship Research*, 4(12), 768–794. *https://doi.org/10.51594/ijmer.v4i12.1473*

Agu, E.E., Abhulimen, A.O., Obiki-Osafiele, A.N., Osundare, O.S., Adeniran, I.A. and Efunniyi, C.P. (2024). Discussing ethical considerations and solutions for ensuring fairness in AI-driven financial services. *International Journal of Frontier Research in Science*, 3(2), 1–9. *https://doi.org/10.56355/ijfrms.2024.3.2.0024*

Anang, A.N., Ajewumi, O.E., Sonubi, T., Nwafor, K.C., Arogundade, J.B. and Akinbi, I.J. (2024). Explainable AI in financial technologies: Balancing innovation with regulatory compliance. *International Journal of Science and Research Archive*, 13(1), 1793–1806. *https://doi.org/10.30574/ijsra.2024.13.1.1870*

Angenent, M. (2022). A Turnkey Explainable AI System for AI Compliance in the Financial Sector. Thesis Master ICT in Business and the Public Sector, LIACS, Leiden University. *https://theses.liacs.nl/2105*

Belanić, L. and Jurić, D. (2019). Transparency in the insurance contract law of Croatia. *Transparency in Insurance Contract Law*, 33–62. *https://doi.org/10.1007/978-3-030-31198-8_2*

Booyse, D. and Scheepers, C.B. (2024). Barriers to adopting automated organisational decision-making through the use of artificial intelligence. *Management Research Review*, 47(1), 64–85. *https://doi.org/10.1108/mrr-09-2021-0701*

Cambier, F. and Poncin, I. (2020). Inferring brand integrity from marketing communications: The effects of brand transparency signals in a consumer empowerment context. *Journal of Business Research*, 109, 260–270. *https://doi.org/10.1016/j.jbusres.2019.11.060*

Campion, A., Gasco-Hernandez, M., Jankin Mikhaylov, S. and Esteve, M. (2022). Overcoming the challenges of collaboratively adopting artificial intelligence in the public sector. *Social Science Computer Review*, 40(2), 462–477. *https://doi.org/10.1177/0894439320979953*

Caporuscio, A., Moran, P. and Simoni, M. (2021). Complexity induced risks posed by upcoming digital ultra-platforms: An agent-based simulation model. *IEEE Transactions on Engineering Management*, 71, 12151–12163. *https://doi.org/10.1109/TEM.2021.3096634*

Ćirić, Z.T. (2024). The importance of customer communication in insurance activities. *Tokovi osiguranja*, 40(1), 211–228. *https://doi.org/10.5937/tokosig2401211c*

Cubric, M. (2020). Drivers, barriers and social considerations for AI adoption in business and management: A tertiary study. *Technology in Society*, 62, 101257. *https://doi.org/10.1016/j.techsoc.2020.101257*

Dexe, J., Franke, U. and Rad, A. (2021). Transparency and insurance professionals: A study of Swedish insurance practice attitudes and future development. *The Geneva Papers on Risk and Insurance—Issues and Practice*, 46(4), 547. *https://doi.org/10.1057/s41288-021-00207-9*

Dhieb, N., Ghazzai, H., Besbes, H. and Massoud, Y. (2020). A secure AI-driven architecture for automated insurance systems: Fraud detection and risk measurement. *IEEE Access*, 8, 58546–58558. *https://doi.org/10.1109/ACCESS.2020.2983300*

Dutt, R. (2020). The impact of artificial intelligence on healthcare insurances. *In:* Artificial Intelligence in Healthcare, 271–293. Academic Press. *https://doi.org/10.1016/b978-0-12-818438-7.00011-3*

Eghaghe, V.O., Osundare, O.S., Ewim, C.P.M. and Okeke, I.C. (2024). Navigating the ethical and governance challenges of AI deployment in AML practices within the financial industry. *International Journal of Scholarly Research and Reviews*, 5(2), 30–51. *https://doi.org/10.56781/ijsrr.2024.5.2.0047*

Filabi, A. and Duffy, S. (2021). AI-enabled underwriting brings new challenges for life insurance: Policy and regulatory considerations. *Journal of Insurance Regulation*, 40(8), 1–20. *https://doi.org/10.52227/25114.2021*

Guruprakash, J., Tokmakov, D., Krithika, L.B., Koppu, S., Srinivasa-Perumal, R., Bekyarova-Tokmakova, A. and Milev, M. (2024). A framework for platform-agnostic blockchain and IoT based insurance system, 12, 64079–64102. *IEEE Access*. *https://doi.org/10.1109/ACCESS.2024.3397059*

Ismail, S.M.G.M. and Sayed Mohamed Gouda Mohammed (2023). Evaluating the use of artificial intelligence in Egyptian insurance companies. *Journal of Financial and Commercial Research* 24(2), 93–117. *https://doi.org/10.21608/jsst.2023.217246.1620*

Kajwang, B. (2022). Insurance opportunities and challenges in an artificial intelligence society. *European Journal of Technology*, 6(3), 15–25. *https://doi.org/10.47672/ejt.1180*

Kelly, C.J., Karthikesalingam, A., Suleyman, M., Corrado, G. and King, D. (2019). Key challenges for delivering clinical impact with artificial intelligence. *BMC Medicine*, 17, 1–9. *https://doi.org/10.1186/s12916-019-1426-2*

Koschel, A., Hausotter, A., Lange, M. and Howeihe, P. (2019). Consistency for Microservices—A legacy insurance core application migration example. *In:* Service Computation 2019, The Eleventh International Conference on Advanced Service Computing, 1–5. IARIA.

Kumar, A., 2024. AI-driven innovations in modern cloud computing. arXiv. *https://doi.org/10.5923/j.computer.20241406.02*

Lee, M.S.A., Floridi, L. and Denev, A. (2021). Innovating with confidence: Embedding AI governance and fairness in a financial services risk management framework. *In:* Ethics, Governance, and Policies in Artificial Intelligence, 353–371, Springer International Publishing. *https://doi.org/10.1007/978-3-030-81907-1_20*

Leff, D. and Lim, K.T.K. (2021). The key to leveraging AI at scale, *Journal of Revenue and Pricing Management*, 20, 376–380, Springer Nature Switzerland. *https://doi.org/10.1057/s41272-021-00320-3*

Lamberton, C., Brigo, D. and Hoy, D. (2017). Impact of robotics, RPA & AI on the insurance industry: Challenges and opportunities. *Journal of Financial Perspectives*, 4(1).

Longo, L., Brcic, M., Cabitza, F., Choi, J., Confalonieri, R., Del Ser, J., Guidotti, R., Hayashi, Y., Herrera, F., Holzinger, A. and Jiang, R. (2024). Explainable artificial intelligence (XAI) 2.0: A manifesto of open challenges and interdisciplinary research directions. *Information Fusion*, 106, 102301. *https://doi.org/10.1016/j.inffus.2024.102301*

Lopez-Garcia, J. and Rojas, E.M. (2024). Barriers to AI adoption and their influence on technological advancement in the manufacturing and finance and insurance industries. *In:* IEEE Colombian Conference on Communications and Computing (COLCOM), 1–6. IEEE. *https://doi.org/10.1109/COLCOM62950.2024.10720309*

Luciano, E., Cattaneo, M. and Kenett, R. (2023). Adversarial AI in insurance: Pervasiveness and resilience. ArXiv. *https://arxiv.org/abs/2301.07520*

Maple, C., Szpruch, L., Epiphaniou, G., Staykova, K., Singh, S., Penwarden, W., Wen, Y., Wang, Z., Hariharan, J. and Avramovic, P. (2023). The AI revolution: Opportunities and challenges for the finance sector. arXiv. *https://doi.org/10.48550/arXiv.2308.16538*

Mateen, A., Khalid, A., Lee, S. and Nam, S.Y. (2023). Challenges, issues, and recommendations for Blockchain-and cloud-based automotive insurance systems. *Applied Sciences*, 13(6), 3561. *https://doi.org/10.3390/app13063561*

Martins, N.M.R. (2023). From on-premise to cloud: Evolving IT infrastructure for the AI age. *World Journal of Advanced Research and Reviews*, 20(3), 1898–1934. *https://doi.org/10.30574/wjarr.2023.20.3.1590.*

Matai, P. (2024). The imperative of AI governance: Steering BFSI towards responsible innovation. *Journal of Artificial Intelligence and Cloud Computing*, 3(1), 1–5. *https://doi.org/10.47363/jaicc/2024(3)319*

Moyo, J., Watyoka, N. and Chari, F. (2022). Challenges in the adoption of artificial intelligence and machine learning in Zimbabwe's insurance industry. *In:* 1st Zimbabwe Conference of Information and Communication Technologies (ZCICT), 1–6. IEEE. *https://doi.org/10.1109/ZCICT55726.2022.10045910*

Murdoch, B. (2021). Privacy and artificial intelligence: Challenges for protecting health information in a new era. *BMC Medical Ethics*, 22, 1–5. *https://doi.org/10.1186/s12910-021-00687-3*

Nair, M., Svedberg, P., Larsson, I. and Nygren, J.M. (2024). A comprehensive overview of barriers and strategies for AI implementation in healthcare: Mixed-method design. *Plos One*, 19(8), 1–27. *https://doi.org/10.1371/journal.pone.0305949*

Owens, E., Sheehan, B., Mullins, M., Cunneen, M., Ressel, J. and Castignani, G. (2022). Explainable artificial intelligence (XAI) in insurance. *Risks*, 10(12), 230. *https://doi.org/10.3390/risks10120230*

Pavlidis, G. (2024). Unlocking the black box: Analysing the EU artificial intelligence act's framework for explainability in AI. *Law, Innovation and Technology*, 16(1), 293–308. *https://doi.org/10.1080/17579961.2024.2313795*

Pertiwi, R.D. (2024). Analysis of consumer perceptions of financial transparency in insurance product marketing practices in Indonesia. *Atestasi: Jurnal Ilmiah Akuntansi*, 7(2), 1288–1303. *https://doi.org/10.57178/atestasi.v7i2.949*

Pradeep, A. and Patil, K. (2022). Use of artificial intelligence in the Indian insurance sector, including healthcare companies. *Cardiometry*, 23, 499–508. *https://doi.org/10.18137/cardiometry.2022.23.499508*

Qureshi, N.I., Choudhuri, S.S., Nagamani, Y., Varma, R.A. and Shah, R. (2024). Ethical considerations of AI in financial services: Privacy, bias, and algorithmic transparency. *In: International Conference on Knowledge Engineering and Communication Systems (ICKECS)*, 1, 1–6. IEEE. *https://doi.org/10.1109/ICKECS61492.2024.10616483*

Raftopoulos, M. (2024). Organizational challenges in adoption and implementation of artificial intelligence, 5786–5795.

Rehman, I.U. (2024). Artificial intelligence (AI) in managing P and C multinational insurance programs. *International Journal of Science and Research (IJSR)*, 13(10), 326–329. *https://doi.org/10.21275/sr241003101503*

Ridzuan, N.N., Masri, M., Anshari, M., Fitriyani, N.L. and Syafrudin, M. (2024). AI in the financial sector: The line between innovation, regulation and ethical responsibility. *Information*, 15(8), 432. *https://doi.org/10.3390/info15080432*

Roski, J., Maier, E.J., Vigilante, K., Kane, E.A. and Matheny, M.E. (2021). Enhancing trust in AI through industry self-governance. *Journal of the American Medical Informatics Association*, *28*(7), 1582–1590. *https://doi.org/10.1093/jamia/ocab065*

Saeed, W. and Omlin, C. (2023). Explainable AI (XAI): A systematic meta-survey of current challenges and future opportunities. *Knowledge-Based Systems*, 263, 0110273. *https://doi.org/10.1016/j.knosys.2023.110273*

Sewada, R., Jangid, A., Kumar, P., and Mishra, N. (2023). Explainable artificial intelligence (XAI). *Journal of Nonlinear Analysis and Optimization*, 13(1), 41–47. https://doi.org/10.36893/jnao.2022.v13i02.041-047.

Singh, M. (2018). Are insurers with legacy IT landscape ready for industry 4.0? *Bimaquest*, 18(3), 35–46.

Śmietanka, M., Koshiyama, A. and Treleaven, P. (2021). Algorithms in future insurance markets. *International Journal of Data Science and Big Data Analytics*, 1(1), 1–19. *https://doi.org/ 10.2139/ssrn.3641518*

Trout, C. (2024). Liability and insurance for catastrophic losses: The nuclear power precedent and lessons for AI. arXiv. *https://doi.org/10.48550/arXiv.2409.06673*

Uzougbo, N.S., Ikegwu, C.G. and Adewusi, A.O. (2024). Legal accountability and ethical considerations of AI in financial services. *GSC Advanced Research and Reviews*, 19(2), 130–142. *https://doi.org/10.30574/gscarr.2024.19.2.0171*

van der Vlist, F., Helmond, A. and Ferrari, F. (2024). Big AI: Cloud infrastructure dependence and the industrialisation of artificial intelligence. *Big Data and Society*, 11(1), 20539517241232630. *https://doi.org/10.1177/20539517241232630*

Vel, D.V.T. (2023). Explainable AI (XAI) for health insurance underwriting, *International Journal on Recent and Innovation Trends in Computing and Communication*, 11(2), 288–307. *https://doi.org/10.17762/ijritcc.v11i2.11160.*

Wang, Y. (2024). Ethical considerations of AI in financial decision. *Computing and Artificial Intelligence*, 2(1), 1290–1290. *https://doi.org/10.59400/cai.v2i1.1290*

Zarifis, A., Kawalek, P. and Azadegan, A. (2021). Evaluating if trust and personal information privacy concerns are barriers to using health insurance that explicitly utilizes AI. *Journal of Internet Commerce*, 20(1), 66–83. *https://doi.org/10.1080/15332861.2020.1832817*

Financial Fraud Mitigation through Advanced AI: Leveraging GANs, XAI, and DL–A 2025 Outlook

7

Mukul Yadav[1], *Vinay Aseri*[2,*], *and Khadija Slimani*[3]

INTRODUCTION

Digital transactions witnessed exponential growth and gave rise to financial fraud, which is an alarming threat to the global financial ecosystem. Internet scams have increased in volume and sophistication, requiring ever more advanced technological interventions (Sood et al. 2023). Traditional detection methods, like manual reviews and rule-based systems, are proving insufficient against increasingly sophisticated fraudulent schemes and growing digital transactions, which surpassed 2.7 billion globally (Du et al. 2024). In this regard, artificial intelligence (AI) has become a transformative force that has the potential to bring fraud detection methods into the next generation. These systems, which utilize a unique blend of machine learning (ML), deep learning (DL), and other AI technologies, are able to identify anomalous patterns in large datasets, detect real-time fraudulent behavior, and ultimately reduce financial losses. Analyzing extensive amounts of data for fraud detection is much easier to accomplish with these systems than with traditional methods due to time savings and improved accuracy (Kumari and Mishra 2019).

The implementation of AI into financial fraud detection systems is highly beneficial. Massive amounts of transactional data that would be impossible for human analysts to process, or even traditional methods, can be dealt with effectively by AI-based systems. Furthermore, these systems are capable of autonomously adapting to historical fraud and enhancing their detection capabilities (Kishan 2024). This adjustment in approach is crucial in the environment of financial fraud, where the casters of such crimes continuously change their approaches in order not to be discovered. These benefits are countered by the negative challenges posed by AI usage for fraud detection. Increased adoption rates are inhibited by issues such as data privacy, discrimination by machine algorithms, moral issues, and even risks

[1] School of Information Technology & Artificial Intelligence, Rashtriya Raksha University, Ministry of Home Affairs, GoI, Gandhinagar, Gujrat, India.
[2] School of Behavioural Sciences & Forensic Investigations, Rashtriya Raksha University, Ministry of Home Affairs, GoI, Gandhinagar, Gujrat, India.
[3] Higher School of Computer Science Electronics and Automation (ESIEA),75005 Paris, France.
[*] *Corresponding author:* vinay4n6@gmail.com

DOI: 10.1201/9781003621119-7

to the systems themselves, which are quite concerning (Kumari and Mishra 2019, Kishan 2024). The reliability of most AI models is also challenged, as it is often difficult to explain and justify their decisions, which can lead to possible violations of recourse regulations (Kishan 2024 and Van Veen 2025).

This chapter sets out to research the extent of use of new AI technologies such as DL, reinforcement learning, generative adversarial networks (GANs), and explainable AI (XAI) to tackle fraud in a range of industries. For the benefit of researchers, practitioners, and policymakers regarding the AI-based fraud detection framework, we sought to highlight the current methods, issues, and, additionally, the expected trend of AI fraud detection by evaluating the recent progress from 2023 to 2025.

LITERATURE REVIEW

Over the last few years, the application of AI in fraud detection has changed greatly, as researchers devise more advanced ways to deal with the problem of fraud detection. This part deals with the evolution of AI in fraud detection and compares various literatures of this domain with a focus on the reliability of different methods, comparative studies, and trends.

Evolution of AI in Fraud Detection

The methods of AI anti-fraud measures have transformed from simple rule-based systems without learning capabilities to more sophisticated systems that learn from historical data and detect anomalies independently. Particularly with the emergence of newer forms of fraud, the limitations of classic rule-based systems led to an unavoidable transition to more advanced AI methods (Seyyede et al. 2023).

Systematic reviews by Chen et al. (2025) mentioned the significant advantages of AI over traditional systems (e.g. for real-time fraud detection, and adaptability to new frauds) (Seyyede et al. 2023). ML was introduced, which made AI systems more flexible; they could analyze past data and seek out anomalies on their own. It is evident that fraudsters are able to outpace financial institutions with their efforts to commit unique types of fraud, and financial institutions are struggling to keep pace (Aldoseri et al. 2023). In a 2025 review, there were the same findings in reviewing 57 publications 2019 to 2024 on DL techniques on financial fraud detection. The review highlighted the tremendous potential of DL techniques to engage in fraud detection by examining credit card transactions, insurance claims, and even audits of financial statements; providing yet another illustration of how AI systems could detect fraud yet precise in their functionality.

Comparative Studies

Recently, there have been some efforts to get an understanding of how AI algorithms perform against traditional methods of fraud detection. Sood et al. (2023) initiated a framework that encompassed over 241 published articles, within a systematic review and network analysis, on AI-based fraud detection over a twenty-year time period. This "meta-analytic" framework combined findings that were otherwise disparate into an overall "meta-analytic" framework, giving a kind of "big-picture" of the various AI methods' diffusion overall. Summarily, the findings indicated, as also noted in previous literature, that DL and advanced methods outperformed older systems, although the findings also highlighted areas for general improvement of traditional methods.

In a comparable research endeavor, the efficiency of nine distinct ML algorithms was investigated in relation to credit card fraud detection by Alfaiz and Fati (2022), employing stratified K-fold cross-validation to validate an overall evaluation matrix of the algorithms. The study concluded with successful results from the CatBoost algorithm, integrating the combined All K-nearest neighbors (KNN) under-sampling technique to improve performance. The highest-performing model in the study returned an Area under the curve of 97.94%, recall of 95.91%, and F1-score of 87.40%.

The second comparative study from the paper by Kumari and Mishra (2019) examined Long Short-Term Network (LSTM) recurrent networks and achieved results approaching those highlighted in the previous examples: one dataset studied returned an accuracy of 96.72%, precision of 98.85%, and recall of 91.91%, and another dataset returned an accuracy of 97.48%, precision of 97.69%, and recall of 97.22%. These results once again demonstrate the performance gain of more complex, advanced AI technology, clearly proving to provide significant improvements over more traditional methods as described in Table 1 (Chen et al. 2025).

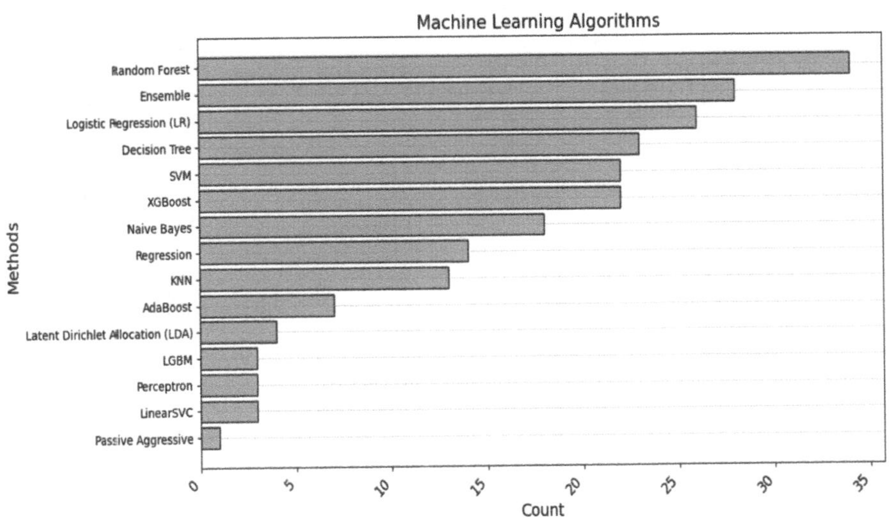

Fig. 1. Distribution of ML Algorithm Application in Fraud Detection from 2019 to 2024 (Chen et al. 2025)

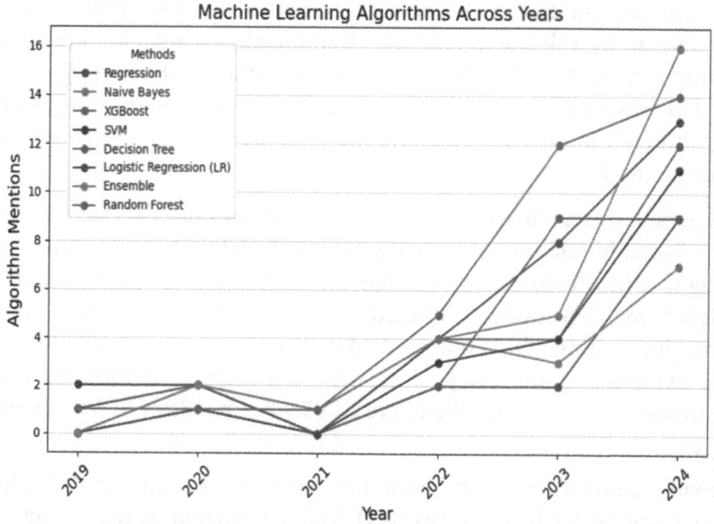

Fig. 2. Yearly Trends of ML Algorithm Application in Fraud Detection from 2019 to 2024 (Chen et al. 2025)

Table 1: Comparative Studies of AI Techniques for Fraud Detection

Study (Reference)	AI Techniques Implemented/ Compared	Traditional Methods Comparison	Key Performance Metrics & Results	Key Findings
(Sood et al. 2023)	Systematic Review & Network Analysis of AI-based Methods	Not explicitly stated, but implies comparisons to non-AI methods	Meta-analytic view of 241 articles (past 20 years)	Presents the strengths and weaknesses of DL and related techniques compared with traditional approaches, taking literature into account.
(Kumari and Mishra 2019)	Nine ML Algorithms	-	CatBoost + KNN: AUC = 97.94%, Recall = 95.91%, F1-score = 87.40%	CatBoost with KNN under-sampling is the best among the installed ML algorithms for credit card fraud detection.
(Kumari and Mishra 2019)	LSTM with Attention Mechanisms	-	Dataset 1: Accuracy = 96.72%, Precision = 98.85%, Recall = 91.91% Dataset 2: Accuracy = 97.48%, Precision = 97.69%, Recall = 97.22%	LSTM with attention mechanisms achieves high accuracy, precision, and recall, demonstrating superior performance.

AI Techniques in Fraud Detection

This section will examine different specific AI techniques in fraud detection through DL, reinforcement learning, GANs and XAI. Each AI method has distinct benefits and challenging attributes in fraud detection, thus much of the recent literature sets out several ways to constructively use these AI methods (Bisen et al. 2024).

Generative Adversarial Networks in Fraud Detection

GANs represent a viable approach to fraud detection, particularly with generating imbalanced datasets and synthetic data to enhance the model's training process. In 2023, a paper was published which discussed a framework using GANs and ensemble models for fraud detection with financial statements (Ahmad et al. 2022). The framework addressed the imbalance of underrepresented fraud detection datasets and enhanced the general performance of the fraud detection model. This is beneficial because GANs are capable of generating realistic synthetic datasets that are useful in fraud detection models due to the challenges that arise in sampling fraudulent transactions in particular areas of endeavor. The capacity to generate synthetic data also addresses the challenge of class imbalance, as highlighted with a bulk of fraud detection datasets where virtually all transactions are legitimate and fraud occurs with much lower frequency (Ali et al. 2024).

Some recent research has looked at GANs out of anomaly detection, whereby GANs can consider any transaction that is outside of what the generator and sample has learned (Bisen et al. 2024), thus identifying anomalies. This also touches on the ability to detect fraud patterns that have not been seen in the past nor captured robustly by the previously sampled data, which also opens up the adaptation of a detection system. GANs are a novel mechanism that address two challenges of fraud detection: class imbalance and anomaly detection. A GAN is composed of two neural networks—a generator and a discriminator—which compete against each other, in the sense that, while the generator creates synthetic data, the discriminator tries to distinguish between the two. Specifically, in fraud detection, the GAN will generate synthetic examples of fraudulent transactions (for example, fraudulent credit cards) as synthetic cases to balance the distribution of legitimate and illegitimate cases in a typical fraud detection task (Dhayanidhi 2022). Thus, the model of generated fraudulent transactions has the potential to improve the training of the fraud detection model by improving the modeling of legitimate (not fraudulent) training cases and benchmarking them against synthetic fraud participants.

In a recent study, a 2023 study implemented a unique approach using GANs and ensemble models to detect fraudulent financial statements (Hassan et al. 2023). As a result, the GAN was able to generate realistic synthetic examples of fraudulent financial statements to reduce the welfare (cost) of an ensemble group model (due to fraudulent activity). The GAN paired with an ensemble model learned to detect the more subtle but prevalent patterns of fraudulent activity in a real-world application. These application studies validate the practical use of GANs to effectively address the imbalance and anomaly detection challenges. Recent studies have shown how effective GANs can be in a variety of fraud detection contexts, like credit card fraud, insurance fraud, and financial statement fraud (Salam et al. 2024). For example, Zhang et al. (2025) built a hybrid ensemble model for detecting Bitcoin fraudulent transactions, in which synthetic data generated by GANs enhanced performance (Salam et al. 2024). This growing field of literature indicates that GANs have a lot of potential for solving problems in the fraud detection domain and maximizing the effectiveness of AI-assisted fraud detection systems.

Explainable AI in Fraud Detection

The "black box" traits of many AI models have sparked backlash around questions of interpretability and trust in their use, especially in sensitive contexts like applications for fraud detection. Some of the recent research has aimed to improve AI performance with XAI techniques that increase interpretability and provide human-comprehensible rationales behind outcomes produced by AI (Dhayanidhi 2022, Hassan et al. 2023).

The 2024 study emphasizes a hybrid DL approach of convolutional neural network (CNN) plus attention-based recurrent networks, which led to the development of high-performance models that are rational and human-comprehensible (Kishan 2024). This illustrated a balance of the two key considerations in fraud detection applications: monitoring behavior with high performance, and the need for explainability in a regulated industry. Similarly, a 2025 study proposed a new way to assess fraud detection, combining causal discovery and XAI techniques to produce a new assessment framework (Hassan et al. 2023). The researchers examined the combination of interpretable ML models such as Shapley Additive Explanations (SHAP), a new causal feature vector, and the use of feature selection techniques, focusing on the tradeoff between interpretability and predictive modeling. The researchers achieved award-winning interpretations by evaluating models based on metrics that distinguish causative features from noise due to correlation. However, challenges remained in validating indicators while preserving anonymity in real-world datasets (Salam et al. 2024). All studies suggest a rapidly growing awareness of the importance of explainability in terms of compliance with the emerging collaborative processes introduced by AI-based fraud detection systems while establishing trust relationships with users and stakeholders. As AI models become increasingly sophisticated, the demand for explanations supporting the AI recommendations grows as well, clearly indicating the importance of trust, fairness, and regulatory requirements in fraud detection. XAI techniques can offer human-interpretable explanations for AI decisions, which are needed in all fields but most notably in the area of fraud detection in finance and insurance. For example, a 2024 study proposed a hybrid DL approach featuring XAI techniques, which increased the level of transparency in fraud detection (Shehnepoor et al. 2022). This study used mixed CNNs for feature extraction with attention-based recurrent networks to develop a hybrid model that not only provided high levels of accuracy but also human-interpretable explanations to support individual decision-making. This study provided a two-fold approach to the need for accuracy, transparency, accountability, and ethics required in fraud detection systems, especially in highly regulated industries such as finance and insurance (Shen and Kurshan 2021).

Research has recently looked at the possibility of integrating XAI with other AI methods to develop more reliable and interpretable fraud tracking systems. This is seen in approaches that incorporate attention models into DL networks to identify the features that had the highest impact on the prediction of fraud (Kumari and Mishra 2019, Kishan 2024). This approach helps to quantify how much each feature contributes to the overall prediction in order to better understand what the more complex models are doing. These two approaches exemplify how XAI can respond to the "black box" dilemma while still maintaining the performance of more advanced AI models.

Deep Learning (Convolutional Neural Networks, Recurrent Neural Networks, Autoencoders)

DL models have shown exceptional success in detecting fraud patterns in multiple fields. These models—such as CNNs, Recurrent Neural Networks (RNNs), and autoencoders—use large quantities of data to develop anomalous patterns that suggest fraud. CNNs were designed for image processing but have been adapted to fraud by viewing transaction data as "images" of features. For example, a 2024 paper proposed a hybrid approach that uses CNNs for feature-based extractions from financial transaction data. CNNs are efficient at recognizing spatial patterns and correlations with features and types of fraud and are suitable for more complex fraud patterns that a simpler model or rule-based system may miss. RNNs, especially LSTM, could be particularly useful for analyzing sequential data (e.g. transaction histories) (Shen and Kurshan 2021, Chen et al. 2025). These models have advantages in capturing temporal dependencies and patterns over time when identifying suspicious behavior that spans across multiple transactions. Kumari and Mishra (2019) added attention mechanisms to LSTM recurrent networks, and the authors obtained strong results: 96.72% accuracy, 98.85% precision, 91.91% recall on one dataset, and 97.48% accuracy, 97.69% precision, 97.22% recall on another (Chen et al. 2025). Autoencoders are another form of neural network used to learn meaningful representations of data and have been used to detect anomalies (i.e. in fraud cases). The idea is that by learning how to reconstruct normal transactions, fraudulent transactions can be detected based on the fact that they would have high reconstruction errors. This is useful because it allows the detection of fraud without historical training data, which adds flexibility and adaptability to fraud detection systems.

Numerous case studies have revealed consistent support for DL models outperforming traditional methods in detecting fraud. These studies demonstrated that DL methods were much more accurate than traditional approaches in detecting fraud, showing suitable applicability for real-world transactions and large-scale data contexts. The main advantage of DL models is the capacity to learn at a deeper level what features are relevant to the nature of the raw data; this is useful for fraud detection studies in which it can be difficult to explicitly define the features of the fraud instance. One key challenge in fraud detection is the class imbalance problem. Class imbalance occurs when the statistical distribution of legitimate versus illegitimate cases skews toward legitimate cases (Sowah et al. 2019).

RESEARCH METHODOLOGY

This investigation undertook an AI-fraud detection method focused on systematized pattern recognition and pattern matching, which are more current in AI technology. The methodology comprised three phases: collection of data, selection and filtering, and analysis and synthesis.

Data Collection Process

We performed an exhaustive review on online platforms that include Scopus, ScienceDirect (Elsevier), Springer Link, and IEEE Xplore. The review included journal articles, conferences, and systematic reviews within the range of January 2023 to March 2025. Some of the keyword phrases used are "anomaly detection", used with "credit card fraud", "financial fraud", "deep learning", "artificial intelligence", "machine learning", "reinforcement learning", "generative adversarial networks", "explainable artificial intelligence". Giving preference to peer-reviewed journals in the beginning of the research helped in the reduction of misinformation and therefore provided more useful answers. Known journals were given more importance (Sowah et al. 2019, Sun et al. 2018).

Filtering Criteria

The first search provided us with an overload of documents, so we narrowed it down according to certain criteria:

1. **Publication date:** In order to capture the most recent advancements in AI-based fraud detection, papers published from 2023 to 2025 were prioritized.
2. **Relevance:** Focus was on the papers which utilized AI for fraud detection, specifically those that applied DL, reinforcement learning, GANs, or XAI.
3. **Quality and authority:** The papers published in peer-reviewed journals and conferences of higher impact were given more weight so that the review was based on proper and worthy research.
4. **Empirical validation:** There was greater preference towards papers that provided some sort of case studies or empirical results, instead of purely theoretical papers. This would help showcase the effectiveness of different usage of AI techniques in the real-life scenarios of fraud detection.
5. **Innovation:** Greater weight was allocated towards papers which proposed fresh AI methods or significant changes to the existing ones and more recent approaches.

This filtering mechanism yielded a collection of documents which presents the advanced AI use cases for fraud detection. These selected documents form the foundation for comprehensive review and analysis of AI in fraud detection and mitigation.

Analysis and Synthesis Approach

Each article underwent a thorough review in terms of its methods, results, and challenges. We focused on analyzing the efficacy of different AI techniques concerning various types of fraud and industries. Special attention was paid to the reported performance metrics: accuracy, precision, recall, F1-score, and AUC-ROC. This step included the analysis of the literature to find recurring patterns, differences, and relationships, which allowed the gaps in the literature to be synthesized in order to develop a holistic picture of AI applications in fraud detection, where innovations and further developments are needed (Tang and Liu 2024).

The results are synthesized on the frameworks of utilized DL techniques, reinforcement learning techniques, the use of GANs, and the application of XAI in fraud detection. Furthermore, as a study of the field, we found the most common and important challenges and limitations in the studies, and at the same time, the most promising ones for future research (Poberezhna and Slimani 2025).

CHALLENGES AND LIMITATIONS

While there have been advances in AI-mediated fraud detection and pre-emption, there are still challenges and limitations that can prevent these systems from being employed more effectively across broader applications. This section describes important challenges related to data privacy, adversarial attack vulnerabilities, scalability, and relevant ethical considerations.

Data Privacy Concerns

As with many AI systems, data privacy is a crucial consideration for AI-driven fraud detection systems, which typically rely on large amounts of personal and/or financial information to develop and deploy their operations. The sensitive nature of these types of information opens the door to privacy concerns, data breaches, and potential implications on compliance with relevant data protection regulations and laws (e.g. General Data Protection Regulation (GDPR)) (Qayoom et al. 2024). Additionally, a relevant area with respect to data privacy is the inherent difficulty of obtaining real-world labeled fraud data, specifically for research and development.

Many studies rely on obtaining synthetic or anonymized datasets, which may not allow for accuracy and complexity of real-world situations when not collected from the last 12–24 months compared to features collected from ID precursors. These issues can ultimately limit the applicability and generalizability of AI models deployed in a production environment (Qayoom et al. 2024).

Protecting guarantees of privacy in using data points for fraudulent transactions will require multi-faceted solutions that balance the tension between needing data access and needing privacy protection (allied with regulatory compliance). As an example, stronger and more sophisticated techniques for anonymizing data, privacy-by-design for AI systems, and new avenues for programming models that pose a lesser risk of requiring sensitive data need further attention. A balanced approach in addressing these issues may support organizations with developing fraud detection systems with more privacy-friendly operational protocols without compromising high performance in the outcome and regulatory compliance.

Adversarial Attacks

AI-based fraud detection systems are still vulnerable to adversarial attacks, where bad actors (of malicious intent) attempt to corrupt input data to frame a false positive or otherwise confuse the models. Adversarial events can be found in pattern-matching approaches in AI models, so fraudsters can create transactions that are algorithmically treated as valid transactions even if they are fraudulent.

Mishra (2023) called for timely standards for rigorous coupling of AI with state-of-the-art cybersecurity practices including adversarial training and emerging evidence-based threat intelligence. Adversarial training involves simulated attacks on the adversarial models to help avoid the models being corrupted through deliberative transactional efforts in attack attempts in real-time. It is difficult to measure the uncertainty of modeled performance in comparison with diagnosis of adversarial logic applications, since adversarial threats continue to evolve, and this is an arduous task for system maintainers (Bisen et al. 2024, Charizanos et al. 2024).

Scholarly literature continues to be a moving target with all kinds of inspiring (as well as receptive) approaches such as robust optimization, adversarial regularization, and appropriate ensemble approaches to incorporate AI models as the basis for developing systems with similar basic frameworks of resilience in practice and high fraud detection diagnostics by adversarial threat design.

Scalability Issues

Scalability is another major challenge for AI-based fraud detection systems, especially for smaller organizations with limited computing capabilities. The complexity of training DL models, the need for ample data, and real-time detection require considerable computing power and, at times, specific hardware options and may represent a significant barrier to adoption for some organizations (Sun et al. 2018).

Scalability is only further complicated by the continual increase in transactional volume as well as the sophistication of fraud, which necessitates more complex models and larger datasets to train. Recent investigations have examined ways to increase the efficiency and scalability of AI models through Neural Architecture Transformation while not sacrificing accuracy of detection. These include model compression techniques, efficient neural network architectures, or cross-domain transfer learning models for smaller organizations to leverage pre-trained models with little-to-no additional training effort (Tang and Liu 2024).

However, these approaches may represent a balance between efficiency and accuracy of detection depending on the specific circumstances and context of each organization. Consideration of what scalability means to AI in fraud detection is crucially important to the possible democratization of access to advanced fraud detection capabilities and touches on the idea that larger organizations have considerable resources (Poberezhna and Slimani 2025, Qayoom et al. 2024).

By providing more streamlined and scalable options for fraud detection, while being a prime focus in cloud AI or pre-trained currency, researchers and practitioners are attempting to overcome the notion of a domain advantage of large organizations to otherwise benefit from the fraud detection capabilities of AI. As AI continues to progress, several promising trends emerge that will build on the fraud detection capabilities mentioned up to this point (Du et al. 2024).

FUTURE DIRECTIONS

As AI continues to progress, several promising trends emerge that will build on the fraud detection capabilities mentioned up to this point. This section examines significant future pathways in AI-based fraud detection, including promising newly developed techniques, predictive methods, and shifting regulatory environments.

Emerging Trends in AI for Fraud Detection

The future of AI-based fraud detection capabilities may be enhanced by implementing several newly emerging AI techniques. Federated learning—training models across a distributed system of devices or servers in a secure environment while not sharing the raw data itself—presents an exciting avenue for enabling technical efficacy without compromising customer data privacy concerns. Federated learning allows training models to keep sensitive structured data local for the end user, while the system transmits updated information about the models. This would enable more collaborative efforts to target fraud across organizations without directly exposing customer data to voluntary disclosure.

Multimodal AI models integrate and analyze data from unique modalities, some of which may be behavioral—such as parsed transaction data combined with customer behavioral data, or related aggregated device behavioral data and context—to effectively learn from all of the information in relation to customer behavior and develop normal behavioral and transaction patterns, as well as anomalous, fraud-related transactions (Poberezhna and Slimani 2025). Use of this type of methodology will improve expected rates of detection, especially as more typical fraud schemes operate across multiple channels and non-channel contexts.

Finally, the overlap of AI with fintech emerging technologies such as blockchain and quantum computing may allow significant advancements and improvements in fraud detection and response. Blockchain technology provides an immutable record of transaction history in effective ways to develop trust and mitigate risk for certain fraud schemes; while quantum computing may, in the longer-term coming years, allow for the design of incredibly powerful AI models capable of processing astronomical amounts of data faster than traditional computing models. These overlaps in technologies may expand financial institutions' capabilities to administer more robust, integrated fraud detection methods in this space.

Predictive Fraud Prevention

One substantial future strategy in fraud detection will be a shift from simply detecting fraud reactively to preventing it actively. State-of-the-art AI approaches, including reinforcement learning and predictive analytics, can predict near-future fraudulent activity by identifying patterns or likely fraud targets or behaviors based on historical data.

Predictive modeling can look at historical data to highlight factors and phenomena associated with future fraud risk, enabling the organization to act and put in place preventative measures. These could include requirements for additional authentication for high-risk transactions or enhanced vigilance on high-fraud-risk accounts. This approach has the potential to drastically reduce losses associated with fraud operations, in contrast to previous reactive and opportunistic methods that only monitor for fraud after its occurrence.

In addition, deep reinforcement learning shows particular promise in the predictive fraud prevention landscape, as it continually learns and adapts over time to evolving fraud practices. It is capable of updating its predictors of normal and fraudulent behavior to allow it to anticipate and respond to new fraudulent activity—an important advantage in the ongoing cat-and-mouse game that fraud detection and prevention represent.

A 2024 study on credit card fraud detection using Deep Q Networks (DQN) emphasizes the potential of reinforcement learning to act as a legitimate fraud detection and prevention tool in real-time. The reinforcement learning model also replaces human intervention by autonomously learning patterns and suggests the potential for more proactive approaches toward preventing fraud from materializing in real time.

Regulatory and Ethical Evolution

In the next few years, it is expected that regulations concerning AI in fraud detection will continue to evolve, with a growing emphasis on accountability, transparency, and fairness. Future changes may lead to more direct requirements for algorithmic impact assessments, fairness testing, and model explainability, particularly in regulated industries such as banking and insurance (Ali et al. 2024, Bisen et al. 2024).

In response to these changing requirements, organizations will need to invest in substantially more robust governance systems for AI. At a minimum, these systems must include processes for documenting model design choices, monitoring for bias, addressing any identified ethical issues, and documenting and providing transparent explanations for fraud detection decisions (Poberezhna and Slimani 2025, Qayoom et al. 2024) .

The development of industry standards or best practices for responsible AI in fraud detection may help organizations manage these complex requirements and maintain trust with customers and content regulators (Slimani et al. 2024). The application of causal modeling in conjunction with XAI techniques represents another promising avenue to address regulatory and ethical pressures. By focusing on causal relationships—not just correlations—these approaches may reduce algorithmic bias and improve interpretability in fraud detection models.

The 2025 study provides encouraging evidence that causal discovery holds promise when combined with XAI techniques to develop fraud detection systems that are both trustworthy and explainable, though challenges remain in applying this line of thinking to real-world data (Adhikari et al. 2024).

CONCLUSION

This extensive literature review has highlighted the changes in AI-driven fraud detection, addressing key developments occurring between 2023 and 2025. Specifically, this review demonstrated how traditional fraud detection systems could be transformed with the implementation of sophisticated AI techniques (e.g. DL, reinforcement learning, GANs, and XAI). It is vital to advance fraud detection systems in response to new forms of financial fraud, especially since fraud is rapidly evolving due to an increasingly digitized world. The literature provides an evidence-based path for key areas of evolution—from rule-based systems to advanced AI-based systems that can detect complex patterns, adapt to novel tactics, and provide explanations. Through a combination of methods, recent studies have demonstrated that DL models, in particular CNNs and RNNs, can offer an effective mechanism for identifying fraudulent activity across disparate areas, with some unsupervised methods reporting more than 97% accuracy.

Reinforcement learning methods, such as deep Q-networks, have the potential to allow fraud detection algorithms to learn and adapt to continuously changing fraud patterns independently of human adjustment or guidance. Specifically, GANs have altered the landscape of fraud detection algorithms and provided novel solutions to the challenges presented by imbalanced datasets and anomaly detection, while XAI techniques provided crucial transparency and interpretability into the decisions made by successful fraud detection systems.

REFERENCES

Adhikari, P., Hamal, P. and Baidoo Jnr., F. (2024). Artificial intelligence in fraud detection: Revolutionizing financial security. *Int. J. Sci. Res. Arch.* 13, 1457–1472.

Ahmad, K., Maabreh, M., Ghaly M., Khan K., Qadir, J. and Al-Fuqaha A. (2022). Developing future human-centered smart cities: Critical analysis of smart city security, data management, and ethical challenges. *Comput. Sci. Rev.* 43, 100452.

Aldoseri, A., Al-Khalifa, K.N. and Hamouda, A.M. (2023). Re-thinking data strategy and integration for artificial intelligence: Concepts, opportunities, and challenges. *Appl. Sci.* 13, 7082.

Alfaiz, N.S. and Fati S.M. (2022). Enhanced credit card fraud detection model using machine learning. *Electronics* 11, 662. *https://doi.org/10.3390/electronics11040662*

Ali, G., Mijwil, M.M., Buruga, B.A., Abotaleb M. and Adamopoulos, I. (2024). A survey on artificial intelligence in cybersecurity for smart agriculture: State-of-the-art, cyber threats, artificial intelligence applications, and ethical concerns. *Mesopotamian J. Comput. Sci.* 2024, 71–121.

Bisen, W., Padwad, H., Keswani, G., Agrawal, Y., Tiwari, R. and Tiwari V. (2024). Autoencoder-driven insights into credit card fraud: A comprehensive analysis. *Int. J. Intell. Syst. Appl. Eng.* (IJISAE), 12(12s), 111–120.

Charizanos, G., Demirhan, H. and İcen, D. (2024). An online fuzzy fraud detection framework for credit card transactions. *Expert Syst. Appl.* 252, 1–15.

Chen, Y., Zhao, C., Xu, Y. and Nie, C. (2025). Year-over-year developments in financial fraud detection via deep learning: a systematic literature review. arXiv. *https://10.48550/arXiv.2502.00201.*

Dhayanidhi, G. 2022. Research on IoT Threats & Implementation of AI/ML to Address Emerging Cybersecurity Issues in IoT with Cloud Computing.

Du, H., Lv, L., Wang, H. and Guo, A. (2024). A novel method for detecting credit card fraud problems. *PLoS One.* 19, e0294537.

Hassan, M., Aziz, L.A.R. and Andriansyah, Y. (2023). The role of artificial intelligence in modern banking: An exploration of AI-driven approaches for enhanced fraud prevention, risk management, and regulatory compliance. *Rev. Contemp. Bus. Anal.* 6, 110–132.

Kishan, P.R. (2024). Explainable AI for financial fraud detection: A hybrid deep learning approach. *Trans. Recent Dev. Health Sectors* 7, 7.

Kumari, P. and Mishra, S. (2019). Analysis of credit card fraud detection using fusion classifiers. *In:* Proceedings of Advances in Intelligent Systems and Computing, 112–118. *https://10.1007/978-981-10-8055-5_11*

Poberezhna, Z. and Slimani, K. (2025). Blockchain technology using for automation of business processes of the enterprise. *CEUR Workshop Proc.* 3912, 37–49.

Qayoom, A., Khuhro, M.A., Kumar, K. et al. (2024). A novel approach for credit card fraud transaction detection using deep reinforcement learning scheme. *PeerJ Comput. Sci.* 10, e1998.

Salam, M.A., Fouad, K.M., Elbably, D.L. and Elsayed, S.M. (2024). Federated learning model for credit card fraud detection with data balancing techniques. *Neural Comput. Appl.* 36, 6231–6256.

Seyyede Z.A., Ahmadi, A. and Farzi, S. 2023. Fraud detection in financial statements using data mining and GAN models. *Expert Syst. Appl.* 227, 120144.

Shehnepoor, S., Togneri, R., Liu, W. and Bennamoun, M. (2022). Spatio-temporal graph representation learning for fraudster group detection. *IEEE Trans. Neural Netw. Learn. Syst.* 4–9.

Shen, H. and Kurshan, E. (2021). Deep Q-network-based adaptive alert threshold selection policy for payment fraud systems in retail banking. *In:* Proc. ACM Int. Conf. AI Finance (ICAIF '20), Article 24, 1–7.

Slimani, K., Khoulji, S., Mortreau, A. and Kerkeb, M.L. (2024). From tradition to innovation: The telecommunications metamorphosis with AI and advanced technologies. *J. Auton. Intell.* 7, 1.

Sood, P., Sharma C., Nijjer, S. and Sakhuja, S. (2023). Review the role of artificial intelligence in detecting and preventing financial fraud using natural language processing. *Int. J. Syst. Assur. Eng. Manag.* 14, 8–9.

Sowah, R.A., Kuuboore, M., Ofoli, A., Kwofie, S., Asiedu, L., Koumadi, K.M. et al. (2019). Decision support system for fraud detection in health insurance claims using genetic support vector machines (GSVMs). *J. Eng.* 10–13.

Sun, C., Li Q., Li, H., Shi, Y., Zhang, S. and Guo, W. (2018). Patient cluster divergence based healthcare insurance fraudster detection, *IEEE Access.*

Tang, Y. and Liu, Z. (2024). A distributed knowledge distillation framework for financial fraud detection based on transformer. *IEEE Access.*

Van Veen, K.Y. (2025). XAI in Fraud Detection: A Causal Perspective. Master's Thesis, University of Twente. *https://essay.utwente.nl/105290/1/Veen_MA_EEMCS.pdf*

Zhang C.J., Gill A.Q., Liu B. and Anwar, M.J. (2025). AI-based identity fraud detection: A systematic review, 7–17. ArXiv preprint arXiv:2501.09239.

8

Challenges and Barriers to AI Adoption

Azadeh Eskandarzadeh

NTRODUCTION

The use of Artificial Intelligence (AI) in multiple industries presents a revolutionary platform for greater efficiency, innovation, and power in making decisions. However, the process towards the universal use of AI is fraught with complex challenges and hurdles to be addressed by organizations in a strategic approach. These barriers cross technological, organizational, ethical, and societal dimensions and require an integrated and multi-faceted approach to overcome them (Murire 2024). Successful adoption of AI requires careful scrutiny of the unique context of each organization in relation to its existing infrastructure, culture, and human resources (Li et al. 2024).

The technology challenges include issues of data quality, model interpretability, and integration into current systems. Organizational challenges include resistance to change, insufficient appropriate skills, and the need for new governance structures and workflows. Ethically, there are concerns regarding bias, privacy, and the potential for AI to exacerbate socioeconomic disparities (Murire 2024). Societal challenges include public distrust, job loss concerns, and regulatory frameworks to enable the development and deployment of AI in a responsible and appropriate manner.

Overcoming the intricate obstacles to AI adoption is as much a technological challenge as it is a strategic imperative requiring firm leadership, clear communication, and an unshakeable commitment to values (Lahlali et al. 2021). Organizations must actively overcome such obstacles through a multi-faceted approach. This entails building an innovation culture in which employees feel empowered to experiment and learn to work with emerging technology, upskilling staff to develop the appropriate technical and analytical capabilities, and collaborating with a cross-section of stakeholders ranging from policymakers and industry experts to the broader public. Through this comprehensive approach, organizations can establish the conditions for an easier and more effective integration of AI, driving innovation, enhancing operational efficiency, and harvesting sustainable competitive advantage. Ultimately, successful

Western Community College, Surrey, Canada
Email ID: azadeh@wcc.ca

DOI: 10.1201/9781003621119-8

AI adoption depends on a strategic, values-based, and collaborative effort to match technological capabilities with the unique needs and values of the organization and its wider ecosystem.

NAVIGATING THE COMPLEX LANDSCAPE OF AI ADOPTION

Successful implementation of AI hinges on a variety of factors, most of them presenting significant challenges in African and other developing economies. A trained indigenous talent pool capable of creating and maintaining AI systems is required, but such specialized technical talent typically remains in short supply (Okolo et al. 2022). Adequate infrastructural capacity to handle the computational burdens of algorithmic training is another requirement, but infrastructural deficiencies can severely stymie AI deployment (Okolo et al. 2022). Access to quality, representative datasets is also necessary, but shortages and biases in data can undermine the success of AI systems (Okolo et al. 2022).

Equally important are supportive government policies and regulations ensuring the responsible and equitable use of AI technology. These regulatory frameworks are typically underdeveloped and expose AI applications to misuse and harmful impacts (Okolo et al. 2022). Moreover, independent civic organizations and policymakers play a very significant role in safeguarding against such harms and ensuring accountability, but such systems are typically missing or insufficient in most parts of the world (Okolo et al. 2022). Upscaling AI applications to a global level and replicating success in multiple geographies and contexts are significant challenges. Context-specific methods and capacity development programs are essential in order to overcome these challenges and enable widespread adoption, particularly in the pursuit of sustainability goals (Olawade et al. 2024).

The implication of AI on job quality cannot be underestimated. Workers who are in direct contact with AI systems need to be involved in order to understand the intricate benefits and limitations such technology poses (Bell 2023). Firms must carefully consider the welfare of workers and the potential for AI transitions to have a detrimental effect on their lives, which might require government intervention to mitigate such effects (Bell 2023). Foreseeable investments in AI workforce development and supporting facilities can lead to the creation of more locally focused solutions rather than dependence on imported technology, which could be counterproductive to local social and economic aspirations (Okolo et al. 2022).

It is essential to prioritize ethics in AI applications. Potential unintended consequences, employment and socioeconomic impacts, and transparency and accountability require thorough examination (Olawade et al. 2024). Engaging a wide range of stakeholders, including communities, policymakers, and experts in the development, implementation, and governance processes of AI systems, ensures their application aligns with society and its vision (Olawade et al. 2024). Standardization and protocols for the evaluation and certification of AI should be established to ensure compliance with ethical, regulatory, and security standards

(Martini et al. 2024). Regulation should facilitate the use of AI for social purposes and place emphasis on workers' welfare in the production process (Martini et al. 2024).

OBSTACLES TO WIDESPREAD AI INTEGRATION

Most individuals viewed working with AI as less skill-demanding in nature compared to the work they had been undertaking prior to the introduction of the AI system. Workers involved in AI implementation reported feeling excluded from key design decisions, which may account for why AI systems can cause problems for frontline workers. Personnel time emerged as the most substantial obstacle, with tasks such as raw data labeling being tiresome and time-consuming, discouraging staff from embracing the novel technology (Ahmed et al. 2023). However, workers are in the best position to know how to avoid such harms and bring recommendations to improve their employers' bottom lines (Bell 2023). Employers stand to gain by leveraging AI to improve job quality and reap the benefits of a satisfied and engaged workforce.

The adoption of AI in the health sector is met with major hurdles due to conservatism in existing medical systems, which favor established practices over innovative technology. This breeds resistance that can significantly hinder AI adoption, as health professionals may be apprehensive of its advantages and concerned with disrupting their established workflow (Li et al. 2024). Technical incompatibilities between health information infrastructure and AI systems, and the need for fundamental changes in underlying technology and infrastructure, present other obstacles to adoption (Li et al. 2024). Despite these hurdles, the adoption of collaborative workplace AI—leveraging the unique strengths and complementary abilities of humans and technology—can enable firms to push their production frontier and achieve greater efficiency, productivity, and decision-making ability (Bell 2023). To address safety concerns in AI properly, it is necessary to work not only on reducing potential risks but also on aligning AI systems with human values and ethics.

EXPLAINABLE AI

Trust in AI systems is needed for widespread adoption, but this can be compromised by a lack of transparency and explainability in the reasoning behind AI algorithms' decisions (Petković 2023). The complexity of most AI models, particularly deep learning (DL) algorithms, often leads to an inability to understand the reasoning behind their predictions—resulting in a "black box" effect. This lack of explainability can be particularly dangerous in domains involving risk, such as healthcare and finance, where it is necessary to understand why an AI system made a particular decision. To overcome this issue, methods for explainable AI (XAI) are emerging to make AI systems more transparent and interpretable. Accuracy and robustness, transparency and explainability, human governance and control, fairness and avoidance of bias, and risk mitigation and safety are all building blocks for trustworthy AI applications (Petković 2023). XAI methods can uncover the factors influencing an AI model's predictions and enable the development of trust and human oversight. Trust typically needs to be established before adoption can occur in highly regulated and risk-averse domains such as healthcare. Gaining the trust of users and stakeholders necessitates transparency and explainability in the AI system's decision-making process.

XAI methods can provide useful insights into why an AI model is making its predictions and can play a role in building confidence and enabling meaningful human oversight. Explainability is most valuable in highly regulated and risk-averse industries such as healthcare, where "trust" typically needs to be established in order for adoption to occur. By making the process of AI system decision-making transparent and explainable, organizations can establish confidence with users and stakeholders by allowing them to understand and verify the reasoning behind the system output in a better way. XAI techniques such as interpretable machine learning (ML) techniques and interactive visualizations can expose the underlying logic and rules being used by AI systems and allow users to work with the technology in a better and more confident way. This added transparency is essential for the trustworthy and responsible use of AI to ensure such powerful systems are in alignment with human values and in the best interests of the people and communities impacted by them (Amann et al. 2020).

Das and Rad (2020) explained that incorporation of AI in health care, especially, needs to include explainability to improve patient care and workflow operations by resolving the challenge of the "black box" and maintaining accountability and transparency of usage of AI. This involves building human-understandable interfaces which unpack the internal decision-making processes of AI, thus enabling doctors to identify and correct possible errors or biases within AI-based health care solutions.

The US National Artificial Intelligence Research and Development Strategic Plan recently stated the perception that "Truly trustworthy AI requires XAI. This requires a comprehensive understanding of the AI system by the human user and the human designer" (Sendak et al. 2019). While "trust" and "adoption" are not synonymous words, in a highly regulated and risk-averse industry such as healthcare, "trust" typically needs to be established in order for adoption to occur (Sendak et al. 2019). Hence, it becomes imperative for end users to understand the underlying working principle of the decision-making process (Haque et al. 2022, Sendak et al. 2019). Only specific individuals who develop the algorithms know how the system works (Bell 2023).

XAI can be a very powerful instrument in building clinicians' confidence in their decision-making by explaining healthcare algorithms in a transparent manner (Muhammad and Bendechache 2024). XAI methods produce valuable information regarding the most significant factors influencing an AI model's predictions and support building and enabling human comprehension and inspection of the underlying reasoning (Muhammad and Bendechache 2024). Transparency becomes very significant in highly regulated and risk-averse domains such as healthcare, where trust typically becomes imperative for successful adoption and deployment of AI systems (Muhammad and Bendechache 2024).

Beyond confidence and trust in AI systems, XAI also plays a key role in explaining and optimizing the performance of AI models. By locating weaknesses, finding latent patterns, and extracting clinically irrelevant features out of the many input parameters and network layers, XAI techniques facilitate developers and auditors in optimizing the accuracy, stability, and reliability of such intelligent systems (Muhammad and Bendechache 2024). This becomes increasingly important in view of the complex "black box" nature of most AI models, especially DL algorithms, where the reasoning process behind the predictions becomes opaque and difficult to interpret.

Though current XAI methods are still far from being able to guarantee an individual decision as accurate, create unshakeable user confidence, or fully vindicate the use of AI recommendations in medical practice, they are highly useful in model debugging and systems auditing (Ghassemi et al. 2021). These capabilities enable organizations to optimize model performance, identify common failure modes or bias, and ultimately facilitate the optimal use of AI technology in high-risk domains such as healthcare.

XAI serves a significant function in responsible and trustworthy AI systems as it enables users to learn the reasoning process of a system and instills confidence and transparency (Muhammad and Bendechache 2024). This becomes extremely significant in those fields where the dependable and accurate working of AI systems plays the most crucial role, such as in healthcare, where the risks are very high and accountability and explainability are a priority.

By making the AI system's process of decision-making transparent and explainable, organizations can empower users to work with the technology in an effective and confident manner, ultimately leading to increased adoption and responsible use of such powerful technology. Moreover, XAI works toward building increasingly interpretable and explainable models with a very high level of efficacy in learning, thereby empowering human users to understand, have suitable confidence in, and properly manage the next-generation artificially intelligent collaborators (Muhammad and Bendechache, 2024). XAI holds the promise of significantly increasing trust and transparency in AI-based systems by explaining how complex models such as deep neural networks arrive at their results (Kale et al. 2022). Further, the use of provenance to explain such complex models can further improve transparency in AI-based systems (Kale et al. 2022).

Despite the immense potential of XAI, the rising level of sophistication in modeling techniques and the black-box nature of deep neural networks present challenges to its use in mission-critical systems, raise issues of ethics and justice, and create a lack of confidence (Rozario and Čevora 2023). XAI offers an appealing solution in the form of a set of tools, techniques, and algorithms with the ability to generate high-quality, intuitive, and human-interpretable explanations of AI decisions.

It should be appreciated how deployment limitations apply to XAI and how transparency and rigorous validation are most appropriate in building confidence in AI systems (Rozario and Čevora 2023). Often end-users of AI systems rather than developers of AI systems want human-like explanations of the decisions made by their machines in many cases, namely in mission-critical applications such as medical diagnoses, legal trials, and military combat (Rozario and Čevora 2023). This points to the importance of carefully considering the intended audience and purpose of explanations when designing and deploying XAI techniques (Muhammad and Bendechache 2024). Implementation of XAI generally prioritizes model performance over explainability of the decision-making process (Muhammad and Bendechache 2024). Explainability can inspect and optimize performance by pointing out weaknesses in the model, extracting patterns in the input data, and distinguishing clinically irrelevant features from many input parameters and network layers (Muhammad and Bendechache 2024).

OVERCOMING THE CHALLENGES AND BARRIERS

Successful leadership helps overcome the obstacles and challenges of adopting AI. Leaders must champion AI programs, clarify the benefits of AI to employees, and create an environment where experimentation and learning are encouraged and supported. This entails championing ethical behavior in the development of AI and actively engaging in conversation on the moral use of AI technology in the context of widespread societal issues (Uddin 2023). Leaders have to overcome employees' resistance and concerns over job loss, loss of autonomy, and loss of power in decision-making as AI systems become more prominent in the workplace. Through open communication, provision of comprehensive training programs, and direct involvement of workers in the development and deployment of AI solutions, leaders can create a culture of cooperation and trust that facilitates the successful integration of AI technology into the organization.

To enable responsible and ethical development and deployment of AI systems, organizations must invest in sound data infrastructure and governance frameworks. This requires having policies and procedures in place for data collection, storage, and use, as well as implementing controls to protect data privacy and prevent data breaches. These data governance practices are imperative in ensuring the quality, integrity, and security of data used to train and operate AI models.

In addition, organizations must actively address the ethical concerns posed by AI technology. This involves implementing strict governance frameworks, performing thorough risk assessments, and providing transparency and explainability in AI systems. By promoting ethical behavior and actively taking into account the moral concerns of AI in the public domain, organizations can align the development and implementation of such technology with ethics and societal values (Uddin 2023). In partnership with advocacy organizations, legislators, and regulatory agencies, this is also necessary in order to address the ethics of AI. These external organizations play a significant role in shaping the use of AI in a responsible and accountable manner and ensuring development and implementation in consonance with ethics and societal needs (Uddin 2023). Through this partnership strategy, organizations can navigate the complex realm of ethics and ensure the reliable and beneficial use of AI technology.

Organizations have to make investments in comprehensive training programs in order to empower workers with the expertise and knowledge to work with AI systems. These programs have to build up the technical competencies such as ML and data analysis, as well as the soft competencies such as problem-solving and critical thinking (Bell 2023). Organizations also have to actively recruit staff from diverse backgrounds to work on AI development and actively retain them as employees upon recruitment (Bell 2023). Representation by itself is not enough, but the relative lack of diversity in AI product teams can result in the development of blind spots that could be mitigated by more diverse teams (Bell 2023). In addition to this, sources of bias in data and algorithms used in AI systems have to be detected and analyzed in order to avoid unfairly disadvantaging any category of people (Harbi et al. 2023). Fairness involves careful examination of data used to train AI models and periodic audits in order to spot and counteract bias (Araujo et al. 2020). Careful monitoring of the AI system's functioning over time is also needed in order to ensure that it operates as intended and does not cause harm or negative impacts (Harbi et al. 2023).

To cultivate a professional disposition toward this, developers must have a thorough comprehension of the fact that the technology they create is inevitably bound up with significant ethical concerns. They need to appreciate, as developers, that they have a significant role in ensuring the responsible and ethical development and deployment of AI systems (Borenstein and Howard 2020). Organizations need to have rigorous red-teaming and harm mitigation practices in place as well, and this may include carefully balancing and possibly scrapping some product ideas where the harms can't be suitably mitigated. Careful attention needs to be paid to ensuring the diversity and heterogeneity of the intended use contexts of such AI technologies (Borenstein and Howard 2020). Ultimately, successful and responsible adoption of AI involves a multi-faceted strategy actively addressing the technical, organizational, and ethical concerns at stake. This integrated approach needs to be pursued in order to achieve the transformative promise of AI and avoid unintended harms.

THE HUMAN DIMENSION OF AI ADOPTION

The human element becomes crucial when implementing AI in the work environment—beyond the technological dimension of algorithms and automation—to consider the workforce's experiences and views. Organizations have to take into account how AI affects workers and their aspirations and concerns. It becomes imperative to manage concerns such as job loss, deskilling, and the requirement for emerging talent in order to facilitate a smooth transition and maintain employee motivation (Ventura-Silva et al. 2024).

Worker involvement in the development and deployment of AI systems is needed in order to adequately address such concerns. Involving employees and soliciting their participation in the decision-making process assists in creating a sense of ownership and cooperation (Bell 2023). If employees are actively involved in the process, they are likely to accept AI and view it as an asset rather than a risk. In addition to this, by incorporating workers in the development of AI solutions, organizations can recognize and avoid harms and risks in circumstances where worker protections may be in short supply (Bell 2023).

AI-driven organizational transformation involves redefinition of job roles, increased collaboration and communication, and management of cultural resistance in a way that preserves core values such as inclusivity and accountability. These are the most important factors in building an environment amenable to AI adoption and protecting the core values of the organization. Human-machine partnership needs to be prioritized by HR executives to manage responsibilities between employees and AI in an efficient manner (Madanchian and Taherdoost 2025). Automation-augmentation dynamics have a significant influence on newer-generation work designs and consequently organizational performance (Madanchian and Taherdoost 2025). Organizations can deploy AI in their workforce in an optimal manner by addressing and resolving such human-oriented issues carefully, resulting in an engaged, empowered, and resilient workforce. Humans and their impact on innovation have developed a variety of cross-functional team skills and perceptual integration, leading to creative solutions, addressing the inherent obstacles associated with team cross-functionality and strategies for overcoming them to achieve optimal inventive outcomes (Eskandarzadeh 2024).

Resistance to change is an inherent human response, most commonly caused by fear of the unknown and concerns over potential repercussions (Murire 2024). Organizations have to address ethical issues, manage successful leadership and communication, and plug gaps in talent and skills in order to achieve cultural transformation in the adoption of AI. Furthermore, organizations have to acknowledge and dispel employees' fears regarding job security, changes in work dynamics, and deskilling risk (Bell 2023). Open channels of communication, education programs, and upskilling and reskilling programs are essential to dispel fears and instill a culture of openness and trust. Organizations have to overcome barriers and facilitate worker adoption of AI and ultimately capitalize on its potential to augment human capacities and organizational success (Madanchian and Taherdoost 2025). Furthermore, prudence and active collaboration with workers are needed in order to prevent workplace AI adoptions from having adverse repercussions (Bell 2023). One of the most significant risks lies in cases where AI systems are deployed in a way that deskills work, amplifies surveillance, or worsens work in a way detrimental to job quality. Managers and executives considering utilizing AI technology to free up their workers to accomplish more "human" or higher-value work should avoid assuming any AI device will serve that purpose (Madanchian and Taherdoost 2025).

ETHICAL LEADERSHIP IN AI ADOPTION

Responsible use of AI in organizations needs to be supported by ethical leadership. Ethical leaders play a significant role in guiding their organizations toward the development and implementation of AI systems in an ethical way and in accordance with societal norms and values (Uddin 2023). Ethical leaders can guide their teams to develop and implement AI in a way that benefits society as a whole.

In addition to this, ethical leaders can take steps toward addressing ethical challenges by investing in upskilling and reskilling programs to facilitate workers in moving into new occupations supporting AI technology and by building a lifelong culture of learning (Brevini 2020). They can also advocate policies supporting equal pay, benefits, and working conditions for all workers, whether they work on AI systems or not (Bell 2023). Organizations also need to facilitate cooperation between workers and AI systems in order to leverage the strengths of both (Brevini 2020). They can also engage in partnerships with schools and other education institutes for education, engage in transparent communication, and have support systems and resources in place (Brevini 2020). Incorporation of workers' and other end-users' perspectives right at the beginning of the product development process is also important (Bell 2023). Ethical leaders also facilitate transparency and accountability in the use of AI by designing and deploying AI systems in a way that makes them explainable, interpretable, and amenable to human scrutiny (Brevini 2020). Through transparency in the functioning of AI systems and in how they are being used, organizations can build stakeholder confidence and ensure AI is used in a responsible and ethical way (Brevini 2020).

STRATEGIES FOR PROMOTING AI ADOPTION IN THE WORKPLACE

It is timely to implement technology-aligned strategies at the organizational level. Leaders must espouse a moral system in alignment with the greater goals and values of society and acknowledge and harness the power of AI in the context of efficiency and enhancing worker productivity (Uddin 2023). A firm's focus on customers does not always translate into a focus on worker end-users (Bell 2023). In order to overcome this, organizations must create better feedback loops and genuinely prioritize workers' needs and opinions and may have to consult workers and their representatives beyond their own organizations (Bell 2023).

Though all workers' needs and preferences are not in agreement with business leaders' and managers' incentives, there are points of alignment where they can be harnessed (Bell 2023). For example, workers may appreciate the efficiency and reduced physical effort brought by AI-enabled tools, and leaders may appreciate the productivity gains. In order to leverage AI opportunities, methods should have a human-centered approach where workers' welfare and satisfaction are prioritized, and innovative and responsible measures are taken for the use of technology in the organization (Shabbir and Answer 2018). This may include investing in upskilling and reskilling programs to allow workers to transition into new roles, enhancing the partnership between workers and AI systems, and building a culture of transparency and accountability in the use of AI technology. By centering workers and promoting ethical leadership, organizations can make AI work in favor of the business and its workers and result in a healthier and more positive work culture (Uddin 2023). Ultimately, organizations have to actively address issues such as cultural resistance and ethics in order to leverage such technological advancements (Murire 2024). This holds particularly in firms with massive numbers of low-wage workers most exposed to AI's negative effects. In order to do this, they should have a human-centered approach where workers' welfare and satisfaction are prioritized and innovative and responsible actions are taken for the use of AI in the organization. This can include investing in upskilling and reskilling programs to allow workers to transition into new roles, enabling cooperation between workers and AI systems, and building a culture of transparency and accountability in AI technology use. By centering workers and promoting ethical leadership, organizations can leverage AI in a way that serves the business and its workers and builds a healthier and more productive work culture (Murire 2024).

Table 1 provides descriptions of the adoption-driving strategies in the workplace. Intelligent machine implementation across various industries needs symbolic structures, the ability to capture people's interest, and the observance of moral and ethical values, resulting in positive feedback and empowering people to leverage their expertise and innovate (Shabbir and Answer 2018). With the appropriate implementation of AI solutions, most industries can achieve higher profitability and economic growth. Organizations typically face massive barriers to AI adoption in spite of the existence of key enablers (Madanchian and Taherdoost 2025). These enablers include advanced technology, an adoption-supporting organizational culture, and leadership (Shabbir and Answer 2018).

Table 1. Strategies for Promoting AI Adoption in the Workplace

Strategy	Description
Promote ethical AI framework	Develop AI policies that align with societal values (Uddin 2023).
Enhance worker involvement	Create feedback loops and include workers' perspectives in AI adoption strategies (Bell 2023).
Align AI benefits with worker needs	Leverage areas where worker needs align with business goals, such as productivity gains (Bell 2023).
Invest in reskilling and upskilling	Provide training programs to help workers transition into AI-assisted roles (Shabbir and Anwer 2018).
Foster human-AI collaboration	Encourage seamless collaboration between employees and AI-powered tools (Shabbir and Anwer 2018).
Ensure transparency and accountability	Establish a transparent AI governance framework to build trust and accountability (Bell 2023).
Address cultural resistance	Mitigate resistance by addressing ethical concerns and low-wage worker vulnerabilities (Murire 2024).
Adopt human-centric AI approaches	Focus on well-being and satisfaction while implementing AI-driven solutions (Murire 2024)

It becomes essential to deploy new technology and support staff in order to overcome resistance to change—an inherent human response based on fear of the unknown and concern over possible negative impacts (Murire 2024). Organizations need to overcome such cultural and attitudinal problems actively in order to develop an AI-friendly work culture while maintaining core values and empowering employees.

By keeping employees' needs and opinions at the center of concern, companies can employ AI in a way that serves both the business and employees, improving the work culture in a positive and productive direction. Therefore, organizations need to overcome problems such as cultural resistance and ethical concerns in an active manner in order to make the deployment of AI technology consistent with established values, promote workforce empowerment, and optimize the possibility of positive organization-wide transformation. Ultimately, successful assimilation of AI hinges on an integrated approach that utilizes technological advancement as much as human-centered methods, maintains ethics standards, and promotes continuous workforce development. Table 1 (Uddin 2023, Bell 2023, Shabbir and Anwer 2018, Murire 2024, Madanchian and Taherdoost 2025) shows the main strategies that help this process.

REGULATORY CHALLENGES OF AI

The demand for accuracy, strength, transparency, explainability, human control and governance, fairness, elimination of bias, and risk and safety mitigation has contributed to the creation of multiple government and regulatory programs. These programs aim to make impactful and risky AI applications trustworthy and ethical. Indeed, workers who work hand in hand with AI systems have a deep sense of their benefits and harms. In the best-case scenario, such workers feel the positive effects of such technology on their work in making it efficient, free of errors, and even enjoyable, as opposed to tiresome, exhausting, and risky (Farhud and Zokaei 2021). In most cases, AI systems can restrict workers' autonomy, invade their private lives, erode their judgment and empathy, and push them to the point of exhaustion and harm (Bell 2023).

Companies outsourcing tasks to AI systems expose workers to binding decisions that are capricious and cruel. On a global scale, increased use of AI systems will accelerate existing problems brought about by economic inequality (Petković 2023). AI raises many ethical and legal concerns and remains inaccessible to all societies despite its contribution to improving treatment procedures. Many low-income and developing countries still lack access to the latest technology. It should be noted that ethical concerns, privacy and data protection, informed consent, social inequalities, medical consultation, empathy, and sympathy are all issues (Farhud and Zokaei 2021). Many people enjoyed the added ease; many others demonstrated that they needed a greater level of challenge. Each of the examples mentioned above can be viewed as a continuum.

AI requires quality data in order to estimate risks accurately and generate successful suggestions. Incomplete data, old data, and incorrect data have a significant effect on AI systems and can result in incorrect predictions and potential safety hazards (El-Helaly 2024). Data on which an AI system is trained should represent a wide range of real-world scenarios so that the system can work effectively. If the data used for training AI systems are biased or do not represent all the scenarios in which the AI system will operate, it can generate incorrect and biased results (El-Helaly 2024).

The AI systems used in their work decreased the level of intellectual demand relative to how it functioned in the absence of AI. Workers in U.S. warehouses with higher degrees of AI adoption had less task variety and higher technological scaffolding to assist them in performing tasks correctly (Bell 2023). While AI promises much in terms of increasing efficiency, productivity, and decision-making, adoption comes at a cost and with some moral issues (El-Helaly 2024). One of the principal obstacles to adoption is the cost of building and implementing AI systems (El-Helaly 2024).

Though AI systems are expensive to buy and deploy in hardware and software and to train on data initially, the long-term advantages can typically pay for such costs (El-Helaly 2024). AI can enable organizations to make improved risk assessments and develop better, data-informed recommendations by rapidly processing and analyzing massive amounts of data at a level beyond human capabilities. This can ultimately result in safer workspaces, increased productivity, and improved efficiency in operations overall (El-Helaly 2024).

One of the major obstacles to the adoption of AI lies in the immense amount of time, cost and effort needed to train such systems in the first place and the subsequent maintenance and adjustment to maintain their effectiveness over time, specifically in the beginning stages of adoption (Ahmed et al. 2023). Spending sufficient amounts of time and resources and involving joint effort between organizations and AI developers is essential to overcome this obstacle and achieve the ultimate benefits of AI adoption in the long run.

ECONOMIC DISPARITIES AND GLOBAL AI ADOPTION

Economic variations in different countries and areas pose a significant barrier to AI adoption. Low-income and developing countries have no access to existing technologies (Farhud and Zokaei 2021). This lack of access is attributed to several factors, including inadequate financial resources, inadequate infrastructure, and a shortage of competent people. Even if AI technologies are within reach, their implementation and upkeep may be too expensive for organizations in these countries. Furthermore, the regulatory and ethical frameworks surrounding AI may not be well developed in these countries, causing uncertainty and hindering adoption. AI implementation entails massive amounts of data collection, which may be time-consuming and exhausting. It is important to engage leaders and practitioners with AI developers and vendors to ensure adequate funding and time commitment to training and implementation. At a societal level, the increased utilization of AI systems is going to accelerate existing problems due to economic disparity (Bell 2023). AI technologies can exacerbate socioeconomic disparities since their benefits may accrue primarily to higher-income individuals and organizations, with lower-income individuals lagging behind (Bell 2023). Companies that delegate managerial tasks to AI systems can subject employees to binding decisions that are arbitrary or severe (Bell 2023), diminishing worker self-governance and agency. AI systems can also constrain workers' autonomy, intrude into their privacy, undermine their judgment and empathy, and push them to the edge of exhaustion or injury (Bell 2023). These negative impacts disproportionately affect the most vulnerable workers.

ADDRESSING ALGORITHMIC BIAS AND ETHICAL CONSIDERATION IN AI DEPLOYMENT

AI algorithms are trained on data, and if the data reflects existing biases, the AI system will mirror and even amplify the biases (Lambert et al. 2023). This can lead to unfair or discriminatory outcomes, particularly in applications such as hiring, lending, and criminal justice. Algorithmic bias can result in variation in diagnosis and treatment and harm vulnerable populations (Nazer et al. 2023). Algorithmic bias can be mitigated by diligent data collection and model development, and ongoing monitoring and assessment of AI systems to maintain fairness and equity (Nazer et al. 2023, Panch et al. 2019). To ensure responsible deployment of AI, there is a need for clear ethical guidelines and regulatory frameworks. These frameworks should address data privacy, transparency, and accountability concerns and be formulated through broad stakeholder involvement. Organizations must invest not only in the adoption of these technologies but also in creating an environment supportive of innovation and the adoption of AI use by professionals (Ventura-Silva et al. 2024). This includes formulating clear policies, fostering a culture of continuous learning, and ensuring that all members of the team are familiar with AI's benefits and limitations.

In addition, ongoing monitoring and assessment of AI systems are required to ensure their effectiveness and fairness. Equity in AI applications entails the fair and just distribution of technologies and their benefits (Dankwa-Mullan 2024). Algorithmic bias that may lead to discrimination and unjust results is a key ethical challenge that needs to be addressed proactively (Panch et al. 2019). AI systems automating or augmenting work tasks are usually evaluated primarily in terms of their impact on business outcomes like productivity, cost savings, or efficiency (Bell 2023). But these evaluations generally do not factor in impacts on workers or otherwise only consider a limited set of impacts that are relatively easy to measure (Bell 2023). Companies may be unaware of the less obvious ways in which AI systems shape the day-to-day experience of those who interact with them directly (Bell 2023). It is necessary to collaborate with workers to identify areas where they would welcome AI or automation assistance, grounded in the complementarity of human and machine capabilities (Bell 2023).

It is thus important to understand the sources of bias inherent in AI-based algorithms (Nazer et al. 2023). Historical biases, which can be inherent in data used for training AI algorithms, may result in discrimination if not checked. It is thus important to devise AI algorithms that minimize bias and promote fairness in decision-making (Elendu et al. 2023). Bias could be from varied sources, including biased data collection, algorithm design, and human interpretation (Ferrara 2023a). Algorithmic transparency can help reveal as well as minimize biases by enabling scrutiny of the training data, algorithm design, and decision-making processes (Dhopte and Bagde

2023). Due consideration of the data used for training AI models and regular audits to detect and minimize bias are important to ensure fairness.

In order to minimize the amount of bias and promote fairness in AI algorithms, AI product teams need to be diverse (Bell 2023). Diversity in this instance is necessary in order to assist in lowering the levels of biased output and also to provide a greater variety of viewpoints (Araujo et al. 2020). Lack of diversity in AI product teams will create blind spots that more diverse teams would minimize (Bell 2023).

This is accomplished through working forward from issue, challenge, and opportunity statements made by those at the front line (Bell 2023). These systems have the potential to encourage unfair outcomes and reinforce existing inequalities (Ferrara 2023b). Additionally, robust AI performance monitoring and assessment mechanisms must be implemented in order to detect and mitigate the implications of biases or unexpected outcomes. Moreover, AI adoption must be done through heterogeneous and inclusive groups in order to minimize one-sided results as well as ensure a balanced set of viewpoints. AI systems are highly dependent on big datasets that often entail sensitive and personal information (Araujo et al. 2020). To mitigate the potential risks and vulnerabilities of such systems, organizations must pursue a proactive and multilayered approach. This includes rigorous testing and validation processes to identify and address biases, errors, or unforeseen results that may arise from the use of AI.

Besides, it is necessary for organizations to incorporate diverse perspectives from diverse disciplines in developing and deploying AI systems, such as ethics, computer science, sociology, and law. This interdisciplinarity can help ensure that AI development and deployment align with ethical principles, promote fairness and equity, and mitigate negative impacts on society (Leavy et al. 2020).

By prioritizing the responsible and ethical use of AI, organizations can reap the full benefits of these technologies without incurring potential harms. This holistic approach, which addresses data privacy, algorithmic fairness, and the societal implications of AI, is essential to bring about maximal benefits of AI adoption and the establishment of public trust in these transformative technologies. This can be achieved by recruiting individuals of varied backgrounds to AI development teams and actively striving to retain them as personnel after being hired (Panch et al. 2019). Having employees as participants and significant stakeholders in creating any company's AI ethics and responsible AI principles is also essential (Araujo et al. 2020).

Organizations must have strict protocols in place that are compliant with the relevant laws and regulations such as the Health Insurance Portability and Accountability Act in order to protect data, ensure privacy, and confidentiality in the process of research (Abujaber and Nashwan 2024). This involves having strong data governance frameworks in place that consist of policies for data collection, storage, and utilization. When AI is used in the decision-making process, there are concerns related to data privacy and security that are evoked (Araujo et al. 2020). Organizations must therefore prioritize having robust data governance policies and security measures in place to enable responsible and ethical handling of sensitive data (Abujaber and Nashwan 2024). Privacy, integrity, and individuality must be assured and possible algorithmic biases or discrimination prevented while using AI (Ventura-Silva et al. 2024).

AI ADOPTION: A HOLISTIC AND STRATEGIC APPROACH

AI adoption is not only a technical task, but a complex organizational transformation involving careful planning, execution, and ongoing monitoring (Ventura-Silva et al. 2024). There is a need to address the numerous challenges and barriers that companies face to unlock AI's transformational potential and to ensure its responsible and ethical use (Lu et al. 2022). One of the fundamental barriers to AI implementation is the impact it will have on workers. AI systems can constrain worker autonomy, invade their privacy, undermine their professional authority and empathy, and even push them to exhaustion or injury (Bell 2023). Workers who directly engage with these technologies are familiar with their pros and cons intimately. In the best-case scenario, AI can do their job more efficiently, perfectly, and even pleasurably. Too often, however, employees are on the receiving end of the negatives, including the removal of their decision-making abilities and the dehumanizing effects of AI-powered management (Farhud and Zokaei 2021). In addition, the increased application of AI systems at the organizational and societal levels can exacerbate current problems resulting from economic inequality (Petković 2023). Organizations that delegate managerial tasks to AI systems can expose workers to binding decisions that are perceived as arbitrary or ruthless, and further degrade worker autonomy and well-being.

Technological limitations, such as the lack of robust algorithms, limited computing power, and the need for specialized hardware, can also hinder the development and deployment of AI systems (Sendak et al. 2019). Data challenges, such as unavailability of data, data quality issues, data silos, and data privacy concerns, can undermine the training and effectiveness of AI models (El-Helaly 2024). Organizational challenges, such as resistance to change, lack of skilled staff, and insufficient funding, can slow the adoption of AI technologies (Sendak et al. 2019).

Ethical concerns surrounding bias, fairness, transparency, and accountability must also be proactively addressed to enable the responsible use of AI (Petković 2023). The social implications of AI, such as job displacement and the possibility of reinforcing existing societal biases, must be carefully considered and remedied (Bell 2023).

Moreover, the economic disparities between countries and regions represent a significant obstacle to the global adoption of AI. Despite the enormous progress in the field, AI is still not within reach for all societies, and large numbers of low- and middle-income countries have no access to existing technologies (Farhud and Zokaei 2021). This lack of access is concerning from an ethical perspective in terms of fairness and equity. To navigate the complex landscape of AI adoption, organizations need to adopt an integrated and holistic approach across technology, people, processes, and ethics. This includes investing in a strong AI infrastructure, creating a data-driven culture, fostering human-machine collaboration, and incorporating ethical considerations across the AI lifecycle (Olawade et al. 2024). By anticipating these challenges and obstacles, organizations can release the transformative potential of AI and ensure its ethical and responsible application, achieving maximum benefits and minimizing risks. This multi-pronged approach is essential for organizations to adopt and implement AI technologies successfully. They need not only to invest in the technical capabilities but also to invest in acquiring the right people and processes, and incorporating ethical considerations across the entire AI lifecycle. This integrated perspective will allow organizations to navigate the complex issues involved in AI adoption and unlock the full potential of these revolutionary technologies while mitigating the risks and guarding against unintended consequences. These ethical issues can only be resolved by an integrated approach involving the promotion of transparency, ensuring fairness, and having accountability mechanisms in place (Farhud and Zokaei 2021).

Global cooperation and coordination are critical in promoting the equitable and ethical development and use of AI at the international level (Ilikhan et al. 2024). This involves sharing best practices, agreeing on shared standards, and addressing the potential risks and unintended consequences of AI technologies. Lastly, effective and responsible AI adoption involves a multi-dimensional strategy that proactively addresses the technical, organizational, and ethical concerns involved. Such a holistic approach is critical in unlocking the transformative potential of AI while guarding against unintended negative effects. Ensuring equitable access and bridging the digital divide remains a fundamental priority, while ethics must remain front and center in the ever-evolving world of technology (Elendu et al. 2023).

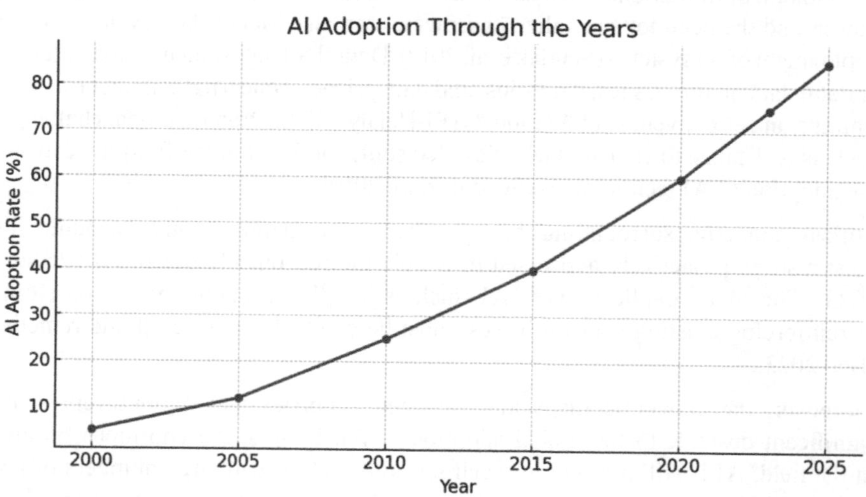

Fig. 1. AI Adoption Through Years

Figure 1 provides an overview of AI adoption rates in various industries and times. The graph easily shows the trajectory of AI adoption, with the accelerated rate of adoption in recent years, particularly in sectors such as healthcare, finance, and manufacturing. Of note is the inflection point at around 2020, which corresponds to increased investments in AI research and development and its impact on industrial practice. The graphic shows the upward trend of AI adoption over the years. This information is useful in strategizing the direction that organizations should take with their technological advancements. It is time to take steps in line with technological advancements at the organizational level. Therefore, leaders must promote a moral framework that will align with the overall objectives and values of society, identifying and harnessing the potential of AI within the framework of enhancing creativity and efficiency (Uddin 2023). Ethical leadership is a pertinent problem with broad practical implications in the era of AI (Uddin 2023).

CONCLUSION

As organizations harness the revolutionary potential of AI, ethical leadership becomes the bedrock of responsible adoption and usage. By prioritizing fairness, transparency, and accountability, ethical leaders can guide their organizations to develop and deploy AI systems that embody ethical values and societal values. Investing in reskilling and upskilling programs, fostering collaboration among workers and AI systems, and establishing a culture of continuous learning are critical actions that ethical leaders can take to cushion the disruptions of AI. Engagement with external stakeholders, such as advocacy groups, legislators, and regulators, is also vital in ensuring that the design and deployment of AI technologies are in alignment with ethical values and societal values. In summary, ethical leadership provides organizations with a blueprint to not only harness the vast potential of AI but also to oversee the associated risks, so that AI becomes a force for progress that is both sustainable and equitable, and contributes to a future where technology augments human capabilities and improves lives for all.

REFERENCES

Abujaber, A.A., and Nashwan, A.J. (2024). Ethical framework for artificial intelligence in healthcare research: A path to integrity. *World Journal of Methodology*, 14(3). *https://doi.org/10.5662/wjm.v14.i3.94071*

Ahmed, M.I., Spooner, B., Isherwood, J., Lane, M.A., Orrock, E., and Dennison, A.R. (2023). A systematic review of the barriers to the implementation of artificial intelligence in healthcare. *Cureus. https://doi.org/10.7759/cureus.46454*

Amann, J., Blasimme, A., Vayena, E., Frey, D., and Madai, V.I. (2020). Explainability for artificial intelligence in healthcare: A multidisciplinary perspective. *BMC Medical Informatics and Decision Making*, 20(1). BioMed Central. *https://doi.org/10.1186/s12911-020-01332-6*

Araujo, T., Helberger, N., Kruikemeier, S., and Vreese, C.H. de. (2020). In AI we trust? Perceptions about automated decision-making by artificial intelligence. *AI and Society,* 35(3), 611. Springer Nature. *https://doi.org/10.1007/s00146-019-00931-w*

Bell, S.A. (2023). AI and job quality: Insights from frontline workers. *SSRN Electronic Journal. https://doi.org/10.2139/ssrn.4337611*

Borenstein, J., and Howard, A. (2020). Emerging challenges in AI and the need for AI ethics education. *AI and Ethics*, 1(1). *https://doi.org/10.1007/s43681-020-00002-7*

Brevini, B. (2020). Black boxes, not green: Mythologizing artificial intelligence and omitting the environment. *Big Data and Society,* 7(2). SAGE Publishing. *https://doi.org/10.1177/2053951720935141*

Dankwa-Mullan, I. (2024). Health equity and ethical considerations in using artificial intelligence in public health and medicine. *Preventing Chronic Disease*, 21. *https://doi.org/10.5888/pcd21.240245*

Das, A., and Rad, P. (2020). Opportunities and challenges in explainable artificial intelligence (XAI): A survey. arXiv. *https://doi.org/10.48550/arxiv.2006.11371*

Dhopte, A., and Bagde, H. (2023). Smart smile: Revolutionizing dentistry with artificial intelligence, *Cureus. https://doi.org/10.7759/cureus.41227*

Elendu, C., Amaechi, D.C., Elendu, T.C., Jingwa, K.A., Okoye, O.K., Okah, M.J., Ladele, J.A., Farah, A.H., and Alimi, H.A. (2023). Ethical implications of AI and robotics in healthcare: A review. *Medicine*, 102(50). Wolters Kluwer. *https://doi.org/10.1097/md.0000000000036671*

El-Helaly, M. (2024). Artificial intelligence and occupational health and safety, benefits and drawbacks. *La Medicina del lavoro*, 115(2). *https://doi.org/10.23749/mdl.v115i2.15835*

Eskandarzadeh, A. (2024). Human elements in innovation. *In:* H. Taherdoost (Ed.), Mastering Innovation in Business, 235–254. IGI Global. *https://doi.org/10.4018/979-8-3693-3759-2.ch010*

Farhud, D.D., and Zokaei, S. (2021). Ethical issues of artificial intelligence in medicine and healthcare. *Iranian Journal of Public Health. https://doi.org/10.18502/ijph.v50i11.7600*

Ferrara, E. (2023a). Fairness and bias in artificial intelligence: A brief survey of sources, impacts, and mitigation strategies. ArXiv. *https://doi.org/10.48550/arxiv.2304.07683*

Ferrara, E. (2023b). Fairness and bias in artificial intelligence: A brief survey of sources, impacts, and mitigation strategies. *Sci*, 6(1). *https://doi.org/10.3390/sci6010003*

Ghassemi, M., Oakden-Rayner, L., and Beam, A.L. (2021). The false hope of current approaches to explainable artificial intelligence in health care. *The Lancet Digital Health*, 3(11). *https://doi.org/10.1016/s2589-7500(21)00208-9*

Haque, A.B., Islam, A.K.M.N., and Mikalef, P. (2022). Explainable artificial intelligence (XAI) from a user perspective: A synthesis of prior literature and problematizing avenues for future research. *Technological Forecasting and Social Change,* 186, 122120. Elsevier BV. https://doi.org/10.1016/j.techfore.2022.122120

Harbi, S.H.A., Tidjon, L.N., and Khomh, F. (2023). Responsible design patterns for machine learning pipelines. arXiv. *https://doi.org/10.48550/arxiv.2306.01788*

Ilikhan, S.U., Özer, M., Tanberkan, H., and Bozkurt, V. (2024). How to mitigate the risks of deployment of artificial intelligence in medicine? *Turkish Journal of Medical Sciences,* 54(3), 483. Scientific and Technological Research Council of Turkey (TUBITAK). *https://doi.org/10.55730/1300-0144.5814*

Kale, A., Nguyen, T., Harris, J.S., Li, C., Zhang, J., and Ma, X. (2022). Provenance documentation to enable explainable and trustworthy AI: A literature review. *Data Intelligence,* 5(1), 139. The MIT Press. *https://doi.org/10.1162/dint_a_00119*

Lahlali, M., Berbiche, N., and Alami, J.E. (2021). How enterprise must be prepared to be "AI first"? *International Journal of Advanced Computer Science and Applications,* 12(5). *https://doi.org/10.14569/ijacsa.2021.0120542*

Lambert, S.I., Madi, M., Sopka, S., Lenes, A., Stange, H., Buszello, C.P., and Stephan, A. (2023). An integrative review on the acceptance of artificial intelligence among healthcare professionals in hospitals. *Npj Digital Medicine,* 6(1). *https://doi.org/10.1038/s41746-023-00852-5*

Leavy, S., O'Sullivan, B., and Siapera, E. (2020). Data, power and bias in artificial intelligence. arXiv. https://doi.org/10.48550/arxiv.2008.07341

Li, Y.H., Li, Y., Wei, M.Y., and Li, G. (2024). Innovation and challenges of artificial intelligence technology in personalized healthcare. *Scientific Reports,* 14(1). *https://doi.org/ 10.1038/s41598-024-70073-7*

Lu, L., D'Agostino, A., Rudman, S.L., Ouyang, D., and Ho, D.E. (2022). Designing accountable health care algorithms: Lessons from covid-19 contact tracing. *NEJM Catalyst,* 3(4). *https://doi.org/10.1056/cat.21.0382*

Madanchian, M., and Taherdoost, H. (2025). Barriers and enablers of AI adoption in human resource management: A critical analysis of organizational and technological factors. *Information,* 16(1), 51. Multidisciplinary Digital Publishing Institute. *https://doi.org/10.3390/info16010051*

Martini, B., Bellisario, D., and Coletti, P. (2024). Human-centered and sustainable artificial intelligence in industry 5.0: Challenges and perspectives. *Sustainability,* 16(13), 5448. Multidisciplinary Digital Publishing Institute. *https://doi.org/10.3390/su16135448*

Muhammad, D., and Bendechache, M. (2024). Unveiling the black box: A systematic review of Explainable Artificial Intelligence in medical image analysis. *Computational and Structural Biotechnology Journal,* 24. *https://doi.org/10.1016/j.csbj.2024.08.005*

Murire, O. (2024). Artificial intelligence and its role in shaping organizational work practices and culture. *Administrative Sciences,* 14(12). *https://doi.org/10.3390/admsci14120316*

Nazer, L., Zatarah, R., Waldrip, S., Ke, J.X.C., Moukheiber, M., Khanna, A.K., Hicklen, R., Moukheiber, L., Moukheiber, D., Ma, H., and Mathur, P. (2023). Bias in artificial intelligence. *PLOS Digital Health,* 2(6). *https://doi.org/10.1371/journal.pdig.0000278*

Okolo, C.T., Aruleba, K., and Obaido, G. (2022). Responsible AI in Africa—Challenges and opportunities. *Social and Cultural Studies of Robots and AI. https://doi.org/10.1007/978-3-031-08215-3_3*

Olawade, D.B., Wada, O.Z., David-Olawade, A.C., Fapohunda, O., Ige, A.O., and Ling, J. (2024). Artificial intelligence potential for net zero sustainability: Current evidence and prospects. *Next Sustainability,* 4. *https://doi.org/10.1016/j.nxsust.2024.100041*

Panch, T., Mattie, H., and Atun, R. (2019). Artificial intelligence and algorithmic bias: implications for health systems. *Journal of Global Health*, 9(2). https://doi.org/10.7189/jogh.09.020318

Petković, D. (2023). It is not "accuracy vs. explainability"—We need both for trustworthy AI systems. *IEEE Transactions on Technology and Society,* 4(1), 46. Institute of Electrical and Electronics Engineers. https://doi.org/10.1109/tts.2023.3239921

Rozario, S., and Čevora, G. (2023). Explainable AI does not provide the explanations end-users are asking for. arXiv. *https://doi.org/10.48550/arxiv.2302.11577*

Sendak, M., Elish, M.C., Gao, M., Futoma, J., Ratliff, W., Nichols, M., Bedoya, A., Balu, S., and O'Brien, C. (2019). "The human body is a black box": Supporting clinical decision-making with deep learning. arXiv. *https://doi.org/10.48550/arxiv.1911.08089*

Shabbir, J., and Anwer, T. (2018). Artificial intelligence and its role in near future. arXiv. *https://doi.org/10.48550/arxiv.1804.01396*

Uddin, A.S.M.A. (2023). The era of AI: Upholding ethical leadership. *Open Journal of Leadership,* 12(4). *https://doi.org/10.4236/ojl.2023.124019*

Ventura-Silva, J.M.A., Martins, M.M., Trindade, L.de L., Faria, A. da C.A., Pereira, S.C. de A., Züge, S.S., and Ribeiro, O.M.P.L. (2024). Artificial intelligence in the organization of nursing care: A scoping review. *Nursing Reports,* 14(4), 2733. Multidisciplinary Digital Publishing Institute. *https://doi.org/10.3390/nursrep14040202*

Note: *AI was used in the preparation of this chapter to enhance language clarity and created Figure 1 with real data from references.*

Index

For Product Safety Concerns and Information please contact our EU representative GPSR@taylorandfrancis.com Taylor & Francis Verlag GmbH, Kaufingerstraße 24, 80331 München, Germany